GOTHIC FICTION

A Master List of Twentieth Century Criticism and Research

Meckler's Bibliographies on Science Fiction, Fantasy and Horror

1. PKD: A Philip K. Dick Bibliography, Revised Edition
   Daniel J. H. Levack and Steven Owen Godersky
   ISBN 0-88736-096-3 1988 CIP

2. DUNE MASTER: A Frank Herbert Bibliography
   Daniel J. H. Levack and Mark Willard
   ISBN 0-88736-099-8 1988 CIP

3. GOTHIC FICTION: A Master List of Twentieth Century Criticism and Research
   Frederick S. Frank
   ISBN 0-88736-218-4 1988 CIP

GOTHIC FICTION
A Master List of Twentieth Century Criticism and Research

Frederick S. Frank

Meckler

Library of Congress Cataloging-in-Publication Data

Frank, Frederick S.
Gothic fiction.

(Meckler's bibliographies on science fiction, fantasy, and horror ; 3)
Bibliography: p.
Includes index.
1. Gothic revival (Literature)—History and criticism—Bibliography.
2. Fiction—History and criticism—Bibliography. I. Title. II. Series.
Z5917.G66F69 1988 016.8093'872 87-24705
[PN3435]
ISBN 0-88736-218-4 (alk. paper)

Meckler Corporation, 11 Ferry Lane West, Westport, CT 06880
Meckler Ltd., Grosvenor Gardens House, Grosvenor Gardens,
London SW1W 0BS, UK

Printed on acid free paper.

Manufactured in the United States of America.

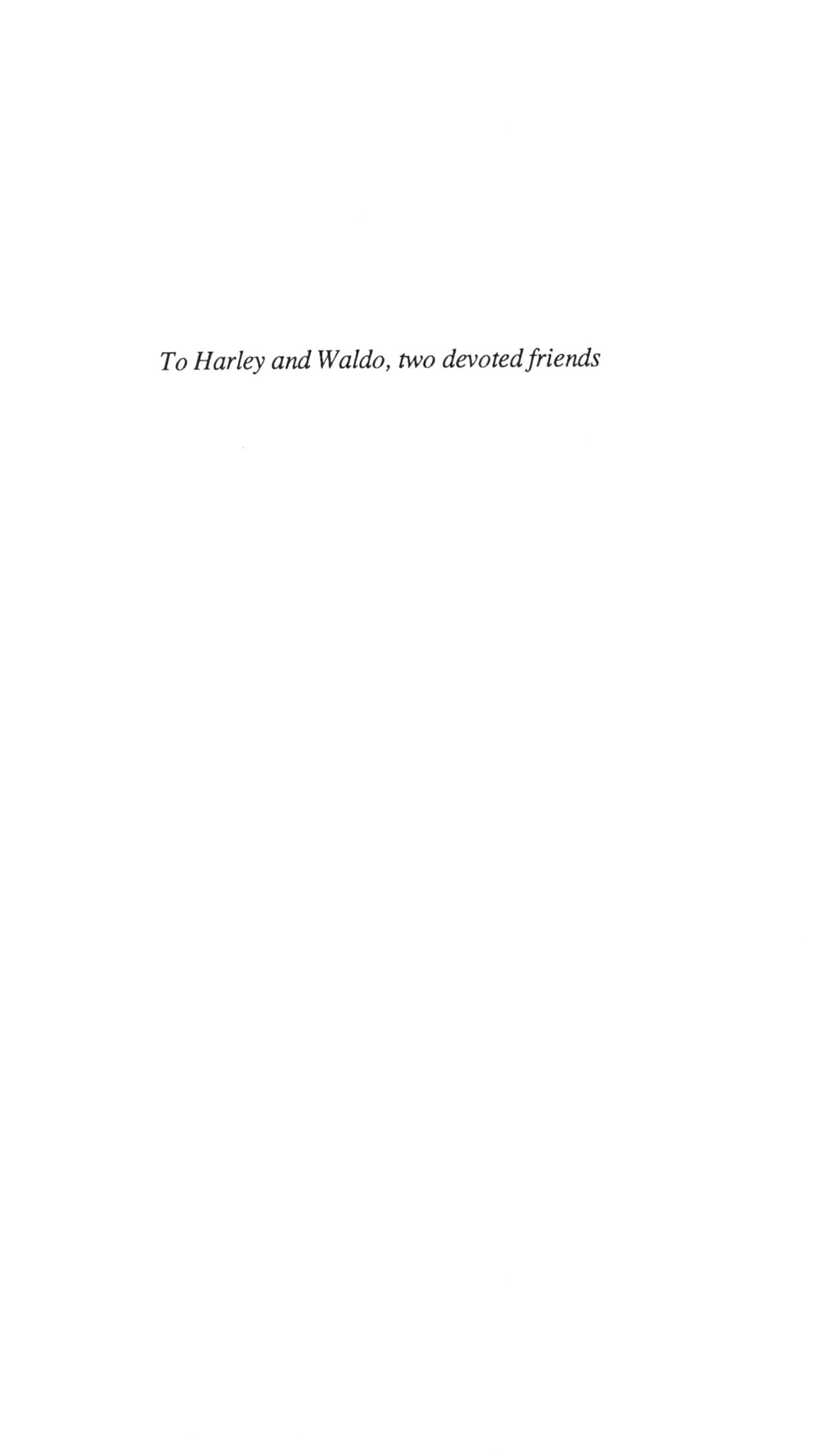

To Harley and Waldo, two devoted friends

Contents

Introduction

The compilation of a reliable master list of criticism and research on Gothic fiction began as an ongoing project in bibliographical surveillance in 1973 when the *Bulletin of Bibliography* [1] published the original checklist of scholarship on the Gothic novel. A sequel bibliography of Gothic studies and research appeared in the *Bulletin of Bibliography* in 1978 in the first number for that year. These two checklists marked the first formal attempt to gather, organize, classify, and evaluate the expanding volume of interpretive writing on the Gothic genre, a critical phenomenon that could be traced back directly to the resurgence of interest in the Gothic reflected in the several book-length studies of the form by Dorothy Scarborough, (*The Supernatural in Modern English Fiction*, 1917) Edith Birkhead, (*The Tale of Terror: A Study of the Gothic Romance*, 1921) Eino Railo, (*The Haunted Castle: A Study of the Elements of English Romanticism*, 1927) and Montague Summers (*The Gothic Quest: A History of the Gothic Novel*, 1938). These early twentieth-century scholarly surveys of the Gothic gave rise to a revitalization of critical inquiry into the nature and purpose of this audacious genre which had been long regarded since its invention by Horace Walpole in the Eighteenth Century as an inconsequential and superficial literary tradition to be scorned and avoided by serious students and real scholars. Except for the nearly universal rage of the Gothic's first reviewers, almost no one had bothered to examine Gothic literature until the tireless and prolific Montague Summers thrust his erudite torch into the dark places of the haunted castle in quest of the lost and forgotten Gothics of the late Eighteenth Century in his exhaustive history of the early Gothic novel.

Summers also laid the foundations for two parallel fields of bibliographical endeavor relating to the Gothic novel and its later manifestations in the short tale of terror. His *Gothic Bibliography* (1941) identified for the first time literally hundreds of Gothic titles and suggested the formidable scope of the field to future researchers. Along with his work on the elusive primary source, the Gothic novel itself, Summers was the first Gothic quester to deplore the absence of sound bibliography in the field and to express the need for valid reference works to cover the mounting backlog of secondary writing on the Gothic, a new and fertile area of studies in the 1930's. "I am very well aware," he wrote, "that full dress Bibliographies of Lewis, of Maturin, and (above all) of Mrs. Radcliffe are badly needed."[2]

However, Summers's challenge and summons to future bibliographers of the Gothic movement was not immediately heeded. On the other hand, a great quantity of critical writing on the Gothic and its influence followed in the wake of Summers's demonstration of the important place of the Gothic in *The Gothic Quest*. Inevitably, much of this criticism was appreciative, apologetic, and even militantly defensive as scholarship tried to compensate for a century of benign neglect of Gothicism. Although Gothic fiction from its beginnings in Walpole's *Castle of Otranto* (1764) had had no difficulty in attracting readers, the genre and its derivative types had generated no intellectual respect and was frequently accused of lacking those qualities of "high seriousness" expected of great literature. Even the acknowledged masterworks of the Gothic movement in its prime, the novels of Mrs. Ann Radcliffe, Monk Lewis, Charles Robert Maturin, and Mary Shelley, received scant mention by literary historians if indeed they were mentioned at all. A typical stricture can be heard in Henry A. Beers's *A History of English Romanticism in the Eighteenth Century* (1899) in which the first Gothic novelist, Horace Walpole, is dismissed as "a trifler and a fribble; and his incurable superficiality, dilettantism, and want of seriousness, made all his real cleverness of no avail when applied to such a subject as 'The Castle of Otranto.'"[3]

This state of scholarly indifference or hostility to the Gothic began to change radically and swiftly in the early 1950's when several American scholars began to take up Summers's challenge for reinvigorated Gothic studies. The influential Edmund Wilson had appraised the power and appropriateness of the Gothic in *Classics and Commercials: A Literary Chronicle of the Forties* (1951), while the Gothic was starting to seep into the academic curriculum. A young scholar, Robert D. Mayo, had written a doctoral dissertation (Princeton, 1938) on the unexplored relationship between Sir Walter Scott and the Gothic novelists. Mayo subsequently published several closely researched studies of the presence of the Gothic in the popular periodical literature of the Eighteenth Century. Thus, he had come into contact with the bleak bibliographical terrain in Gothic scholarship and when he came later to write a long essay entitled "Gothic Romance in the Magazines" for *Publications of the Modern Language Association* in 1950,[4] he was fully convinced of the critical need for a coherent bibliographical tool which would enable researchers to locate the widely scattered and proliferating body of writing on the subject. Nevertheless, no bibliography of secondary materials on the Gothic was forthcoming throughout the 1950's and 1960's while in the meantime interpretive writing about the Gothic had advanced into its major phase and was undergoing a kind of international explosion as books, articles, dissertations, and monographs multiplied and reeditions of the minor Gothic authors of the Eighteenth Century began to appear. By 1973 when the first checklist appeared the Gothic renaissance which Summers had anticipated and helped to launch and that Mayo had recognized in the early 1950's as already extensive enough to require bibliographical control was now swarming with scholarly activity. The sheer volume of writing on Gothicism was strangely reminiscent of the flood of Gothics in their hundreds at the end of the Eighteenth Century when Gothic fiction glutted the literary marketplace. The age of critical approval had arrived and students of the Gothic eagerly rushed to express their scholarly views or to react to the views of others in an effort to redefine, reassess, reread, or reinterpret Gothic fiction and its influence.

The prerequisite model study for bibliographers of the Gothic during the period of the 1970's was an article by the Poe scholar, Richard Benton, published in a double issue of the renamed *Emerson Society Quarterly* (now called *ESQ: A Journal of the American Renaissance*) for 1972. The issue itself was exclusively devoted to questions of interpretation raised by the matter and modes of American Gothicism. In Benton's important bibliographical essay, entitled "The Problems of Literary Gothicism,"[5] he summed up the contemporary state of Gothic studies, repeated the need for a solid book on Gothicism's distinctive American strain, and urged further efforts at bibliographical governance of the growing body of scholarship. Benton also aptly and accurately described some of the reasons behind the new emphasis on Gothic studies by observing that for many new critics Gothicism was "symbolic of the primordial content of man's unconscious." The psychological validity which had always lain at the core of the Gothic had gone undetected by outraged reviewers and had also been overlooked by cultural and literary historians who "have treated [Gothic fiction] with indifference or condescension, especially in its popular as opposed to its serious form."

The manifest necessity for up-to-date inventories and tabulations of writing on Gothic fiction was first satisfied in book form in Dan J. Mc Nutt's *The Eighteenth Century Gothic Novel: An Annotated Bibliography*, issued by Garland in 1975. Mc Nutt's bibliography is carefully segmented, historically selective, and impeccably thorough in its listings of work done on six major Gothic novelists of the Eighteenth Century, Horace Walpole, Clara Reeve, Charlotte Turner Smith, Ann Radcliffe, Matthew Gregory Lewis, and William Beckford. Scholarship on the American Goths and the Nineteenth-Century English Gothic writers including the Shelleys, Maturin, and later figures such as Joseph Sheridan Le Fanu was to have been collected in a projected second volume by Mc Nutt, but this addendum has not yet been published. Other secondary bibliographies of note are: B.F. Fisher's "Ancilla to the Gothic Tradition" (1976),[6] a checklist somewhat marred by lax criteria of selectivity, the annual bibliographies of Gothic studies appearing in the journal, *Gothic: The Review of Supernatural Horror Literature* (1978-1980),[7] and a superlative series of bibliographical essays together with checklists by Robert D. Spector in his recent *The English Gothic: A Bibliographical Guide to Writers from Horace Walpole to Mary Shelley*, published by Greenwood Press in 1984. Of marginal value are the seriously flawed secondary bibliographies of Narda L. Schwartz[8] and the bibliographical chapter on "Reference Sources" compiled by Mike Ashley in *Horror Literature: A Core Collection and Reference Guide* (1981).

In its inclusion of special subject areas and its coverage of German, French, and American and Canadian Gothic sources, this *Master List* attempts to be more comprehensive and international in scope than any of these prior bibliographies. The bibliography is logically structured and sub-divided to permit ease and rapidity of consultation for the researcher. Its fundamental organization is by author, then by various national divisions with other large areas of data made accessible to the researcher by means of directive chapter headings. For the researcher who is interested in acquiring the scholarship on a Gothic figure or period, the logical point of entry is the "Index of Authors and Artists," which collates all references to a Gothic writer occurring outside that writer's special segment of the bibliography if such a segment has been allotted. Thus, scholarship of importance on the American Gothic novelist, Charles Brockden Brown, is easily located by consulting the index in conjunction with the special Charles Brockden Brown bibliographical subdivision under "American Gothic Fiction: Individual Author Studies." Material on Gothic authors such as Bram Stoker and William Faulkner who have not been given separate subdivisions can be found by means of the index in which all names and titles are followed by item numbers which direct the user to the entry numbers assigned to each item in the text of the bibliography. "The Index of Critics" enables the researcher to assemble the critical opinions of any critic who has written extensively about the Gothic over a period of time or to isolate specific pieces of criticism when only the critic's name is known.

The preparation of doctoral dissertations on Gothic subjects can be used as one reliable index to the enduring appeal of the subject for professional and casual researchers. All doctoral dissertations cited throughout the *Master List* contain vital data about the year of the publication of the abstract and the sponsoring university in cases where such data is available. This procedure allows the investigator instantaneous access to the essential contents of the work as well as the means of obtaining the entire dissertation should the user wish to examine the whole study. Nearly one quarter of the approximately 2,500 entries are doctoral dissertations on the Gothic. This trend in Gothic criticism focuses in large part on the search for a satisfactory definition of the elusive term "American Gothic" or on questions of structure and symbolism in English Gothic fiction. Perhaps one out of every three dissertations studies the form from a feminist perspective. Presently, there is so much doctoral level writing on Gothic themes and variations that what was once only a segment of a brief bibliography in the 1973 checklist now deserves a separate bibliography of its own.

If there is any salient pattern to emerge from the multifarious analyses of Gothic fiction published during the last decade, this tendency involves the effort to address problems of taxonomy and generic classification raised by post-Romantic or "modernist" considerations of what the Gothic is and does. Is Gothic fiction best defined by its content (the so-called machinery or parts such as the haunted castle) or by intent (the evocation of a Gothic aesthetic of deep pleasure in fear and admiration for the supernatural)? Or is the genre best defined by a critical synthesis of content with intent? Furthermore, why should the American Gothic, a powerful tributary of the form which drew so liberally upon the technology of English Gothicism in its earliest phase, retain such a potent place in American letters all the way from the nightmares of Charles Brockden Brown to the rural Gothic of Flannery O'Connor and urban horrors of Joyce Carol Oates? The hermeneutics of horror and the semiotics of terror have also become favorite critical approaches for deciphering the irrational symbols of the Gothic world. The deconstructionist perspectives of Lacan and Derrida have also recently been brought to bear on the dissolving architecture and frenzied characters of the typical Gothic tale. Clearly, this once-lonely literary field is now quite overrun with sophisticated methodologies of every type and discipline. Summing up the situation in Gothic criticism today, one of the best modern bibliographers, R.D. Spector, has remarked: "Structuralists, deconstructionists, semiologists, Marxists, and feminists in surprising numbers now attempt to explain how and what the Gothic communicates."[9]

The primary task of the bibliographer is to systematize the large library of criticism of Gothic literature for the researcher's inspection and selection. The bibliographer cannot and indeed should not perform the duties of the critic in trying to explain the popularity of the Gothic as an object of intense analysis in recent years. Yet, one fact is inescapable in the compilation of the listings. Whatever the causes for a resurgence of interest in Gothicism might be, the passion to pursue the subject has apparently not yet peaked and shows no signs of abatement. In the introduction to the 1973 checklist, the bibliographer offered one speculation about the surge of interest in Gothic literature which began in the 1930's and intensified following the second World War. "Enormous social catastrophes which bring mankind to the margin of permanent disaster are apparently responsible for such Gothic revivals. But whether the Gothic novel is read for amoral diversion, for escapist release from dull reality, or as social prophecy about a world gone mad, the genre and its many mutations are here to stay. For, just as certainly as we are living beneath the atomic shadow, so we are also entering upon the Frankensteinian Renaissance."[10] If, like nature itself, any concentrated study of a literary movement also abhors a vacuum, then we may expect the renaissance in Gothic studies to continue undiminished into the next century.

Notes

1. Frederick S. Frank, "The Gothic Novel: A Checklist of Modern Criticism," *Bulletin of Bibliography*, 30 (1973): 45-54. The initial bibliography was updated by a second compilation in 1978: Frederick S. Frank, "The Gothic Novel: A Second Bibliography of Criticism," *Bulletin of Bibliography*, 35 (1978): 1-14, 52.

2. Montague Summers, *A Gothic Bibliography*. (London: Fortune Press, 1941; Rpt. New York: Russell & Russell, 1964), p. viii. Since the publication of Summers's exploratory bibliography, bibliographical description of the primary source,

the Gothic novels themselves, has advanced slowly, but much work remains to be done. Since 1978, there have appeared: Allen J. Hubin, *The Bibliography of Crime Fiction, 1749-1975: Listing All Mystery, Detective, Suspense, Police, and Gothic Fiction in Book Form Published in the English Language* (Del Mar, CA: Publisher's, 1979); Elsa J. Radcliffe, *Gothic Novels of the Twentieth Century: An Annotated Bibliography* (Metuchen, NJ: Scarecrow Press, 1979); Kay J. Mussell, *Women's Gothic and Romantic Fiction: A Reference Guide* (Westport, CT: Greenwood Press, 1981); Ann B. Tracy, *The Gothic Novel 1790-1830: Plot Summaries and Index to Motifs* (Lexington, KY: Kentucky UP, 1981); Frederick S. Frank, "The Gothic Romance: 1762-1820," in *Horror Literature: A Core Collection and Reference Guide*, ed. Marshall B. Tymn (New York: R.R. Bowker, 1981), pp. 3-175; Frederick S. Frank, *The First Gothics: A Critical Guide to the English Gothic Novel* (New York: Garland Publishing, 1987).

3. Henry A. Beers, "The Gothic Revival," in *A History of English Romanticism in the Eighteenth Century* (New York: Henry Holt, 1899), p. 240.

4. Robert D. Mayo, "Gothic Romance in the Magazines," *Publications of the Modern Language Association*, 65 (1950): 762-789.

5. Richard P. Benton, "The Problems of Literary Gothicism," ESQ: *A Journal of the American Renaissance*, 18 (1972): 5-9.

6. Benjamin Franklin Fisher IV, "Ancilla to the Gothic Tradition: A Supplementary Bibliography," *American Transcendental Quarterly*, 30 (1976): 22-36. A similar fragmentary effort is John A. Stoler, "One Hundred Years of English Gothic Fiction from Walpole's *Castle of Otranto* (1764) to Le Fanu's *Uncle Silas* (1864): *A Selected Annotated Bibliography of Criticism* (Erasmus Press Microfilm Series, 1975).

7. See various references in Chapter I of the *Master List* under "Gary W. Crawford," founder of the journal, *Gothic: The Review of Supernatural Horror Fiction*, and publisher-owner of The Gothic Press, Baton Rouge, LA. Annual bibliographies of Gothic studies are now published in pamphlet form.

8. Narda L. Schwartz, *A Selected, Annotated Bibliography of Literary History and Criticism of the English Gothic Novel (1764-1820) from 1956 Through 1971* (Fullerton, CA: No Publisher Indicated, 1973).

9. Robert D. Spector, *The English Gothic: A Bibliographic Guide to Writers from Horace Walpole to Mary Shelley* (Westport, CT: Greenwood Press, 1984). The

bibliographer gratefully acknowledges the indispensable value of Spector's work in the compilation of the *Master List*.

10. F. S. Frank, "The Gothic Novel: A Checklist of Modern Criticism," p. 46.

I. ENGLISH GOTHIC FICTION
Primary and Secondary Bibliographies, Special Collections, Research and Reference Works

0001. BLACK, Robert K. *The Sadleir-Black Gothic Collection*. *An Address Before the Bibliographical Society of the University of Virginia on May 12, 1949*. Charlottesville, VA : Pamphlet published by the Alderman Library of the University of Virginia, 1949, 15 pp.

0002. BLAKEY, Dorothy. *The Minerva Press, 1790-1820*. London : Printed for the Bibliographical Society by Oxford UP, 1939.

0003. BLEILER, E.F. *The Checklist of Science-Fiction and Supernatural Fiction*. Glen Rock, NJ : Firebell Books, 1978.

0004. _______. *The Guide to Supernatural Fiction. A Full Description of 1,775 Books From 1750 to 1960. Including Ghost Stories, Weird Fiction, Stories of Supernatural Horror, Fantasy, Gothic Novels, Occult Fiction, and Similar Literature*. Kent, OH : Kent State UP, 1983.

0005. _______. *Supernatural Fiction Writers*. 2 vols. New York : Charles Scribner's Sons, 1985.

0006. BLOCK, Andrew. *The English Novel; A Catalogue: 1740-1850*. London: Grafton, 1939.

0007. BRAUCHLI, Jakob. *Der Englische Schauer-roman um 1800. Unter Berücksichtigung der Unbekannten Bücher; Ein Beitrag zur Geschichte der Volksliteratur*. Weida, Germany : Thomas & Hubert, 1928.

0008. CRAWFORD, Gary William. "The Modern Masters 1920-1980," in *Horror Literature: A Core Collection and Reference Guide*, ed. Marshall B. Tymn. New York : R.R. Bowker, 1981, pp.276-369.

0009. CRAWFORD, Gary William, Frederick S. Frank, Benjamin Franklin Fisher IV, Kent Ljungquist. *The 1980 Bibliography of Gothic Studies*. Baton Rouge, LA : Gothic Press, 1983, pp.1-20.

0010. ENG, Steve. "Supernatural Verse in English," in *Horror Literature: A Core Collection and Reference Guide*, ed. Marshall B. Tymn. New York: R.R. Bowker, 1981, pp.401-452.

0011. FISHER, Benjamin Franklin IV. "Ancilla to the Gothic Tradition: A Supplementary Bibliography," American Transcendental Quarterly, 30 (1976): 22-36.

0012. ________. "The Residual Gothic Impulse: 1824-1873," in Horror Literature: A Core Collection and Reference Guide, ed. Marshall B. Tymn. New York : R.R. Bowker, 1981, pp.176-220.

0013. ________. The Gothic's Gothic: Study Aids to the Tale of Terror. New York : Garland Publishing, 1987.

0014. FRANK, Frederick. "The Gothic Novel: A Checklist of Modern Criticism," Bulletin of Bibliography, 30 (1973): 45-54.

0015. ________. "Correspondence--From Frederick S. Frank and John A. Stoler," Papers of the Bibliographical Society of America, 70 (1976): 513-515.

0016. ________. "The Gothic Novel: A Second Bibliography of Criticism," Bulletin of Bibliography, 35 (1978): 1-14, 52.

0017. FRANK, Frederick, Gary W. Crawford, Benjamin Franklin Fisher IV. "The 1978 Bibliography of Gothic Studies," Gothic: The Review of Supernatural Horror Fiction, 1 (1979): 65-67.

0018. ________. "The 1979 Bibliography of Gothic Studies," Gothic: The Review of Supernatural Horror Fiction, 2 (1980): 48-52.

0019. FRANK, Frederick S. "The Gothic Romance: 1762-1820," in Horror Literature: A Core Collection and Reference Guide. New York : R.R. Bowker, 1981, pp.3-175.

0020. ________. Guide to the Gothic: An Annotated Bibliography of Criticism. Metuchen, NJ : Scarecrow Press, 1984.

0021. ________. The First Gothics: A Critical Guide to the English Gothic Novel. New York : Garland Publishing, 1987.

0022. HAWKINS, Jean. "Ghost Stories and Tales of the Supernatural," Bulletin of Bibliography, 5 (1909): 142-145; 168-171.

0023. HUBIN, Allen J. The Bibliography of Crime Fiction: 1749-1975. Listing All Mystery, Detective, Suspense, Police, and Gothic Fiction in Book Form Published in the English Language. Del Mar, CA : Publisher's, 1979.

0024. LÉVY, Maurice. "Bibliographie Chronologique du Roman 'Gothique' 1764-1824," in Le Roman 'Gothique' Anglais 1764-1824. Toulouse, France : Association des Publications de la Faculté des Lettres et Sciences Humaines de Toulouse, 1968, pp.684-708.

0025. ________. "English Gothic and the French Imagination: A Calendar of Translations, 1767-1828," in The Gothic Imagination: Essays in Dark Romanticism, ed. G.R. Thompson. Pullman, WA : Washington State UP,

1974, pp.150-176.

0026. MAYO, Robert D. The English Novel in the Magazines, 1740-1815: With a Catalogue of 1,375 Magazine Novels and Novelettes. Evanston, IL : Northwestern UP, 1963.

0027. MC NUTT, Dan J. The Eighteenth-Century Gothic Novel: An Annotated Bibliography of Criticism and Selected Texts, foreword by Devendra P. Varma and Maurice Lévy. New York : Garland Publishing, 1974.

0028. MUSSELL, Kay J. "Gothic Novels," in Handbook of American Popular Culture, ed. M. Thomas Inge. Westport, CT : Greenwood Press, 1978, pp. 151-169.

0029. ______. Women's Gothic and Romantic Fiction: A Reference Guide. Westport, CT : Greenwood Press, 1981.

0030. RADCLIFFE, Elsa J. Gothic Novels of the Twentieth Century: An Annotated Bibliography. Metuchen, NJ : Scarecrow Press, 1979.

0031. RICHTER, David H. "The Gothic Impulse: Recent Studies," Dickens Studies Annual: Essays on Victorian Fiction, 11 (1983): 279-311.

0032. Sadleir-Black Gothic Collection. Charlottesville, VA : Mimeographed Listing of the Holdings in the Collection printed by the Alderman Library of the University of Virginia, n.d., 100 pp.

0033. SCHWARTZ, Narda Lacey. A Selected, Annotated Bibliography of Literary History and Criticism of the English Gothic Novel (1764-1820) from 1956 Through 1971. Fullerton, CA : No publisher indicated, 1973.

0034. SIEMON, Fred. Ghost Story Index: An Author-Title Index to More Than 2,200 Stories of Ghosts, Horrors, and the Macabre Appearing in 190 Books and Anthologies. San Jose, CA and Monroe, NY : Library Research Associates, 1967.

0035. SMITH, Warren H. "Recent Acquisitions in Gothic Fiction," Yale University Library Gazette, 8 (1934): 109-111.

0036. SPECTOR, Robert D. The English Gothic: A Bibliographic Guide to Writers from Horace Walpole to Mary Shelley. Westport, CT : Greenwood Press, 1984.

0037. STOLER, John A. "One Hundred Years of English Gothic Fiction from Walpole's Castle of Otranto (1764) to Le Fanu's Uncle Silas (1864): A Select Annotated Bibliography of Criticism," Erasmus Press Microfilm Series, 1975.

0038. STREETER, Harold W. "The Gothic Romance in France: Walpole, Reeve, Lewis, Radcliffe," in The Eighteenth Century English Novel in French Translation, A Bibliographical Study. New York : Columbia University Institute of French Studies, 1936; Rpt. New York : Benjamin Blom, 1970, pp.117-123.

0039. SULLIVAN, Jack. "Psychological, Antiquarian, and Cosmic Horror 1872-

1919," in Horror Literature: A Core Collection and Reference Guide, ed. Marshall B. Tymn. New York : R.R. Bowker, 1981, pp.221-275.

0040. SUMMERS, Montague. A Gothic Bibliography. London : Fortune Press, 1941; Rpt. New York : Russell & Russell, 1964.

0041. TRACY, Ann B. The Gothic Novel 1790-1830: Plot Summaries and Index to Motifs. Lexington, KY : Kentucky UP, 1981.

0042. TYMN, Marshall B., ed. Horror Literature: A Core Collection and Reference Guide, foreword by Peter Haining. New York : R.R. Bowker, 1981.

0043. VARMA, Devendra P. "The Starhemberg Collection," Illustrated London News, Christmas Number, 1983, pp.67-68.

0044. VINSON, James and D.L. Kirkpatrick. Twentieth-Century Romance and Gothic Writers. Detroit, MI : Gale, 1982.

II. ENGLISH GOTHIC FICTION

Literary Histories, Theories and Formal Definitions, Genre Studies

0045. ANDERSON, Howard. "Gothic Heroes," in The English Hero, 1660-1800, ed. Robert Folkenflik. Newark, DE : Delaware UP, 1982, pp.205-221.

0046. ANGLO, Michael. "Gothic Foundations," in Penny Dreadfuls and Other Victorian Horrors. London : Jupiter Press, 1978.

0047. ARNAUD, Pierre. "Crime et Châtiment dans le Roman Romantique," in La Mort, le Fantastique, le Surnaturel du XVIe Siècle à l'Époque Romantique, ed. Michele Plaisant. Villeneuve d'Ascq, France : Centre de Recherches sur l'Angleterre des Tudors à la Régence, Université de Lille III, PU Lille, 1981, pp.165-171.

0048. ASTLE, Richard Sharp. "Structures of Ideology in the English Gothic Novel," Dissertation Abstracts International, 38 (1978): 5490A (University of California at San Diego).

0049. BAKER, Donald Whitelaw. "Themes of Terror in Nineteenth-Century English Fiction: The Shift to the Internal," Dissertation Abstracts, 16 (1956): 118-119 (Brown University).

0050. BAKER, Ernest. "The Novel of Sentiment and the Gothic Romance," in The History of the English Novel. 11 vols. New York : Barnes & Noble, 1924-39; Rpt. 1975, V, 175-227.

0051. BARCLAY, Glen St. John. Anatomy of Horror: The Masters of Occult Fiction. New York : St. Martin's Press, 1979.

0052. BASSIN, Henry A. "The Gothic Transformation: Developments in the British Gothic Romance," Dissertation Abstracts International, 35 (1974): 6700A (University of Indiana).

0053. BAYER-BERENBAUM, Linda. "The Expansion of Consciousness in Gothic Literature and Art," Dissertation Abstracts International, 37 (1977): 4361A-4362A (Florida State University).

0054. ______. The Gothic Imagination: Expansion in Gothic Literature and Art. Rutherford, Madison, and Teaneck, NJ : Fairleigh Dickinson UP,

1982.

0055. BEERS, Henry A. "The Gothic Revival," in *A History of English Romanticism in the Eighteenth Century*. New York : Henry Holt, 1926, pp.221-264.

0056. BELSEY, Catherine. "The Romantic Construction of the Unconscious," in *1789: Reading, Writing, Revolution: Proceedings of the Essex Conference on the Sociology of Literature*, July 1981, eds. Francis Barker, Jay Bernstein, Peter Hulme, Margaret Iverson, Jennifer Stone. Colchester, England : Essex UP, 1982, pp.67-80.

0057. BHALLA, Alok. "Shades of the Preternatural: Thematic and Structural Essays on the Gothic Novel," *Dissertation Abstracts International*, 39 (1978): 2948A-2949A (Kent State University).

0058. BIERWIRTH, Gerhard. "Die Problematik des Englischen Schauerromans: Ein Kritisches Modell zur Behandlung Diskriminierter Literatur," Unpublished Doctoral Dissertation, Frankfurt/M, 1970.

0059. BIRKHEAD, Edith. *The Tale of Terror: A Study of the Gothic Romance*. London : Constable, 1921; Rpt. New York : Russell & Russell, 1963.

0060. ______. "Sentiment and Sensibility in the Eighteenth-Century Novel," *Essays and Studies*, 11 (1925): 22-116.

0061. BLAND, D.S. "Endangering the Reader's Neck: Background Description in the Novel," *Criticism*, 3 (1961): 121-139.

0062. BLEILER, E.F., ed. *Supernatural Fiction Writers: Fantasy and Horror*. New York : Charles Scribner's Sons, 1985.

0063. BLONDEL, Jacques. "On 'Metaphysical Prisons,'" *Durham University Journal*, 32 (1971): 133-138.

0064. BOWMAN, Barbara. "The Gothic Novel: A Structuralist Inquiry," *Dissertation Abstracts International*, 38 (1978): 4175A (University of Maryland).

0065. BUNNELL, Charlene. "The Gothic: Its Worlds and Visions," Master's Thesis, Western Illinois University, 1982.

0066. BURRA, Peter. "Baroque and Gothic Sentimentalism," *Farrago*, 3 (1930): 159-182.

0067. CARTER, Mary Louise. "'Fiend, Spectre, or Delusion?': Narrative Doubt and the Supernatural in Gothic Fiction," *Dissertation Abstracts International*, 47 (1986): 908A (University of California, Irvine).

0068. CHURCH, Elizabeth. "The Gothic Romance: Its Origins and Development," Unpublished Doctoral Dissertation, Harvard University, 1913.

0069. CHURCH, Reginald C. "Classic History and Gothic Romance," in *English Literature in the Eighteenth Century; With a Preface on the Relations Between Literary History and Literary Criticism*. London : University Tutorial Press, 1953.

0070. COLEMAN, William E. "On the Discrimination of Gothicisms," Dissertation Abstracts International, 31 (1970): 2871A (City University of New York).

0071. ______. On the Discrimination of Gothicisms. New York : Arno Press, 1980.

0072. COOKE, Arthur. "Some Side-lights on the Theory of Gothic Romance," Modern Language Quarterly, 12 (1951): 429-436.

0073. DAY, Patrick. In the Circles of Fear and Desire: A Study in Gothic Fantasy. Chicago : Chicago UP, 1985.

0074. DOODY, Margaret Anne. "Deserts, Ruins, and Troubled Waters: Female Dreams in Fiction and the Development of the Gothic Novel," Genre, 10 (1977): 529-572.

0075. DUFFY, Maureen. "Gothick Horror," in The Erotic World of Faery. London: Hodder & Stoughton, 1972.

0076. EHLERS, Leigh Ann. "From Polarity to Perspective: The Development of Structure and Character in Gothic Fiction," Dissertation Abstracts International, 39 (1978): 294A (University of Florida).

0077. ENGEL, Leonard. "The Role of the Enclosure in the English and American Gothic Romance," Essays in Arts and Sciences, 11 (1982): 59-68.

0078. ENOMOTO, Futoshi. "Gothic Shosetsu Shikan: Jinbutsu Wo Chushin to Shite," in Eikoku Shosetsu Kenkyu: Dai 12 Satsu. Tokyo, Japan : Shinozaki Shorin, 1977, pp.1-42.

0079. FIEROBE, Claude. "Le Portrait dans le Récit Fantastique," in Vivante Tradition, Sources et Racines: Evolution de Quelques Formes et Forces en Littérature et Civilisation Anglaises, eds. Olivier Lutuad, Marie-Madeleine Martinet, Roger Lejosne. Paris : Centre d'Histoire des Idées dans les Britanniques, 1982, pp.43-52.

0080. FISKE, Christabel. "The Tales of Terror," Conservative Review, March, 1900, pp.37-74.

0081. FLEENOR, Juliann E., ed. The Female Gothic. Montreal, Canada : Eden Press, 1983.

0082. FOSTER, James R. The History of the Pre-Romantic Novel in England. London : Oxford UP, 1949.

0083. GARBER, Frederick. "Meaning and Mode in Gothic Fiction," in Racism in the Eighteenth Century. Cleveland, OH : Case Western Reserve UP, 1973, pp.155-169.

0084. GARRETT, John. "The Eternal Appeal of the Gothic," The Sphinx: A Magazine of Literature and Society, 2, number 4 (1977): 1-7.

0085. GARTE, Haujörg. Kunstform Schauerroman. Eine Morphorlbegriffsbestimmung die Sensationromans in 18. Jahrhunderts von Walpole's "Castle of Otranto" bis Jean Pauls "Titan!". Leipzig : Garte, 1935.

0086. GOULD, Ellen Yvette. "The Gothic Novel: An Exercise in Definition," Dissertation Abstracts International, 38 (1977): 3514A (SUNY at Buffalo).

0087. "The Gothic Spell," Times Literary Supplement, March 8, 1941, p.115.

0088. GRAHAM, John. "Character and Description in the Romantic Novel," Studies in Romanticism, 5 (1966): 208-218.

0089. HAGGERTY, George Edgar. "Gothic Fiction from Walpole to James: A Study of Formal Development," Dissertation Abstracts International, 40 (1980): 4036A (University of California at Berkeley).

0090. ______. "Fact and Fantasy in the Gothic Novel," Nineteenth-Century Fiction, 39 (1985): 379-391.

0091. HARING-SMITH, Tori. "The Gothic Novel: A Tale of Terrors Tamed," Wissenschaftliche Zeitschrift der Wilhelm-Pieck-Universität (Rostock), 31, number 8 (1982): 49-55.

0092. HART, Francis R. "The Experience of Character in the English Gothic Novel," in Experience in the Novel, ed. Roy Harvey Pearce. New York: Columbia UP, 1968, pp.83-105.

0093. ______. "The Limits of the Gothic: The Scottish Example," in Racism in the Eighteenth Century. Cleveland, OH : Case Western Reserve UP, 1973, pp.137-153.

0094. ______. "Scottish Variations of the Gothic Novel," in The Scottish Novel from Smollett to Spark. Cambridge, MA : Harvard UP, 1976, pp. 13-30.

0095. HASLAG, Josef. "Gothic" in 17 und 18 Jahrhundert. Eine Wort-und-Ideengeschichtliche Untersuchung. Köln, West Germany : Böhlau, 1963.

0096. HENDERSON, James. "The Gothic Novel in Wales, 1790-1820," National Library of Wales Journal, 11 (1960): 244-254.

0097. HENNESSY, Brendan. The Gothic Novel. London : Longman for the British Book Council, 1978.

0098. ______. "The Gothic Novel," in British Writers, ed. Ian Scott-Kilvert. New York : Charles Scribner's Sons, 1980, III, 324-346.

0099. HOFMANN, Otto. Studien zum Englischen Schauerroman. Halle, Germany : H. John, 1915.

0100. HOGLE, Jerrold E. "The Restless Labyrinth: Cryptonymy in the Gothic Novel," Arizona Quarterly, 36 (1980): 330-358.

0101. HOLBROOK, William C. "The Adjective 'Gothique' in the Eighteenth Century," Modern Language Notes, 56 (1941): 498-503.

0102. HOLLAND, Norman and Leona F. Sherman. "Gothic Possibilities," New Literary History, 8 (1977): 278-294.

0103. HORWITZ, Sylvia. "A Study of the Nature and Function of the Devices Used in Gothic Fiction in England (1764-1820)," Unpublished Doctoral Dissertation, University of Virginia, 1958.

0104. HOWELLS, Coral Ann. "The Presentation of Emotion in the English Gothic Novels of the Late Eighteenth and Early Nineteenth Centuries, With Particular Reference to Ann Radcliffe's Mysteries of Udolpho, Matthew G. Lewis's The Monk, Mary Shelley's Frankenstein, Charles Robert Maturin's Melmoth the Wanderer, Charlotte Bronte's Jane Eyre, and Works by the Minor Minerva Press Novelists Regina Maria Roche and Mary Anne Radcliffe, Doctoral Dissertation, London University, 1969.

0105. _______. Love, Mystery, and Misery: Feeling in Gothic Fiction. London : Athlone Press, 1979.

0106. HUDSON, Randolph Hoyt. "'Hence Vain Deluding Joys': The Anatomy of Eighteenth-Century English Gothicism," Dissertation Abstracts, 22 (1962): 4344 (Stanford University).

0107. HUME, R.D. "Gothic Versus Romantic: A Revaluation of the Gothic Novel," Publications of the Modern Language Association, 84 (1969): 282-290.

0108. _______. "Lévy on the Gothic Novel," Poe Studies, 4 (1971): 58-59.

0109. IDE, Hiroyuki. "Gendai Igirisu; u Genso Shosetsu to Goshikku," in Shiro to Memai: Goshikku o Yomu. Tokyo, Japan : Kokusho Kankokai, 1982, pp.119-138.

0110. JACOBS, Maureen Sheehan. "Beyond the Castle: The Development of the Paradigmatic Female Story," Dissertation Abstracts International, 41 (1980): 679A-680A (American University).

0111. JACQUETTE, Arlene. "'Vile Pruriency for Fresh Adventures': Sexuality and Storytelling in Selected Eighteenth-Century and Gothic Novels," Dissertation Abstracts International, 38 (1977): 783A (Vanderbilt University).

0112. JENNINGS, Richard Jerome. "La Fenêtre Gothique: The Influence of Tragic Form on the Structure of the Gothic Novel," Dissertation Abstracts International, 44 (1983): 760A (Ball State University).

0113. KANJI, M. "The Irrational and Supernatural in the English Novel, 1780-1891," Unpublished Doctoral Dissertation, Sheffield University, 1980.

0114. KAUFMAN, Pamela. "Burke, Freud, and the Gothic," Studies in Burke and His Time, 13 (1972): 2178-2192.

0115. KEECH, James M. "The Survival of the Gothic Response," Studies in the Novel, 6 (1974): 130-144.

0116. KEELING, Thomas Harvey. "The Grotesque Vision: Structure and Aesthetics in the British Gothic Novel," Dissertation Abstracts International, 38 (1977): 2809A (University of California at Los Angeles.

0117. KIELY, Robert. The Romantic Novel in England. Cambridge, MA : Harvard UP, 1972.

0118. KILLEN, Alice M. Le Roman Terrifiant ou Roman Noir de Walpole à Anne Radcliffe et son Influence sur la Littérature Française Jusqu'en 18-40. Paris, France : G. Cèes, 1915; Rpt. Geneva, Switzerland : Slatkine, 1984.

0119. KLEIN, Jürgen. Der Gotische Roman und die Ästhetik des Bösen. Darmstadt, West Germany : Wissenschaftliche, 1975.

0120. ______. "Introduction," to England Zwischen Aufklärung und Romantik: Studien zur Literatur und Gesellschaft einer Übergangsepoche. Tübingen, West Germany : Narr, 1983, pp.11-20.

0121. KOIKE, Shigeru. "Identity no Jikenbo: Goshikku Shosetsu to Suiri Shosetsu," in Shiro to Memai: Goshikku o Yomu. Tokyo, Japan : Kokusho Kokusho Kankokai, 1982, pp.359-373.

0122. KOIKE, Shigeru, Masao Shimura, Takao Tomiyama, eds. Shiro to Menai: Goshikku o Yomu. Tokyo, Japan : Kokusho Kankokai, 1983.

0123. LADYGIN, M.B. "K Voprusu ob Evoliutsii Zhanra 'Romana Uzhasa' v Angliiskoi Literature Vtoroi Poloviny XVIII-Nachalo XIX vv," Sbornik Nauchchnykh Trudov Sverdlovskogo Pedagogicheskogo Institituta (Sverdlovsk), 319 (1979): 3-15.

0124. LANG, Andrew. "The Supernatural in Fiction," in Adventures Among Books. London : Longman, Green, 1905, pp.273-276.

0125. LEA, Sydney L.W. "Gothic to Fantastic: Readings in Supernatural Fiction," Dissertation Abstracts International, 34 (1972): 323A (Yale University).

0126. ______. Gothic to Fantastic: Readings in Gothic Fiction. New York : Arno Press, 1980.

0127. LEEUWEN, Frederike van. "Female Gothic: The Discourse of the Other," Revista Canaria de Estudios Ingleses, 4 (1982): 33-44.

0128. LE TELLIER, Robert I. "The Intensifying Vision of Evil: The Gothic Novel (1760-1820) as a Self-Contained Literary Cycle," Unpublished Master's Thesis, Rhodes University, 1977.

0129. ______. An Intensifying Vision of Evil: The Gothic Novel (1764-1820) as a Self-Contained Literary Cycle. Salzburg, Austria : Institut für Anglistik & Amerikanistik, Universität Salzburg, 1980.

0130. LEVY, Maurice. "Le Premier Renouveau et la Sensibilité Anglaise au Milieu du Dix-Huitième Siècle," Etudes Anglaises, 14 (1961): 349-349-350.

0131. ______. Le Roman "Gothique" Anglais, 1764-1824. Toulouse, France : Association des Publications de la Faculté des Lettres et Sciences Humaines de Toulouse, 1968.

0132. ______. "Images du Roman Noir," in Die Buchillustration im 18. Jahrhundert: Colloquium der Arbeitsstelle 18. Jahrhundert Gesamthochschule Wuppertal Universität Münster Düsseldorf vom 3. bis 5. Oktober, 1978. Heidelberg, West Germany, 1980, pp.156-165.

0133. ______. "Gothique et Fantastique," Europe, 611 (1980): 41-48.

0134. ______. "Les Illustrations du Roman 'Noir' en France à la Fin du XVIIIe Siècle," in L'Illustration du Livre et la Littérature an XVIIIe Siècle France et en Pologne, ed. Zdislaw Libera. Warsaw, Poland : U de Varsovie, 1982, pp.123-134.

0135. ______. "Le Roman Gothique: Genre Anglais," Europe, 659 (March, 1984): 5-13.

0136. LEWIS, Paul. "Fearful Questions, Fearful Answers: The Intellectual Functions of Gothic Fiction," Dissertation Abstracts International, 38 (1977): 2791A-2792A (University of New Hampshire).

0137. ______. "Fearful Lessons: The Didacticism of the Early Gothic Novel," College Language Association Journal, 23 (1980): 470-484.

0138. ______. "Beyond Mystery: Emergence from Delusion as a Pattern in Gothic Fiction," Gothic: The Review of Supernatural Horror Fiction, 2 (1980): 7-13.

0139. ______. "Mysterious Laughter: Humor and Fear in Gothic Fiction," Genre, 14 (1981): 309-327.

0140. LONGUEIL, Alfred E. "The Word 'Gothic' in Eighteenth Century Criticism," Modern Language Notes, 38 (1923): 453-460.

0141. LOVECRAFT, Howard Phillips. Supernatural Horror in Literature. New York : Ben Abramson, 1945; Rpt. New York : Dover Publications, 1973.

0142. LÜSEBRINK, Hans-Jürgen. "La Bastille: Château Gothique," Europe, 659 (1984): 104-112.

0143. LYDENBERG, Robin. "Gothic Architecture and Fiction: A Survey of Critical Responses," Centennial Review, 22 (1978): 95-109.

0144. MAC ANDREW, Elizabeth. The Gothic Tradition in Fiction. New York : Columbia UP, 1979.

0145. MADOFF, Mark Samuel. "Ambivalent and Nostalgic Attitudes in Selected Gothic Novels," Dissertation Abstracts International, 38 (1977):

284A-285A (University of British Columbia).

0146. ______. "The Chief of Conspiracies," English Studies in Canada, 6 (1980): 409-420.

0147. MATHEWS, John Robert. "Ghostly Language: A Theory of Gothic Discourse," Dissertation Abstracts International, 45 (1984): 529A (Cornell University).

0148. MAYERSBERG, Paul. "The Corridors of the Mind," The Listener, 74 (1965): 959-960.

0149. MAYO, Robert D. "How Long Was Gothic Fiction in Vogue?" Modern Language Notes, 58 (1943): 58-64.

0150. MC CARTHY, Mary. "Can There Be a Gothic Literature?" Johan Huizinga Lecture. Amsterdam, The Netherlands : Uitgeverij De Harmonie, 1973.

0151. MC INTYRE, Clara. "Were the Gothic Novels Gothic?" Publications of the Modern Language Association, 36 (1921): 644-667.

0152. MISE, Raymond W. "The Gothic Heroine and the Nature of the Gothic Novel," Dissertation Abstracts International, 31 (1970): 3513A (University of Washington).

0153. ______. The Gothic Heroine and the Nature of the Gothic Novel. New York : Arno Press, 1980.

0154. MÖBIUS, Hans. The Gothic Romance. Leipzig, Germany : Grimme und Treomel, 1902.

0155. MOERS, Ellen. "Traveling Heroinism: Gothic for Heroines," in Literary Women. Garden City, NY : Doubleday, 1976, pp.122-140.

0156. MORRIS, D.B. "Gothic Sensibility," New Literary History, 16 (1985): 299-319.

0157. MORSE, David. "The Social Novel and the Gothic," and "The Transposition of the Gothic," in Romanticism: A Structural Analysis. Totowa, NJ : Barnes & Noble, 1982, pp.13-49; pp.50-103.

0158. NAPIER, Elizabeth R. The Failure of the Gothic: Problems of Disjunction in an Eighteenth-Century Literary Form. New York : Oxford UP, 1986.

0159. NEILL, S. Diana. "The Gothic Romances," in A Short History of the English Novel. London : Jarrolds, 1951.

0160. NELSON, Lowry Jr. "Night Thoughts on the Gothic Novel," Yale Review, 52 (1963): 236-257; Rpt. in Pastoral and Romance, ed. Eleanor Terry Lincoln. Englewood Cliffs, NJ : Prentice-Hall, 1969, pp.259-267.

0161. NOCHIMSON, Martha. "Gothic Novel," in Critical Survey of Long Fiction, ed. Frank Magill. Englewood Cliffs, NJ : Salem Press, 1983, VIII, pp.3121-3131.

0162. NOJIMA, Hidekatsu. "Eikoku Roman ha to Goshikku Shosetsu Hiraita Shizen to Tojita Shizen," in Shiro to Memai: Goshikku o Yomu. Tokyo, Japan : Kokusho Kankokai, 1982, pp.11-34.

0163. NOLLEN, Elizabeth Mahn. "The Gothic Experience: Female Imprisonment, Madness, and Escape in Selected Texts by Women Writers," Dissertation Abstracts International, 46 (1985): 159A (University of Indiana).

0164. NORTON, Rictor. "Aesthetic Gothic Horror," Yearbook of Comparative and General Literature, 21 (1972): 31-40.

0165. NOVAK, Maximillian E. "Gothic Fiction and the Grotesque," Novel: A Forum on Fiction, 13 (1979): 50-67.

0166. OATES, Joyce Carol. "Wonderlands," Georgia Review, 38 (1984): 487-506.

0167. ONOCHIE, B.C. "Changing Expressions of Gothicism in English Fiction from The Castle of Otranto to Wuthering Heights," Unpublished Doctoral Dissertation, University of Ibadan, 1972.

0168. OTTEN, Kurt. "Neuansätze zur Interpretation des Gotischen Romans," in Literatur als Kritik des Lebens. Heidelberg, West Germany : Quelle und Meyer, 1975, pp.137-147.

0169. ______. "Der Englische Schauerroman," in Europäische Romantik II, ed. Klaus Heitmann. Wiesbaden, West Germany : Athenaion, 1982, pp. 215-242.

0170. PAULSON, Ronald. "Gothic Fiction and the French Revolution," Journal of English Literary History, 48 (1981): 532-554.

0171. ______. "Review of 'Gothic Novels. Series III,'" Eighteenth-Century Studies, 16 (1982): 427-432.

0172. PEAVOY, John Roger. "Artificial Terrors and Real Horrors: The Supernatural in Gothic Fiction," Dissertation Abstracts International, 42 (1981): 714A-715A (Brandeis University).

0173. PENZOLDT, Peter. The Supernatural in Fiction. London : P. Nevill, 1952; Rpt. New York : Humanities Press, 1965.

0174. PETERSON, Clell T. "Spotting the Gothic Novel," Graduate Student of English, 1 (1957): 14-15.

0175. PLATZNER, Robert L. and Robert D. Hume. "'Gothic Versus Romantic': A Rejoinder," Publications of the Modern Language Association, 86 (1971): 266-274.

0176. ______. "The Metaphysical Novel in England: The Romantic Phase," Dissertation Abstracts International, 33 (1972): 2390A (University of Rochester).

0177. _______. The Metaphysical Novel in England: The Romantic Phase. New York : Arno Press, 1980.

0178. POOVEY, Mary Louise. "The Novel as Imaginative Order," Dissertation Abstracts International, 37 (1977): 4374A (University of Virginia).

0179. PRAZ, Mario. The Romantic Agony, trans. Angus Davidson. London : Oxford UP, 1933; Rpt. New York : Meredian Books, 1960.

0180. PREU, James A. "The Tale of Terror," English Journal, 47 (1958): 243-247.

0181. PRICE, Frederick W. "The Concept of Character in the Eighteenth-Century Gothic Romance," Dissertation Abstracts International, 32 (1972): 6388A-6389A (Princeton University).

0182. PUNTER, David. The Literature of Terror: A History of Gothic Fiction from 1765 to the Present Day. London and New York : Longman, 1980.

0183. QUENNELL, Peter. "The Moon Stood Still on Strawberry Hill," Horizon Magazine, 11 (1969): 113-119.

0184. RAILO, Eino. The Haunted Castle: A Study of the Elements of English Romanticism. London : E.P. Dutton, 1927; Rpt. New York : Humanities Press, 1964; Rpt. New York : Gordon Press, 1974.

0185. REDDIN, Chitra Pershad. "Forms of Evil in the Gothic Novel," Unpublished Doctoral Dissertation, Dalhousie University, 1977.

0186. _______. Forms of Evil in the Gothic Novel. New York : Arno Press, 1980.

0187. REED, Ronald L. "The Function of Folklore in Selected English Gothic Novels," Dissertation Abstracts International, 33 (1972): 284A (Texas Technological University).

0188. REILLY, Donald T. "The Interplay of the Natural and the Unnatural: A Definition of the Gothic Romance," Dissertation Abstracts International, 31 (1970): 2353A (University of Pittsburgh).

0189. ROBERTS, Bette B. "The Gothic Romance: Its Appeal to Women Writers and Readers in Late Eighteenth-Century England," Dissertation Abstracts International, 36 (1975): 6119A (University of Massachusetts).

0190. _______. The Gothic Romance: Its Appeal to Women Writers and Readers in Late Eighteenth-Century England. New York : Arno Press, 1980.

0191. ROBERTS, R. Ellis. "The Other Side," Life and Letters, 10 (1934): 691-701.

0192. ROGERS, Winfield H. "The Reaction Against Melodramatic Sentimentality in the English Novel, 1796-1830," Publications of the Modern Language Association, 49 (1934): 98-122.

0193. RONALD, Margaret A. "Functions of Setting in the Novel: From Mrs. Radcliffe to Charles Dickens," *Dissertation Abstracts International*, 31 (1971): 5373A (Northwestern University).

0194. _______. *Functions of Setting in the Novel: From Mrs. Radcliffe to Charles Dickens*. New York : Arno Press, 1980.

0195. RUSTOWSKI, Adam. "Angielska Powiesc Grozy Lat 1760-1800: Proba Redefinicji," *Acta Philologica*, 6 (1974): 201-242.

0196. _______. "Convention and Generic Instability of the English Gothic Novel," *Studia Anglica Posnaniensia: An International Review of English Studies*, 8 (1976): 175-187.

0197. SAAGPAKK, Paul F. "A Survey of Psychopathology in British Literature from Shakespeare to Hardy," *Literature and Psychology*, 18 (1968): 135-165.

0198. SANDY, Stephen Merrill. "Studies in the Form of the Romantic Novel: *Otranto* to *Waverley*," Doctoral Dissertation, Harvard University, 1963.

0199. _______. *The Raveling of the Novel: Studies in Romantic Fiction from Walpole to Scott*. New York : Arno Press, 1980.

0200. SCARBOROUGH, Dorothy. *The Supernatural in Modern English Fiction*. New York : G.P. Putnam's Sons, 1917; Rpt. New York : Octagon Books, 1967.

0201. SEDGWICK, Eve Kosofsky. "The Coherence of Gothic Conventions," *Dissertation Abstracts International*, 37 (1976): 301A (Yale University).

0202. _______. *The Coherence of Gothic Conventions*. New York : Arno Press, 1980.

0203. SHERBURN, George. "Gothic Romance and the Novel of Doctrine," in *A Literary History of England*, ed. Albert C. Baugh. New York : Appleton-Century-Crofts, 1948, pp.1192-1199.

0204. SKILTON, David. "Gothic, Romantic, and Heroic," in *The English Novel: Defoe to the Victorians*. New York : Barnes & Noble, 1977, pp.59-79.

0205. STEEVES, Harrison R. *Before Jane Austen: The Shaping of the English Novel in the Eighteenth Century*. New York : Holt, Rinehart, and Winston, 1965.

0206. STERN, Philip Van Doren. "Tales of Terror," *Saturday Review*, March 14, 1942, pp.3-4, 20.

0207. STEVENS, L. Robert. "The Exorcism of England's Gothic Demon," *Midwest Quarterly*, 14 (1973): 151-164.

0208. STEVENSON, Lionel. "Terror and Edification," in *The English Novel: A Panorama*. Cambridge, MA : Harvard UP, 1960, pp.148-176.

0209. SUMMERS, Montague. "The Illustrations of the Gothick Novels," Connoisseur, 98 (1936): 266-271.

0210. ______. The Gothic Quest: A History of the Gothic Novel. London : Fortune Press, 1938; Rpt. New York : Russell & Russell, 1964.

0211. SUZUKI, Hiroyuki. "Goshikku Bungaku to Kenchiku to Fukko," in Shiro to Memai: Goshikku o Yomu, eds. Shigeru Koike, Masao Shimura, Takao Tomiyama. Tokyo, Japan : Kokusho Kankokai, 1982, pp.93-118.

0212. TAKAYAMA, Osamu. "A Background of Literary Gothicism in Eighteenth-Eighteenth-Century England," Annual Reports, Doshisha Women's College, Kyoto, Japan, 25 (1974): 48-64.

0213. THOMPSON, G.R., ed. The Gothic Imagination: Essays in Dark Romanticism. Pullman, WA : Washington State UP, 1974.

0214. ______. "Romanticism and the Gothic Tradition," in The Gothic Imagination: Essays in Dark Romanticism. Pullman, WA : Washington State UP, 1974, pp.1-10.

0215. ______. "Gothic Fiction and the Romantic Age," in Romantic Gothic Tales, 1790-1840. New York : Harper & Row, 1979, pp.1-54.

0216. THORNBURG, Thomas R. "The Quester and the Castle: The Gothic Novel as Myth, With Special Reference to Bram Stoker's Dracula," Dissertation Abstracts International, 31 (1970): 4752A (Ball State University).

0217. TOMPKINS, J.M.S. The Popular Novel in England, 1770-1800. London : Constable, 1932; Rpt. London : Methuen, 1969.

0218. TRACY, Ann Blaisdell. "Patterns of Fear in the Gothic Novel, 1790-1830," Dissertation Abstracts International, 38 (1977): 3460A (University of Toronto).

0219. ______. "Gothic, Had-I-But-Known, Damsel-in-Distress: Stalking the Elusive Distinction," in Murderess Ink, ed. Dilys Winn. New York : Workman Publishing, 1979, pp.14-17.

0220. ______. Patterns of Fear in the Gothic Novel, 1790-1830. New York : Arno Press, 1980.

0221. TWITCHELL, James B. Dreadful Pleasures: An Anatomy of Modern Horror. New York : Oxford UP, 1985.

0222. VAN LUCHENE, Stephen Robert. "Essays in Gothic Fiction: From Horace Walpole to Mary Shelley," Dissertation Abstracts International, 34 (1974): 4220A-4221A (Notre Dame University).

0223. ______. Essays in Gothic Fiction: From Horace Walpole to Mary Shelley. New York : Arno Press, 1980.

0224. VARMA, Devendra P. The Gothic Flame: Being a History of the Gothic Novel in England: Its Origins, Efflorescence, Disintegration and Residuary Influences, intro. J.M.S. Tompkins, foreword by Herbert

Read. London : A. Barker, 1957; Rpt. New York : Russell & Russell, 1966.

0225. _______. "The Gothic Fantasy, Or Landscape of Dreams," An Address at the Gothic Symposium of the Modern Language Association of America, December 28, 1973. Halifax, NS : Printed as a pamphlet by Dalhousie University, 1973, pp.1-11.

0226. _______. "The Ripples from 'Otranto,'" Folio Magazine, Winter, 1976, pp.10-18.

0227. _______. "On Field Researches in Gothicism," The Sphinx: A Magazine of Literature and Society, 2, number 4 (1977): 17-24.

0228. VARNADO, S.I. "The Idea of the Numinous in Gothic Literature," in The Gothic Imagination: Essays in Dark Romanticism, ed. G.R. Thompson. Pullman, WA : Washington State UP, 1974, pp.11-21.

0229. VERZEA, Ileana. "Intre Modern si Moda: Note Asupra Romanului 'Gothic' in Anglia Secolului XVIII," Revista de Istorie si Teorie Literara, 30 (1981): 521-528.

0230. WAGENKNECHT, Edward. "The Renascence of Wonder," in Cavalcade of the English Novel. New York : Henry Holt, 1954, pp.110-133.

0231. WATT, William Whyte. Shilling Shockers of the Gothic School: A Study of Chapbook Gothic Romances. Cambridge, MA : Harvard UP, 1932; Rpt. New York : Russell & Russell, 1967.

0232. WILSON, Angus. "Evil in the English Novel," The Listener, 69 (January 10, 1963): 63-65.

0233. _______. "Evil in the English Novel," Kenyon Review, 29 (1967): 167-194.

0234. WILSON, Edmund. "A Treatise on the Tales of Horror," in Classics and Commercials: A Literary Chronicle of the Forties. London : Allen, 1951, pp.172-181.

0235. WILT, Judith. Ghosts of the Gothic: Austen, Eliot, and Lawrence. Princeton, NJ : Princeton UP, 1980.

0236. WOLF, Leonard. "Review of Gothic Novels Edited by Sir Devendra Varma," New York Times Book Review, January 14, 1973, pp.2, 28.

0237. WOOLF, Virginia. "Gothic Romances," in Collected Essays. London : Hogarth Press, 1966, I, pp.131-133.

0238. WRIGHT, Walter Francis. Sensibility in English Prose Fiction, 1760-1814: A Reinterpretation. Urbana, IL : Illinois UP; Illinois Studies in Language and Literature Number 22, Numbers 3-4, (1937).

0239. ZIRKER, Joan Mc Tigue. "The Gothic Tradition in English Fiction, 1764-1824," Dissertation Abstracts International, 35 (1974): 422A (University of Indiana).

III. ENGLISH GOTHIC FICTION

Individual Author Studies

William Beckford
(1760-1844)

0240. ALEXANDER, Boyd. "William Beckford: Man of Taste," History Today, 10 (1960): 686-694.

0241. _______. "The Decay of Beckford's Genius," in William Beckford of Fonthill, 1760-1844. Bicentenary Essays, ed. Fatma Moussa Mahmoud. Cairo, Egypt : C. Tsoumas, 1960; Rpt. Port Washington, NY : Kennikat Press, 1972.

0242. _______. "William Beckford of Fonthill," Yale University Library Gazette, 35 (1961): 161-169.

0243. _______. England's Wealthiest Son: A Study of William Beckford. London : Centaur Press, 1962.

0244. ANDERSON, Jorgen. "Giant Dreams: Piranesi's Influence in England," English Miscellany, 3 (1952): 49-59.

0245. ARMOUR, Richard W. "The Caliph of Fonthill," Reading and Collecting, 1 (1937): 9-10.

0246. BABB, James T. "William Beckford of Fonthill," Yale University Library Gazette, 41 (1966): 60-69.

0247. "Beckford the Caliph: A Traveller of Two Worlds, Passion and Fantasy," Times Literary Supplement, May 6, 1944, p.222.

0248. BELL, C.F. "William Beckford," Times Literary Supplement, May 13, 1944, p.235.

0249. BELLOC, Hilaire. "On Vathek," in A Conversation with an Angel and Other Essays. New York : Harper, 1929.

0250. BLOOM, Margaret. "William Beckford's Vathek," University of California Chronicle, 33 (1931): 424-431.

0251. BORGES, Jorge Luis. "About William Beckford's Vathek," in Other Inquisitions, 1937-1952, trans. Ruth L.C. Sims. Austin, TX : Texas UP, 1964.

0252. BROCKMAN, Harold A.N. The Caliph of Fonthill, intro. Nikolaus Pevsner. London : Werner Laurie, 1956.

0253. BRULÉ, A. "Une Visite à Fonthill en 1792," Revue Anglo-Américaine, 10 (1933): 33-42.

0254. CANNON, Peter. "The Influence of Vathek on H.P. Lovecraft's The Dream-Quest of Unknown Kadath," in H.P. Lovecraft: Four Decades of Criticism, ed. S.T. Joshi. Athens, OH : Ohio UP, 1980, pp.153-157.

0255. CARNERO, Guillermo. "William Beckford (1760-1844) o el Erotismo de Fina Estampa," Insula, 24 (Oct-Nov, 1969): 18-19.

0256. CARTER, John. "Two Beckford Collections," Colophon, New Graphic Series, 1 (1939): 67-74.

0257. ______. "Beckford and Vathek: God and Stereotype," Library, 18 (1963): 308-309.

0258. CARTER, Lin. Introduction to The History of the Caliph Vathek, Including "The Episodes of Vathek" by William Beckford. New York : Ballantine Books, 1971.

0259. CHADOURNE, Marc. "L'Incroyable William Beckford," Revue de Paris, 69 (1962): 43-58.

0260. ______. Eblis, ou L'Enfer de William Beckford: L'Homme et L'Oeuvre. Paris : Jean-Jacques Pauvert, 1967.

0261. CHAPMAN, Guy. Introduction to Vathek, with the Episodes of Vathek by William Beckford. Cambridge : Constable, 1929.

0262. ______. "The Nonesuch Vathek," Times Literary Supplement, January 2, 1930, p.12.

0263. CHAPMAN, Guy and John Hodgkin. A Bibliography of William Beckford of Fonthill. London : Constable, 1930.

0264. CHAPMAN, Guy. Beckford. London : Rupert Hart-Davis, 1952.

0265. CONANT, Martha Pike. The Oriental Tale in England in the Eighteenth Century. New York : Columbia University Studies in Comparative Literature Number 9, 1908; Rpt. New York : Octagon Books, 1966.

0266. CRAIG, Randall. "Beckford's Inversion of Romance in Vathek," Orbis Litterarum, 39 (1984): 95-106.

0267. DE GRAAF, D.A. "Potgieter en Vathek," Revue des Langues Vivantes, 24 (1958): 469-475.

0268. DE MEESTER, Marie E. "Vathek and Its Influence," in Oriental Influences in English Literature of the Nineteenth Century. Heidelberg, Germany : Winters, 1915.

0269. DIDIER, Béatrice. "L'Exotisme et la Mise en Question du Système Familial et Moral dans le Roman à al Fin du XVIIIe Siècle: Beckford, Sade, Potocki," in Transactions of the Fourth International Congress of the Enlightenment. Oxford : Voltaire Foundation, 1976, pp.571-586.

0270. FARRELL, John T. "A Reinterpretation of the Major Literary Works of William Beckford," Dissertation Abstracts International, 45 (1984): 1758A (University of Delaware).

0271. FOLSOM, James K. "Beckford's Vathek and the Tradition of Oriental Satire," Criticism, 6 (1964): 53-69.

0272. FOTHERGILL, Brian. "William Beckford, Prince of Amateurs," Essays by Divers Hands, 38 (1975): 33-47.

0273. _______. Beckford of Fonthill. London : Faber & Faber, 1979.

0274. FRANK, Frederick S. "William Beckford's Vathek: An Arabian Tale," in Survey of Modern Fantasy Literature, ed. Keith Neilson. Englewood Cliffs, NJ : Salem Press, 1983, pp.2023-2027.

0275. GARBER, Frederick. "Beckford, Delacroix, and Byronic Orientalism," Comparative Literature Studies, 18 (1981): 321-332.

0276. GARNETT, Richard. "Beckford's Vathek," in Essays of an Ex-Librarian. London : William Heinemann, 1901; Rpt. Freeport, NY : Books for Libraries, 1970.

0277. GEMMETT, Robert James. "William Beckford and the Picturesque: A Study of Fonthill," Dissertation Abstracts, 28 (1967): 1740A-1741A (Syracuse University).

0278. _______. "An Annotated Checklist of the Works of William Beckford," Papers of the Bibliographical Society of America, 61 (1967): 243-258.

0279. _______. "William Beckford: Bibliographical Addenda," Bulletin of Bibliography, 25 (1967): 62-64.

0280. _______. "The Caliph Vathek from England and the Continent to America," American Book Collector, 18 (1968): 12-19.

0281. _______. "The Critical Reception of William Beckford's Fonthill," English Miscellany, 19 (1968): 133-151.

0282. _______. Introduction to Vathek by William Beckford. Delmar, NY : Scholar's Facsimiles and Reprints, 1972.

0283. _______. William Beckford. Boston : Twayne; Twayne English Authors Series Number 204, 1977.

0284. GIDDEY, Ernest. Introduction to Vathek et les Episodes by William Beckford. Lausanne, Switzerland : Rencontre, 1962.

0285. ________. "Beckford and Byron," Byron Journal, 6 (1978): 38-47.

0286. GIDE, André, Lucien Lavault, Lewis Melville, and Valery Larbaud. "Le Dossier Vathek," Nouvelle Revue Française, 54 (1913): 1044-1050.

0287. GIFFORD, Stephanie. "Genesis of a Caliph," John O'London's, 5 (August 24, 1961): 221.

0288. GOTLIEB, Howard B. William Beckford of Fonthill, Writer, Traveller, Collector, Caliph, 1760-1844: A Brief Narrative and Catalogue of an Exhibition to Mark the Two Hundreth Anniversary of Beckford's Birth, ed. Boyd Alexander. New Haven, CT : Yale UP, 1960.

0289. GRAHAM, Kenneth W. "Beckford's Vathek: A Study in Ironic Dissonance," Criticism, 14 (1972): 243-252.

0290. ________. "Who Revised the 1823 Vathek?" Papers of the Bibliographical Society of America, 67 (1973): 315-322.

0291. ________. "Beckford's Adaptation of the Oriental Tale in Vathek," Enlightenment Essays, 5, number 1 (1974): 24-33.

0292. ________. "Vathek in English and French," Studies in Bibliography, 28 (1975): 153-166.

0293. ________. "Implications of the Grotesque: Beckford's Vathek and the Boundaries of Fictional Reality," Tennessee Studies in Literature, 23 (1978): 61-74.

0294. ________. "'Inconnue dans les Annales de la Terre': Beckford's Benign and Demonic Influence on Poe," The Sphinx: A Magazine of Literature and Society, 4, number 4 (1985): 226-240.

0295. GREEN, Andrew J. "Essays in Miniature: Vathek," College English, 3 (1942): 723-724.

0296. GRIMM, Reinhold. "Vathek in Deutschland: Zwei Zwischenfälle ohne Folgen?" Revue de Littérature Comparée, 38 (1964): 127-135.

0297. GRIMSDITCH, Herbert B. Introduction to Vathek by William Beckford, illustrated with lithographs by Edward Bawden. London : Folio Press, 1958.

0298. GUERRA, Oliva. "Sintra e Lord Beckford," Coloquio, 46 (1967): 14-16.

0299. HEPPENSTALL, Rayner. "The Palace of Subterranean Fire," in The Fourfold Tradition. Notes on the French and English Literatures, With Some Ethnological and Historical Asides. London : Barrie & Rockliff, 1961.

0300. HERRICK, George H. "Fabulous Fonthill," College Art Journal, 12 (19-

53): 128-131.

0301. HODGKIN, John. "*Vathek*: The Henley Letters," *Athenaeum*, December 25, 1909, pp.789-790.

0302. ________. "The Nonesuch *Vathek*," *Times Literary Supplement*, December 26, 1929, p.1097.

0303. HOLLINGSWORTH, Keith. "*Vathek* and 'The Ode to a Nightingale,'" *Times Literary Supplement*, October 27, 1961, p.771.

0304. HUNTER, A.O. "Le *Vathek* de William Beckford: Historique des Editions Françaises," *Revue de Littérature Comparée*, 15 (1935): 119-126.

0305. HUSSAIN, Imdad. "Beckford, Wainewright, De Quincey, and Oriental Exoticism," *Venture*, 1 (1960): 234-248.

0306. HYLAND, Peter. "*Vathek*, Heaven and Hell," *Research Studies*, 50 (1982): 99-105.

0307. JANTZEN, Hermann. "Source of 'The Hall of Eblis' by B. Cornwall," *Archiv für das Studium der Neueren Sprachen und Literaturen*, 107 (1902): 318-323.

0308. JEAN-AUBRY, G. "Autour de *Vathek* de William Beckford," *Revue de Littérature Comparée*, 16 (1936): 549-562.

0309. JOHNSON, R. Brimley. Introduction to *Vathek* by William Beckford. Boston : Small, Maynard; Abbey Classics, 1922.

0310. KNIPP, Charles C. "Types of Orientalism in Eighteenth-Century England," *Dissertation Abstracts International*, 35 (1974): 2944A-2945A (University of California at Berkeley).

0311. LANE-POOLE, Stanley. "The Author of *Vathek*," *Quarterly Review*, 213 (October, 1910): 377-401.

0312. LANGE, Bernd-Peter. "Orientierungsarbeit: Radikale Fantasie in William Beckfords *Vathek*," *Zeitschrift für Anglistik und Amerikanistik*, 33 (1985): 33-43.

0313. LEES-MILNE, James. *William Beckford*. Tisbury, England : Compton Russell, 1976; Rpt. Montclair, NJ : Allanheld and Schram, 1979.

0314. LE YAOUANC, Collette. "Le Thème Sexuel dans *Vathek*," in *Liguistique, Civilisation, Littérature*, ed. André Bordeaux. Paris : Didier, 1980, pp.257-264.

0315. LIU, Alan. "Toward a Theory of Common Sense: Beckford's *Vathek* and Johnson's *Rasselas*," *Texas Studies in Literature and Language*, 26 (1984): 183-217.

0316. LOCKHART, John Gibson. Introduction to *Vathek* by William Beckford. London : Allan, 1923.

0317. LONSDALE, Roger. Introduction to Vathek by William Beckford. London : Oxford UP, 1970, pp.vii-xxxi.

0318. MAHMOUD, Fatma Moussa. "Beckford, Vathek, and the Oriental Tale," in William Beckford of Fonthill, 1760-1844. Bicentenary Essays, ed. Fatma Moussa Mahmoud. Cairo, Egypt : C. Tsoumas, 1960; Rpt. Port Washington, NY : Kennikat Press, 1972, pp.63-121.

0319. ________. "Rasselas and Vathek," in Bicentenary Essays on Rasselas, ed. Magdi Wahba. Cairo, Egypt : Studies in English, 1960.

0320. ________. "A Monument to the Author of Vathek," Etudes Anglaises, 25 (1962): 138-147.

0321. MANZALAOUI, Mahmoud. "Pseudo-Orientalism in Transition: The Age of Vathek," in William Beckford of Fonthill, 1760-1844. Bicentenary Essays, ed. Fatma Moussa Mahmoud. Cairo, Egypt : C. Tsoumas, 1960; Rpt. Port Washington, NY : Kennikat Press, 1972.

0322. MARLOW, Harriet. "Beckford's Vathek, 'Londres 1791,'" Book Collector, 11 (1962): 211.

0323. MAY, Marcel. La Jeunesse de William Beckford et la Genèse de son "Vathek". Paris : Presses Universitaires de France, 1928.

0324. MAYNARD, Temple. "The Landscape of Vathek," Transactions of the Samuel Johnson Society of the Northwest, 7 (1974): 79-98.

0325. MAYOUX, Jean-Jacques. "La Damnation de Beckford," English Miscellany, 12 (1961): 41-77.

0326. MELVILLE, Lewis. Introduction to The Episodes of Vathek by William Beckford, trans. Sir Frank T. Marzials. London : Stephen Swift, 1912.

0327. MOCHI, Giovanna. "L'Inferno Rassicurante di Vathek," Paragone, 350 (1979): 64-102.

0328. MORE, Paul Elmer. "William Beckford," in The Drift of Romanticism. Boston : Houghton, Mifflin, 1913, pp.1-36.

0329. MOURET, François J.L. "Le Vathek de William Beckford et le 'Voyage d'Urien' d'André Gide," Modern Language Review, 64 (1969): 774-776.

0330. OLIVER, John W. The Life of William Beckford. London : Oxford UP, 1932.

0331. PARREAUX, André. "Beckford and Byron," Etudes Anglaises, 8 (1955): 11-31, 113-132.

0332. ________. "Un Vathek Ignoré," Bulletin de Bibliophile et du Bibliothecairé, 5 (1957): 176-179.

0333. ________. "Beckford's Vathek, 'Londres 1791,'" Book Collector, 7 (1958): 297-299.

0334. ________. "Beckford en Italie: Rêve et Voyage in XVIIIe Siècle," *Revue de Littérature Comparée*, 33 (1959): 321-347.

0335. ________. *William Beckford Auteur de "Vathek" (1760-1844): Etude de la Création Littéraire*. Paris : Nizet, 1960.

0336. ________. "The Caliph and the Swinish Multitude," in *William Beckford of Fonthill, 1760-1844. Bicentenary Essays*, ed. Fatma Moussa Mahmoud. Cairo, Egypt : C. Tsoumas, 1960; Rpt. Port Washington, NY : Kennikat Press, 1972.

0337. ________. "Beckford: Bibliographie Sélective et Critique," *Bulletin de la Société d'Etudes Anglo-Américaines des XVIIIe Siècles*, 3 (1976): 45-55.

0338. PRAZ, Mario. "Il Califfo Beckford," in *Studi e Svaghi Inglesi* by Mario Praz. Firenzi, Italy : Sansoni, 1937.

0339. ________. "Swift, Johnson, Beckford: Tre Inglesi Pazzi," *Tempo*, February 9, 1977, p.3.

0340. PRITCHETT, V.S. "Vile Body," *New Statesman*, February 23, 1962, pp.265-266.

0341. PRYCE-JONES, Alan. "William Beckford, Dilletante," *New York Times Book Review*, February 16, 1969, pp.2, 40.

0342. REDMAN, Ben Ray. Introduction to *Vathek* by William Beckford, illustrated by Mahlon Blaine. New York : John Day, 1928.

0343. REVAUGER, Marie-Cécile. "L'Unique et le Multiple dans le *Vathek* de William Beckford: Folie du Mimétisme," in *Folie, Folies, Folly dans le Monde Anglo-Américain aux XVIIe et XVIIIe Siècles*. Aix-en-Provence, France : PU de Provence, 1984, pp.71-80.

0344. RIEGER, James Henry. "Au Pied de la Lettre: Stylistic Uncertainty in *Vathek*," *Criticism*, 4 (1962): 302-312.

0345. SENA, John F. "Drawing From Blots: The Landscapes of *Vathek* and the Paintings of Alexander Cozens," *Etudes Anglaises*, 26 (1973): 210-215.

0346. SITWELL, Sacherverell. *Beckford and Beckfordism*. London : Duckworth, 1930.

0347. THOMPSON, Karl F. "Henley's Share in Beckford's *Vathek*," *Philological Quarterly*, 31 (1952): 75-80.

0348. ________. "Beckford, Byron, and Henley," *Etudes Anglaises*, 14 (1961): 225-228.

0349. VARMA, Devendra P. "William Beckford," in *Supernatural Fiction Writers*, ed. E.F. Bleiler. New York : Charles Scribner's Sons, 1985, I, 139-144.

0350. VIGIL, Julian Josue. "A Nightmare in Literary Criticism," New Mexico Highlands University Journal, 1 (1979): 48-50.

0351. WHIBLEY, Charles. "The Caliph of Fonthill," in The Pageantry of Life. New York : Harper, 1900, pp.81-96.

0352. "William Beckford and Islam," Connoisseur, 191 (1976): 250-253.

0353. WILSON, Edmund. "Firbank and Beckford," in The Shores of Light: A Literary Chronicle of the Twenties and Thirties. New York : Farrar, Straus, and Young, 1952, pp.264-266.

0354. ZEIDLER, Karl. "Beckford, Hope und Morier als Vertreter des Orientalischen Romans," Unpublished Doctoral Dissertation, University of Leipzig, 1908.

William Godwin
(1756-1836)

0355. ABREU, John Warren. "Philosophy into Fiction: The Novels of William Godwin" Dissertation Abstracts International, 39 (1979): 4263A (City University of New York).

0356. ARNAUD, Pierre. "William Godwin: Caleb Williams: Bibliographie Sélective et Critique," Bulletin de la Société d'Etudes Anglo-Américaines des XVIIe et XVIIIe Siècles, 7 (1978): 37-60.

0357. BARKER, Gerard A. "Justice to Caleb Williams," Studies in the Novel, 6 (1974): 377-388.

0358. _______. "Fernando Falkland's Fall: Grandison in Disarray," Papers on Language and Literature, 16 (1980): 376-386.

0359. BATTILLANA, M. "'The Castaway,' Caleb Williams, The Mysteries of Udolpho: The Story Behind the Page," in Itinerari Negati Momenti della Tradizione Inglese e Scozzese nel Settecento e Letterature Moderne, eds. Eiulio Marra, M.V. Lorenzoni, E. Paganelli, M. Battillana. Brescia, Italy : Phideia, 1981.

0360. BECKETT, Juliet. Introduction to St. Leon: A Tale of the Sixteenth Century by William Godwin, foreword by Devendra P. Varma. New York : Arno Press, 1972.

0361. BROOKS, Van Wyck. Introduction to Caleb Williams; or, Things As They Are by William Godwin. New York : Greenberg, 1926, pp.v-viii.

0362. BUTLER, Marilyn. "Godwin, Burke, and Caleb Williams," Essays in Criticism, 32 (1982): 237-257.

0363. CLIFFORD, Gay. "Caleb Williams and Frankenstein: First-Person Narrative and 'Things As They Are,'" Genre, 10 (1977): 601-617.

0364. COBB, Joann P. "Godwin's Novels and Political Justice," Enlightenment

Essays, 4, (1973): 15-28.

0365. CRUTWELL, Patrick. "On Caleb Williams," Hudson Review, 11 (1958): 87-95.

0366. DE PORTE, Michael. "The Consolations of Fiction: Mystery in Caleb Williams," Papers on Language and Literature, 20 (1984): 154-164.

0367. DREXLER, Peter. "'An unconquerable spirit of curiosity': William Godwins Caleb Williams in der Vorgeschichte des Detektivromans," Braunschweiger Anglistische Arbeiten, 7 (1981): 67-89.

0368. DUMAS, D. Gilbert. "Things As They Were: The Original Ending of Caleb Williams," Studies in English Literature, 1500-1900, 6 (1966): 575-597.

0369. ELDER, T.B. "Change and Development in the Works of William Godwin," Dissertation Abstracts International, 43 (1982): 1575C (University of Liverpool).

0370. EVEREST, Kevin and Gavin Edwards. "William Godwin's Caleb Williams: Truth and 'Things As They Are,'" in Reading, Writing, Revolution: Proceedings of the Essex Conference on the Sociology of Literature, July 1981, eds. Francis Barker, Jay Bernstein, Peter Hulme, Margaret Iverson, Jennifer Stone. Colchester, England : University of Essex, 1982, pp.129-146.

0371. FAROUK, Marion O. "Mandeville, A Tale of the Seventeenth Century: Historical Novel or Psychological Study?" in Essays in Honor of Will Gallacher, ed. Brika Lingner. Berlin, East Germany : Humboldt, 1966, pp.111-117.

0372. FLANDERS, Wallace A. "Godwin and Gothicism: St. Leon," Texas Studies in Language and Literature, 8 (1967): 533-545.

0373. FURBANK, P.N. "Godwin's Novels," Essays in Criticism, 5 (1955): 214-228.

0374. GOLD, Alex Jr. "'It's Only Love': The Politics of Passion in Godwin's Caleb Williams," Texas Studies in Literature and Language, 19 (1977): 135-160.

0375. GRAHAM, Kenneth W. "The Gothic Unity of Godwin's Caleb Williams," Papers on Language and Literature, 20 (1984): 47-59.

0376. GROSS, Harvey. "The Pursuer and the Pursued: A Study of Caleb Williams," Texas Studies in Literature and Language, 1 (1959): 401-411.

0377. HARVEY, A.D. "The Nightmare of Caleb Williams," Essays in Criticism, 26 (1976): 236-249.

0378. HOGLE, Jerrold E. "The Texture of the Self in Godwin's Things As They Are," Boundary, 7 (1979): 261-281.

0379. HUGHES, Dean T. "Romance and Psychological Realism in William Godwin's Novels," Dissertation Abstracts International, 33 (1972): 2330A (University of Washington).

0380. ______. Romance and Psychological Realism in William Godwin's Novels. New York : Arno Press, 1980.

0381. JUROE, James G. "St. Leon: A Tale of the Sixteenth Century by William Godwin, A Critical and Annotated Edition," Dissertation Abstracts International, 32 (1972): 3954A (University of Nebraska).

0382. KELLY, Gary. "History and Fiction: Bethlem Gabor in Godwin's St. Leon," English Language Notes, 14 (1976): 117-120.

0383. ______. The English Jacobin Novel (1780-1805). London : Oxford UP, 1976.

0384. ______. "Convention and Criticism in William Godwin's Early Novels," Keats-Shelley Journal, 33 (1984): 52-69.

0385. KROPF, C.R. "Caleb Williams and the Attack on Romance," Studies in the Novel, 8 (1976): 81-87.

0386. LAMOINE, Georges. "Caleb Williams, le Mythe de Faust, et l'Intention Morale," Bulletin de la Société d'Etudes Anglo-Américaines des XVII et XVIII Siècles, 9 (1979): 91-110.

0387. LANG, Hans-Joachim. "Godwin's Caleb Williams as Political Allegory," in Literatur als Kritik des Lebens. Heidelberg, Germany : Quelle und Meyer, 1975, pp.148-166.

0388. MARSHALL, Peter. William Godwin. New Haven, CT : Yale UP, 1984.

0389. MARSHALL, William H. "Caleb Williams and The Cenci," Notes & Queries, 7 (1960): 260-263.

0390. MC CELVEY, George Edward III. "William Godwin's Novels: Theme and Craft," Dissertation Abstracts, 25 (1964): 1215-1216 (Duke University).

0391. MC CRACKEN, David. "Godwin's Caleb Williams: A Fictional Rebuttal of Burke," Studies in Burke and His Time, 11 (1969-1970): 1442-1452.

0392. ______. "Godwin's Literary Theory: The Alliance Between Fiction and Political Philosophy," Philological Quarterly, 49 (1970): 113-133.

0393. ______. Introduction to Caleb Williams; or, Things As They Are by William Godwin. New York : W.W. Norton, 1977, pp.vii-xxii.

0394. MC KINLEY, Virginia S.G. "Rendering Up 'The Tale of What We Are': Gothic Narrative Methods in Selected Novels of Godwin, Brown, and Shelley," Dissertation Abstracts International, 47 (1987): 2597A (Michigan State University).

0395. MEYER, Johannes. William Godwins Romane: Ein Beitrag zur Geschichte des Englischen Romans. Weida, Germany : Thomas & Hubert, 1906.

0396. MILLER, Jacqueline T. "The Imperfect Tale: Articulation, Rhetoric, and Self in Caleb Williams," Criticism, 20 (1978): 366-382.

0397. MYERS, Mitzi. "Godwin's Changing Conception of Caleb Williams," Studies in English Literature, 1500-1900, 12 (1972): 591-628.

0398. PALACIO, Jean de. William Godwin et son Monde Intérieur. Lille, France : PU de Lille, 1980.

0399. PESTA, John. "Caleb Williams: A Tragedy of Wasted Love," Tennessee Studies in Literature, 16 (1971): 67-76.

0400. POLLIN, Burton. Godwin Criticism: A Synoptic Bibliography. Toronto : Toronto UP, 1967.

0401. ROEMER, Donald. "William Godwin's Caleb Williams: The Idealogue as Novelist," Dissertation Abstracts International, 32 (1970): 2705A-2706A (Brandeis University).

0402. ______. "The Achievement of Godwin's Caleb Williams: The Proto-Byronic Squire Falkland," Criticism, 18 (1976): 43-56.

0403. ROGERS, Deborah D. "Caleb Williams: Things As They Are Not," American Notes & Queries, 13 (1975): 133.

0404. ROTHSTEIN, Eric. "Allusion and Analogy in the Romance of Caleb Williams," University of Toronto Quarterly, 37 (1967): 18-30.

0405. ______. "Caleb Williams: I. History into Romance II. Romance into History III. A Conclusion in Which Everything and Nothing is Concluded," in Systems of Order and Inquiry in Late Eighteenth Century Fiction. Berkeley, CA : California UP, 1975, pp.208-242.

0406. SCHEIBER, Andrew. "Falkland's Story: Caleb Williams' Other Voice," Studies in the Novel, 17 (1985): 255-266.

0407. SCHEUERMANN, Mona. "The Novels of William Godwin and Those of His Contemporaries," Dissertation Abstracts International, 35 (1974): 7269A (SUNY at Stony Brook).

0408. ______. "From Mind to Society: Caleb Williams as Psychological Novel," Dutch Quarterly Review of Anglo-American Letters, 7 (1977): 115-127.

0409. ______. The Novels of William Godwin and Those of His Contemporaries. New York : Arno Press, 1980.

0410. ______. "The Study of Mind: The Later Novels of William Godwin," Forum for Modern Language Studies, 19 (1983): 16-30.

0411. SHERBURN, George. Introduction to Caleb Williams; or, Things As They Are. New York : Rinehart, 1960, pp.vii-xiv.

0412. ______. "Godwin's Later Novels," Studies in Romanticism, 1 (1962): 65-82.

0413. SMITH, Elton Edward and Esther Greenwell Smith. William Godwin. New York : Twayne; Twayne English Authors Series 27, 1965.

0414. STAMPER, Rexford. "Caleb Williams: The Bondage of Truth," Southern Quarterly, 12 (1973): 39-50.

0415. STORCH, Rudolf F. "Metaphors of Private Guilt and Social Rebellion in Godwin's Caleb Williams," Journal of English Literary History, 34 (1967): 188-207.

0416. TYSDAEL, B.J. William Godwin as Novelist. London : Athlone Press,1981; Atlantic Highlands, NJ : Humanities Press, 1981.

0417. UPHAUS, Robert. "Godwin's Epoch of the Mind," Studies in the Novel, 9 (1977): 279-296.

0418. WALTON, James. "'Mad Feary Father': Caleb Williams and the Novel Form," Salzburg, Austria : Salzburg Studies in English Literature Number 47, 1975.

0419. WILSON, Angus. "The Novels of William Godwin," World Review, 28 (1951): 37-40.

0420. WOODCOCK, George. "Things As They Might Be: Things As They Are: Notes on the Novels of William Godwin," Dalhousie Review, 54 (1975): 685-697.

James Hogg
(1770-1835)

0421. BENEDICT, Williston R. "A Study of the 'Second Self' in James Hogg's Fiction with Reference to its Employment in German Romantic Literature," Dissertation Abstracts International, 34 (1973): 2606A-2607A (Columbia University).

0422. ______. "A Story Replete with Horror," Princeton University Library Chronicle, 44 (1983): 246-251.

0423. BLOEDÉ, Barbara R. "James Hogg's Private Memoirs and Confessions of a Justified Sinner: The Genesis of the Double," Etudes Anglaises, 26 (1973): 174-186.

0424. BRUDER, Charles Harry. "Structuralism, Form, and the Individual Text: An Initial Reading of James Hogg's Confessions of a Justified Sinner," Dissertation Abstracts International, 37 (1976): 2888A (University of Nebraska).

0425. CAMPBELL, Ian. "Hogg's Confessions and The Heart of Darkness," Studies in Scottish Literature, 15 (1980): 187-201.

0426. CAREY, John. Introduction to The Private Memoirs and Confessions of a

Justified Sinner by James Hogg. New York : Oxford UP, 1969, pp.xi-xxiii.

0427. CHIANESE, Robert L. "James Hogg's Confessions of a Justified Sinner: An Anatomy of Terror," Mystery and Detection Annual, 1973, 97-112.

0428. EGGENSCHWILER, David. "James Hogg's Confessions and the Fall into Division," Studies in Scottish Literature, 9 (1971): 29-39.

0429. GIDE, André. Introduction to The Private Memoirs and Confessions of a Justified Sinner by James Hogg. New York : Grove Press, 1959, pp.ix-xvi.

0430. HARRIES, Elizabeth W. "Duplication and Duplicity: James Hogg's Private Memoirs and Confessions of a Justified Sinner," Wordsworth Circle, 10 (1979): 187-196.

0431. KEARNS, Michael S. "Intuition and Narration in James Hogg's Confessions," Studies in Scottish Literature, 13 (1978): 91-91.

0432. LEE, L.L. "The Devil's Figure: James Hogg's Justified Sinner," Studies in Scottish Literature, 3 (1966): 230-239.

0433. MACK, Donald S. "Hogg's Religion and The Confessions of a Justified Sinner," Studies in Scottish Literature, 7 (1970): 272-275.

0434. _______. "The Devil's Pilgrim: A Note on Wringham's Private Memoirs in James Hogg's Confessions of a Justified Sinner," Scottish Literary Journal, 2, number 1 (1975): 36-40.

0435. MASON, Michael York. "The Three Burials in Hogg's Justified Sinner," Studies in Scottish Literature, 13 (1978): 15-23.

0436. REDEKOP, Magdalene Falk. "The Narrative Art of James Hogg," Dissertation Abstracts International, 39 (1978): 1525A-1526A (University of Toronto).

0437. _______. "Beyond Closure: Buried Alive with Hogg's Justified Sinner," Journal of English Literary History, 52 (1985): 159-184.

0438. RIESE, Teut. "James Hogg und der Roman der Englischen Romantik," Archiv für das Studium der Neueren Sprachen und Literaturen, 198 (1961): 145-164.

0439. SMITH, Nelson C. James Hogg. Boston : Twayne; Twayne English Authors Series Number 311, 1977.

0440. _______. "James Hogg," in Supernatural Fiction Writers, ed. E.F. Bleiler. New York : Charles Scribner's Sons, 1985, I, 177-183.

Sophia Lee
(1750-1824)

0441. ROBERTS, Bette B. "Sophia Lee's The Recess (1785): The Ambivalence of

Female Gothicism," Massachusetts Studies in English, 6, numbers 3-4 (1979): 68-82.

0442. VARMA, Devendra P. Introduction to The Recess; or, A Tale of Other Times by Sophia Lee, foreword J.M.S. Tompkins. New York : Arno Press, 1972.

Thomas Leland
(1722-1807)

0443. HARP, Richard L. "Goldsmith's College Tutor: The Malicious Monk in Leland's Longsword, Earl of Salisbury," Moderna Sprak, 76 (1982): 241-242.

0444. HUME, Robert D. Introduction to Longsword, Earl of Salisbury; An Historical Romance by Thomas Leland, foreword by Devendra P. Varma. New York : Arno Press, 1974.

0445. STEPHENS, John C. Jr. Introduction to Longsword, Earl of Salisbury; An Historical Romance by Thomas Leland. New York : New York UP, 1957.

Matthew Gregory "Monk" Lewis
(1775-1818)

0446. ABENSOUR, Liliane. "Limites--Non Frontières d'une Oeuvre: Le Moine de M.G. Lewis," Europe, 659 (1984): 13-18.

0447. ANDERSON, Howard. "The Manuscript of M.G. Lewis's The Monk: Some Preliminary Notes," Papers of the Bibliographical Society of America, 62 (1968): 427-434.

0448. _______. Introduction to The Monk by Matthew G. Lewis. New York : Oxford UP, 1973, pp.vii-xix.

0449. ARNAUD, Pierre. "Le Double dans le Roman Gothique: The Monk de Matthew Gregory Lewis," in Le Double dans le Romanticisme Anglo-Américain. Clermont-Ferrand, France : Faculté des Lettres & Sciences Humaines de l'Université de Clermont-Ferrand II, 1984, pp.131-142.

0450. BAKER, Ernest A. Introduction to The Monk by Matthew G. Lewis. New York : Dutton, 1906.

0451. BALDENSPERGER, Fernand. "Le Moine de Lewis dans le Littérature Française," Journal of Comparative Literature, 1 (1903): 201-219.

0452. BAYFORD, E.G. "Lewis's Monk," Times Literary Supplement, March 28, 1935, p.216.

0453. BERRYMAN, John. Introduction to The Monk by Matthew Gregory Lewis, ed. Louis Peck. New York : Grove Press, 1959, pp.11-28.

0454. BROOKS, Peter. "Virtue and Terror: The Monk," Journal of English Literary History, 40 (1973): 249-263.

0455. BROOKS, Philip. "Notes on Rare Books," New York Times Book Review, January 27, 1935, p.21.

0456. COYKENDALL, Frederick. "A Note on 'The Monk,'" Colophon, new series, 1 (1935): 87-96.

0457. ________. "Lewis's Monk," Times Literary Supplement, April 25, 1935, p.276.

0458. EMERSON, Oliver Farrar. "'Monk' Lewis and the Tales of Terror," Modern Language Notes, 38 (1923): 154-159.

0459. FAURE, Alain. "Du Simple au Double: Du Moine de M.G. Lewis aux Elixirs du Diable d'E.T.A. Hoffmann," Europe, 659 (1984): 54-62.

0460. FERGUSON, Mary. "Ambrosio: or, The Monk," in Survey of Modern Fantasy Literature, ed. Frank Magill. Englewood Cliffs, NJ : Salem Press, 1983, I, pp.36-41.

0461. FIEROBE, Claude. "Le Moine Gothique ou la Parodie du Sacré," in Aspects du Sacré dans la Littérature Anglo-Américaine. Reims, France: Publications du Centre Recherche sur l'Imaginaire dans les Littératures de Langue Anglaise, 1979, pp.33-45.

0462. FOGLE, Richard H. "The Passions of Ambrosio," in The Classic British Novel, eds. Howard M. Harper, Jr., Charles Edge. Athens, GA : Georgia UP, 1972, pp.36-50.

0463. FONGARO, Antoine. "Baudelaire, L'Aminta, et Le Moine," Bulletin Baudelairien, 17 (1982): 5-8.

0464. A FRIEND OF ACCURACY. "M.G. Lewis," Notes & Queries, 204 (1957): 389.

0465. GOSE, Elliott B. "The Gothic Novel" and "The Monk," in Imagination Indulged: The Irrational in the Nineteenth-Century Novel. Montreal : Mc Gill-Queen's UP, 1972, pp.19-40.

0466. GRUDIN, Peter. "The Monk: Matilda and the Rhetoric of Deceit," Journal of Narrative Technique, 5 (1975): 136-146.

0467. GUTHKE, Karl S. "C.M. Wieland and M.G. Lewis," Neophilologus, 40 (1956): 231-233.

0468. ________. "Some Unpublished Letters of M.G. Lewis," Notes & Queries, 202 (1957): 217-219.

0469. ________. "Some Bibliographical Errors Concerning the Romantic Age," Papers of the Bibliographical Society of America, 51 (1957): 159-162.

0470. ________. Englische Vorromantik und Deutscher Sturm und Drang, M.G. Lewis' Stellung in der Geschichte des Deutsch-Englischen Literaturbeziehungen. Göttingen, West Germany : Vandenhoeck und Ruprecht; Band 223, 1958.

0471. _______. "M.G. Lewis' *The Twins*," *Huntington Library Quarterly*, 25 (1962): 189-223.

0472. _______. "F.L. Schroeder, J.F. Regnard, and M.G. Lewis," *Huntington Library Quarterly*, 27 (1963): 79-82.

0473. HEIM, William J. "Matthew Gregory Lewis," in *Critical Survey of Long Fiction*, ed. Frank Magill. Englewood Cliffs, NJ : Salem Press, 1983, IV, pp.1661-1667.

0474. HERZFELD, Georg. "Eine Neue Quelle für Lewis' *Monk*," *Archiv für das Studium der Neueren Sprachen und Literaturen*, 104 (1900): 310-312.

0475. _______. "Die Eigentliche Quelle von Lewis' 'Monk,'" *Archiv für das Studium der Neueren Sprachen und Literaturen*, 111 (1903): 316-323.

0476. _______. "Noch Einmal die Quelle von Lewis' *Monk*," *Archiv für das Studium der Neueren Sprachen und Literaturen*, 115 (1905): 70-73.

0477. IRWIN, Joseph James. *M.G. "Monk" Lewis*. Boston : Twayne; Twayne English Author Series Number 198, 1976.

0478. JANSEN, Peter K. "'Monk Lewis' und Heinrich von Kleist," *Kleist-Jahrbuch* (1984): 25-54.

0479. KNOWLTON, Edgar Jr. "Lewis's *The Monk* and *Tirant lo Blanc*," *Notes & Queries*, 30 (1983): 64-65.

0480. LÉVY, Maurice. "Le Manuscrit du *Moine* de M.G. Lewis," *Caliban*, 3 (1966): 129-131.

0481. _______. "*Le Moine* (1796)," in *Roman et Société en Angleterre au XVIIIe Siècle*. Paris : Presses Université, 1978, pp.197-231.

0482. LYDENBERG, Robin. "Ghostly Rhetoric: Ambivalence in M.G. Lewis's *The Monk*," *Ariel*, 10 (1979): 65-79.

0483. MAGNIER, M. "*Le Moine* et les Superstitions Papistes," *Myths, Croyances et Religions dans le Monde Anglo-Saxon*, 1 (1983): 95-105.

0484. MARROT, H.V. "Lewis's *Monk*," *Bibliographical Notes and Queries*, 1 (1935): 4.

0485. MC ALLISTER, Harold S. "Apology for Bad Dreams: A Study of Characterization and the Use of Fantasy in *Clarissa*, *Justine*, and *The Monk*," *Dissertation Abstracts International*, 32 (1972): 6383A (University of New Mexico).

0486. MC NAMEE, Lawrence F. "Monk Lewis and the Gothic Novel," in *Dissertations in English and American Literature. Theses Accepted by American, British, and German Universities, 1865-1964*. New York : R.R. Bowker, 1968.

0487. PARREAUX, André. *The Publication of the Monk: A Literary Event, 1796-*

1798. Paris : Marcel Didier, 1960.

0488. PECK, Louis F. "Lewis's Monk," Times Literary Supplement, March 4, 1935, p.148.

0489. ______. "M.G. Lewis and the Larpent Catalogue," Huntington Library Quarterly, 5 (1942): 382-384.

0490. ______. "Act III of Lewis's Venoni," Modern Language Notes, 58 (1943): 265-268.

0491. ______. "An Adaptation of Kleist's Die Familie Schroffenstein," Journal of English and Germanic Philology, 44 (1945): 9-11.

0492. ______. "The Monk and Musäus' Die Entführung," Philological Quarterly, 32 (1953): 346-348.

0493. ______. "The Monk and Le Diable Amoureux," Modern Language Notes, 68 (1953): 406-408.

0494. ______. A Life of Matthew G. Lewis. Cambridge, MA : Harvard UP, 1961.

0495. ______. "An Early Copy of The Monk," Papers of the Bibliographical Society of America, 57 (1963): 350-351.

0496. ______. "On the Date of Tales of Wonder," English Language Notes, 2 (1964): 25-27.

0497. ______. "New Poems by Matthew G. Lewis," Archiv für das Studium der Neueren Sprachen und Literaturen, 203 (1967): 189-194.

0498. PICHOIS, Claude. "Actualité du Moine," Mercure de France, 334 (1958): 512-516.

0499. PICOT, Jean-Pierre. "Lewis, Hoffmann, Gogol, Gautier: Du Status de l'Identité au Cérémonial de la Mort dans le Récit Fantastiques," Littératures, 5 (1982): 19-35.

0500. POUND, Louise F. "'Monk' Lewis in Nebraska," Southern Folklore Quarterly, 9 (1945): 107-110.

0501. PRAZ, Mario. "Matthew Gregory Lewis's 'Gothic Novel': The Monk," in Le Romantisme Anglo-Américain: Mélanges Offerts à Louis Bonnerot. Paris : Marcel Didier, 1971, pp.21-34.

0502. RENO, Robert P. "James Boaden's Fontainville Forest and Matthew G. Lewis' The Castle Spectre: Challenges of the Supernatural Ghost on the Late Eighteenth-Century Stage," Eighteenth-Century Life, 9 (1984): 95-106.

0503. RENTSCH, Max. Matthew Gregory Lewis: Mit Besonderer Berücksichtigung seines Romans "Ambrosio, or the Monk". Leipzig, Germany : Pöschel & Trepte, 1902.

0504. RITTER, Otto. "Studien zu M.G. Lewis' Roman 'Ambrosio, or the Monk,'" Archiv für das Studium der Neueren Sprachen und Literaturen, 111 (1903): 106-121.

0505. ________. "Die Angebliche Quelle von M.G. Lewis' Monk," Archiv für das Studium der Neueren Sprachen und Literaturen, 13 (1904): 56-65.

0506. ROBERTS, W. "Lewis's Monk," Times Literary Supplement, March 14, 1935, p.164.

0507. ROMERO, Christiane Z. "M.G. Lewis' The Monk and E.T.A. Hoffmann's Die Elixiere des Teufels: Two Versions of the Gothic," Neophilologus, 63 (1979): 574-582.

0508. SABBADINI, Tiziana. "The Monk di M.G. Lewis e l'Attesa di s/Velamento," Il Lettore di Provincia, 15 (1984): 69-73.

0509. SADLEIR, Michael. "Tales of Terror," Times Literary Supplement, January 7, 1939, pp.9-10.

0510. SCHNEIDER, Rudolf K. Der Mönch in der Englischen Dichtung bis auf Lewis's "Monk," 1795. Leipzig, Germany : Mayer und Müller; Band 155, 1928.

0511. STALHAM, Francis Reginald. Introduction to The Monk by Matthew Gregory Lewis. London : Gibbings, 1906.

0512. SUMMERS, Montague. "Santon Barsisa," Notes & Queries, 175 (1938): 174-175.

0513. SWOYER, Ardeth G. "Matthew Gregory Lewis and his Contributions to the Gothic Novel," Unpublished Doctoral Dissertation, University of Virginia, 1944.

0514. TAYLOR, Archer. "The Three Sins of the Hermit," Modern Philology, 20 (1922): 61-94.

0515. THOMAS, William. "The Called Him 'Monk,'" Personalist, 47 (1966): 81-90.

0516. TODD, William B. "The Early Editions and Issues of The Monk, with a Bibliography," Studies in Bibliography, 2 (1949): 3-24.

0517. "Trollope on The Monk," Nineteenth-Century Fiction, 4 (1949): 167.

0518. TRACY, Ann B. "M.G. Lewis," in Supernatural Fiction Writers, ed. E.F. Bleiler. New York : Charles Scribner's Sons, 1985, I, 153-160.

0519. TROSTANIECKI, Ignacy. "La Poétique du Caché dans Le Moine de M.G. Lewis," Recherches Anglaises et Américaines, 6 (1973): 43-59.

0520. VARMA, Devendra P. Introduction to The Bravo of Venice: A Romance by Matthew Gregory Lewis. New York : Arno Press, 1972.

0521. ________. Introduction to The Monk by Matthew Gregory Lewis, with wood engravings by George Tute. London : Folio Society, 1984, pp.vii-xvi.

0522. VOLKER, Klaus. "Der Mönch," Neue Rundschau, 82 (1971): 774-779.

0523. WATKINS, Daniel P. "Social Hierarchy in Matthew Lewis's The Monk," Studies in the Novel, 18 (1986): 115-124.

0524. WENDELL, John R. "E.T.A. Hoffmann's Die Elixiere des Teufels and its Dependence on Matthew G. Lewis' The Monk," Dissertation Abstracts, 28 (1967): 699A (University of Connecticut).

0525. WYPLEL, L. "Ein Schauerroman als Quelle Die Ahnfrau," Euphorion, 7 (1903): 718-731.

Charles Robert Maturin
(1780-1824)

0526. ASTLE, Richard. "Melmoth the Wanderer," Survey of Modern Fantasy Literature, ed. Frank Magill. Englewood Cliffs, NJ : Salem Press, 1983, II, pp.998-1003.

0527. AXTON, William F. Introduction to Melmoth the Wanderer by Charles Robert Maturin. Lincoln, NE : Nebraska UP, 1961, pp.vii-xviii.

0528. _______. "Charles Robert Maturin," in Supernatural Fiction Writers, ed. E.F. Bleiler. New York : Charles Scribner's Sons, 1985, I, 161-168.

0529. BLEILER, E.F. Introduction to The Wild Irish Boy by Charles Robert Maturin. New York : Arno Press, 1977.

0530. BUCHAN, A.M. "Maturin's Birthday," Notes & Queries, 114 (1950): 302.

0531. CHADOURNE, Marc. "Melmoth et le Pacte Infernal," Revue de Paris, 75 (1968): 8-14.

0532. CLAPTON, G.T. "Balzac, Baudelaire and Maturin," French Quarterly, 12 (1930): 66-84, 97-115.

0533. CLYNE, Anthony. "Maturin (1782-1824)," Bookman, 67 (November, 1924): 103-105.

0534. CONGER, Syndy M. "Matthew G. Lewis, Charles Robert Maturin, and the Germans: An Interpretive Study of the Influence of German Literature on Two Gothic Novels," Dissertation Abstracts International, 37 (1977): 7733A (University of Iowa).

0535. _______. Matthew G. Lewis, Charles Robert Maturin, and the Germans: An Interpretive Study of the Influence of German Literature on Two Gothic Novels. New York : Arno Press, 1980.

0536. CRAMPTON, Hope. "Melmoth in La Comédie Humaine," Modern Language Review, 61 (1966): 42-50.

0537. D'AMICO, Diane. "Christina Rossetti: The Maturin Poems," Victorian Poetry, 19 (1981): 117-137.

0538. _______. "Charles Robert Maturin," in Critical Survey of Long Fiction, ed. Frank Magill. Englewood Cliffs, NJ : Salem Press, 1983, V, pp.1834-1842.

0539. _______. "Feeling and Conception of Character in the Novels of Charles Robert Maturin," Massachusetts Studies in English, 9, number 3 (1984): 42-54.

0540. DAWSON, Leven M. "Melmoth the Wanderer: Paradox and the Gothic Novel," Studies in English Literature, 1500-1900, 8 (1968): 621-632.

0541. DEMIROVIC, Hamdija. "Okretja Zavrtnja: Skica 12 Psihologije Uzasa u Djelu 'Melmoth the Wanderer' Charlesa Maturina," Delo (Belgrade), 27, numbers 1-2 (1981): 253-261.

0542. DE TERNANT, Andrew. "Maturin and the Novel of Terror," Times Literary Supplement, September 2, 1920, p.568.

0543. DURKAN, Michael J. "A Checklist of Works by Charles Robert Maturin," Eire (University of Florida), 1 (1977): 133-146.

0544. EGGENSCHWILER, David. "Melmoth the Wanderer: Gothic on Gothic," Genre, 8 (1975): 165-181.

0545. EHLERS, Leigh A. "The 'Incommunicable Condition' of Melmoth," Research Studies, 49 (1981): 171-182.

0546. FERNSEMER, Oscar F.W. Die Dramtischen Werke Charles Robert Maturins, mit einer Kurzen Lebensbeschreibung des Dichters. München, Germany : Oldenbourg, 1913.

0547. FIEROBE, Claude. "L'Univers Fantastiques de Melmoth the Wanderer," in La Raison et l'Imaginaire. Actes du Congrès de Rennes. Paris : Marcel Didier, 1970, pp.105-116.

0548. _______. "France in the Novels of Charles Robert Maturin," Cahiers I, 2-3 (1974): 119-131.

0549. _______. Charles Robert Maturin (1780-1824): L'Homme et l'Oeuvre. Lille, France : Presse de l'Université de Lille III, 1974.

0550. _______. "A Propos de Maturin: Ni Vrai Ni Faux, Mais Fantastique," Etudes Irlandaises, 3 (1974): 23-28.

0551. _______. "Quelques Images de la Nature Irlandaise dans l'Oeuvre de C. R. Maturin," in Autour de l'Idée de Nature: Histoire des Idées et Civilisation: Pédagogie et Divers. Paris : Marcel Didier, 1977, pp. 117-124.

0552. _______. "Les Derniers Feux 'Gothiques' in Angleterre," Dix-Huitième Siècle, 14 (1982): 391-406.

0553. ______. "C.R. Maturin: Nationalisme et Fantastique," Etudes Irlandaises, 9 (1984): 43-55.

0554. FOWLER, Kathleen. "Hieroglyphics in Fire: Melmoth the Wanderer," Studies in Romanticism, 25 (1986): 521-539.

0555. GRANT, Douglas. "Maturin's Melmoth the Wanderer," Notes & Queries, 212 (1967): 386.

0556. ______. Introduction to Melmoth the Wanderer by Charles Robert Maturin. London : Oxford UP, 1968, pp.iii-xiv.

0557. GRIGORESCU, Dan. Introdution to Melmoth Ratacitorul by Charles Robert Maturin. Budapest, Hungary : Minerva, 1983.

0558. HAMMOND, Muriel E. "C.R. Maturin and Melmoth the Wanderer," English, 11 (1956): 97-101.

0559. HARRIS, John Bernhard. "Charles Robert Maturin: A Study," Dissertation Abstracts, 30 (1965): 282A (Wayne State University).

0560. ______. Charles Robert Maturin: The Forgotten Imitator. New York : Arno Press, 1980.

0561. HAYTER, Alethea. "Coleridge, Maturin's Bertram, and Drury Lane," in New Approaches to Coleridge: Biographical and Critical Essays, ed. Donald Sultana. New York : Barnes & Noble, 1981, pp.17-37.

0562. ______. Introduction to Melmoth the Wanderer by Charles Robert Maturin. Harmondsworth, England : Penguin, 1977.

0563. HENDERSON, Peter Mills. "A Nut Between Two Blades: The Novels of Charles Robert Maturin," Dissertation Abstracts International, 35 (1974): 6668A (Mc Master University).

0564. ______. A Nut Between Two Blades: The Novels of Charles Robert Maturin. New York : Arno Press, 1980.

0565. HENNELLY, Mark M. Jr. "Melmoth the Wanderer and Gothic Existentialism," Studies in English Literature, 1500-1900, 21 (1981): 665-679.

0566. HINCK, Henry W. "Three Studies on Charles Robert Maturin," Dissertation Abstracts, 15 (1955): 1062-1063 (University of Iowa).

0567. ______. Three Studies on Charles Robert Maturin. New York : Arno Press, 1980.

0568. IDMAN, Niilo. Charles Robert Maturin, His Life and Works. London : Constable, 1923.

0569. KENNEDY, Veronica M.S. "Myth and the Gothic Dream: C.R. Maturin's Melmoth the Wanderer," Pacific Coast Philology, 4 (1969): 41-47.

0570. KOSOK, Heinz. "Charles Robert Maturin: Melmoth the Wanderer," in Der

Englische Roman im 19. Jahrhundert: Interpretationen. Berlin, East Germany : E. Schmidt, 1973, pp.56-75.

0571. KRAMER, Dale. Charles Robert Maturin. New York : Twayne; Twayne English Authors Series Number 156, 1973.

0572. ______. Introduction to The Albigenses: A Romance by Charles Robert Maturin, foreword by James Gray. New York : Arno Press, 1974.

0573. LAYMAN, Beverley J. "Charles Robert Maturin and the Romance of Terror," Unpublished Doctoral Dissertation, University of Virginia, 1973.

0574. LÉVY, Maurice. Introduction to The Fatal Revenge; or, The Family of Montorio by Charles Robert Maturin, foreword by Henry D. Hicks. New York : Arno Press, 1980.

0575. LE YAOANC, Moise. "Melmoth et les Romans du Jeune Balzac," in Balzac and the Nineteenth Century: Studies in French Literature Presented to Herbert J. Hunt by Pupils, Colleagues, and Friends. Leicester, England : Leicester University Press, 1972, pp.35-45.

0576. LLOYD, Rosemary. "Melmoth the Wanderer: The Code of Romanticism," in Baudelaire, Mallarmé, Valéry: New Essays in Honour of Lloyd Austin, eds. Malcolm Bowie, Alison Fairlie, Alison Finch. Cambridge, England : Cambridge UP, 1982, pp.80-94.

0577. LOUGY, Robert E. Charles Robert Maturin. Lewisburg, PA : Bucknell UP, 1974.

0578. LOVELL, Ernest J. Jr. "Byron's 'The Island' and Maturin's Melmoth the Wanderer," Notes & Queries, 194 (1949): 497-499.

0579. "Maturin and the Novel of Terror," Times Literary Supplement, August 26, 1920, p.548.

0580. "Maturin's Melmoth the Wanderer," Notes & Queries, 214 (1969): 465.

0581. MAYOUX, Jean-Jacques. "La Grand Création Satanique du Révérend Maturin," Etudes Anglaises, 22 (1969): 393-396.

0582. MENASCÉ, Esther. "Il Tragico Errare de Faust: Melmoth," Studi di Letteratura Francese (Milan), 9 (1983): 103-127.

0583. MERLE, Robert. "Maturin, ou le Roman Noir," Revue de Paris, March, 1957, pp.20-25.

0584. MONROE, Judson T. "Tragedy in the Novels of the Reverend Charles Robert Maturin," Dissertation Abstracts International, 32 (1972): 6991A (University of California at Davis).

0585. ______. Tragedy in the Novels of the Reverend Charles Robert Maturin. New York : Arno Press, 1980.

0586. MOYNAHAN, Julian. "The Politics of Anglo-Irish Gothic: Maturin, Le Fanu and 'The Return of the Repressed,'" in Studies in Anglo-Irish Literature, ed. Heinz Kosok. Bonn, West Germany : Bouvier, 1982, pp. 43-53.

0587. MÜLLER, W. Charles Robert Maturins Romane "The Fatal Revenge" und "Melmoth the Wanderer", Ein Beitrag zur Gothic Romance. Weida, Germany : Thomas & Hubert, 1908.

0588. NULL, Jack. "Structure and Theme in Melmoth the Wanderer," Papers on Language and Literature, 13 (1977): 136-147.

0589. O'HARA, James. "Maturin and the Novel of Terror," Times Literary Supplement, September 9, 1920, p.584.

0590. O'NEILL, Patrick. "Image and Reception: The German Fortunes of Maria Edgeworth, Lady Morgan, Thomas Moore, and Charles Maturin," Canadian Journal of Irish Studies, 6, number 1 (1980): 36-49.

0591. PETERFREUND, Stuart. "Keats's Debt to Maturin," Wordsworth Circle, 13 (1982): 45-49.

0592. PIPER, H.W. and Norman Jeffares. "Maturin the Innovator," Huntington Library Quarterly, 21 (1958): 261-284.

0593. RATCHFORD, Fannie E. and William H. Mc Carthy, eds. The Correspondence of Sir Walter Scott and Charles Robert Maturin, With a Few Allied Letters. Austin, TX : Texas UP, 1937; Rpt. New York : Garland Publishing, 1980.

0594. REBOUL, Pierre. "Villiers de l'Isle-Adam et le Melmoth de Maturin," Revue de Littérature Comparée, 25 (1951): 479-481.

0595. RUFF, Marcel A. "Maturin et les Romantiques Français," Introduction to Bertram; ou, Le Château de St. Aldobrand by Charles Robert Maturin. Paris : Corti, 1956, pp.7-66.

0596. SCHOLTEN, Willem. Charles Robert Maturin, The Terror Novelist. Amsterdam, Netherlands : H.J. Paris, 1933; Rpt. New York : Garland Publishing, 1981.

0597. SCOTT, Shirley S.C. "Myths of Consciousness in the Novels of Charles Maturin," Dissertation Abstracts International, 34 (1974): 5929A (Kent State University).

0598. ______. Myths of Consciousness in the Novels of Charles Maturin. New York : Arno Press, 1980.

0599. SHIPPS, Anthony W. "Maturin's Melmoth the Wanderer," Notes & Queries, 212 (1967): 475.

0600. ______. "Maturin's Melmoth the Wanderer," Notes & Queries, 213 (1968): 108.

0601. ______. "Maturin's Melmoth the Wanderer," Notes & Queries, 214 (1969): 146.

0602. TRAUTWEIN, Wolfgang. Erlesene Angst: Schauerliteratur um 18. und 19. Jahrhundert: Systematischer Aufriss: Untersuchungen zu Bürger, Maturin, Hoffmann, Poe, und Maupassant. Munich, West Germany : Hanser, 1980.

0603. TREMAYNE, Peter. "Charles Robert Maturin," in Irish Masters of Fantasy. Portmarnock, Ireland : Wolfhound Press, 1979, pp.13-60.

0604. WOLFF, Robert Lee. Introduction to The Milesian Chief by Charles Robert Maturin. New York : Garland Publishing, 1979.

0605. ZEENDER, Marie-Noelle. "Le Miroir dans l'Oeuvre de Maturin, de Le Fanu, de Wilde, et de Stoker," Unpublished Doctoral Dissertation, Université de Reims, 1982.

John William Polidori
(1795-1821)

0606. ADAMS, Donald K. Introduction to The Vampyre; A Tale Written by Doctor Polidori, Pasadena, CA : G. Dahlström, 1968, pp.3-37.

0607. ASH, Russell. Introduction to The Vampyre; A Tale by John Polidori. Tring, England : Gubblecote Press, 1963.

0608. ASTLE, Richard S. "Ontological Ambiguity and Historical Pessimism in Polidori's 'The Vampyre,'" The Sphinx: A Magazine of Literature and Society, 2, number 4 (1977): 8-16.

0609. BLEILER, E.F. Introduction to The Vampyre by Dr. John Polidori in Three Gothic Novels. New York : Dover Publications, 1966, pp.xxxi-xl.

0610. RIEGER, James. "Dr. Polidori and the Genesis of Frankenstein," Studies in English Literature, 1500-1900, 3 (1963): 461-472.

0611. SKARDA, Patricia L. and Nora Crow Jaffe. Introduction to The Vampyre by Dr. John Polidori in The Evil Image: Two Centuries of Gothic Short Fiction and Poetry. New York : New American Library, 1981, pp. 91-94.

0612. VIETS, Henry R. "The London Editions of Polidori's The Vampyre," Papers of the Bibliographical Society of America, 63 (1969): 93-103.

Ann Radcliffe
(1764-1823)

0613. ADICKES, Sandra Elaine. "The Social Quest: The Expanded Vision of Four Women Travelers in the Era of the French Revolution," Dissertation Abstracts International, 38 (1978): 7308A (New York University).

0614. ALBERTAZZI, Silvia. "Figurazinoni Oniriche nel Romance 'Italiano' di Ann Radcliffe," Spicilegio Moderno, 9 (1978): 146-153.

0615. ARNAUD, Pierre. "Un Document Inédit: Le Contrat des Mysteries of Udolpho," Etudes Anglaises, 20 (1967): 55-57.

0616. ______. Ann Radcliffe et le Fantastique: Essai de Psychobiographie. Paris : Aubier Montaigne, 1976.

0617. ______. "Les Jardins dans les Romans de Mrs. Radcliffe," in Autour de l'Idée de Nature: Histoire des Idées et Civilisation: Pédagogie et Divers. Paris : Marcel Didier, 1977, pp.83-89.

0618. BEATY, Frederick L. "Mrs. Radcliffe's Fading Gleam," Philological Quarterly, 42 (1963): 126-129.

0619. BERTHIER, Philippe. "Stendhal, Mme. Radcliffe et l'Art du Paysage," Stendhal-Club, 17 (1975): 305-307.

0620. BREY, Joseph. Die Naturschilderungen in den Romanen und Gedichten der Mrs. Ann Radcliffe, Nebst einem Rückblick auf die Entwicklung der Naturschilderung im Englischen Romane des 18. Jahrhunderts. Nürnberg, Germany : F. Korn, 1911.

0621. BROADWELL, Elizabeth P. "The Veil Image in Ann Radcliffe's The Italian," South Atlantic Bulletin, 40, number 4 (1975): 76-87.

0622. BUTLER, Marilyn. "Ann Radcliffe in the Novels of Mary Wollstonecraft and Jane Austen," Women & Literature, 1 (1980): 128-148.

0623. CAPONE, Giovanna. "'What Do I See?. . .': Un Paradigma nel Romanzo Gotico," Spicilegio Moderno, 10 (1978): 96-114.

0624. CHRISTIENSEN, Merton A. "Udolpho, Horrid Mysteries, and Coleridge's Machinery of the Imagination," Wordsworth Circle, 2 (1971): 153-159.

0625. COOLIDGE, Archibald C. Jr. "Charles Dickens and Mrs. Radcliffe: A Farewell to Wilkie Collins," Dickensian, 58 (1962): 112-116.

0626. COTTOM, Daniel. "Ann Radcliffe: The Figure in the Landscape," and "Ann Radcliffe: The Labyrinth of Decorum," in The Civilized Imagination: A Study of Ann Radcliffe, Jane Austen, and Sir Walter Scott. Cambridge, England : Cambridge UP, 1985, pp.35-67.

0627. DECOTTIGNIES, Jean. "A l'Occasion Centenaire de la Naissance d'Anne Radcliffe: Un Domaine 'Maudit' dans les Lettres Françaises aux Environs de 1800," Revue des Sciences Humaines, 116 (1964): 447-475.

0628. DE GATEGNO, Paul J. "Ann Radcliffe," in Critical Survey of Long Fiction, ed. Frank Magill. Englewood Cliffs, NJ : Salem Press, 1983, VI, pp.2195-2204.

0629. DOBRÉE, Bonamy. Introduction to The Mysteries of Udolpho by Ann Radcliffe. London : Oxford UP, 1966, pp.vii-xvi.

0630. DURANT, David S. Jr. "Ann Radcliffe's Novels: Experiments in Setting,"

Dissertation Abstracts International, 32 (1972): 5225A-5226A (University of North Carolina).

0631. _______. Ann Radcliffe's Novels: Experiments in Setting. New York : Arno Press, 1980.

0632. _______. "Aesthetic Heroism in The Mysteries of Udolpho," The Eighteenth Century: Theory and Interpretation, 22 (1981): 175-188.

0633. _______. "Ann Radcliffe and the Conservative Gothic," Studies in English Literature, 1500-1900, 22 (1982): 519-530.

0634. ELLIS, Stewart Marsh. "Ann Radcliffe and Her Literary Influence," Contemporary Review, 123 (1923): 188-197.

0635. EPSTEIN, Lynne. "Mrs. Radcliffe's Landscapes: The Influence of Three Landscape Painters on Her Nature Descriptions," Hartford Studies in Literature, 1 (1969): 107-120.

0636. _______. "Ann Radcliffe's Gothic Landscape of Fiction and the Various Influences Upon It," Dissertation Abstracts International, 32 (1972): 5735A (New York University).

0637. "Extricating Emily," Time Magazine, April 22, 1966, p.88.

0638. FARRAND, Margaret L. "Udolpho and Childe Harold," Modern Language Notes, 45 (1930): 220-221.

0639. FAWCETT, Mary Laughlin. "Udolpho's Primal Mystery," Studies in English Literature, 1500-1900, 23 (1983): 481-494.

0640. FRANK, Frederick S. "A Bibliography of Writings About Ann Radcliffe," Extrapolation, 17 (1975): 54-62.

0641. FREEMAN, R. Austin. Introduction to The Mysteries of Udolpho by Ann Radcliffe. New York : Dent & Dutton, 1959, pp.v-xi.

0642. GARBER, Frederick. Introduction to The Italian; or, The Confessional of the Black Penitents by Ann Radcliffe. London : Oxford UP, 1968, pp.iii-xxii.

0643. GARRETT, John. "Gothic Strains and Bourgeois Sentiments in the Novels of Mrs. Radcliffe and Her Imitators," Unpublished Doctoral Dissertation, Dalhousie University, 1973.

0644. _______. Gothic Strains and Bourgeois Sentiments in the Novels of Mrs. Radcliffe and Her Imitators. New York : Arno Press, 1980.

0645. GRANT, Aline. Ann Radcliffe. Denver, CO : Alan Swallow, 1951.

0646. GREENER, Amy. "Ann Radcliffe, Novelist," in A Lover of Books: The Life and Literary Papers of Lucy Harrison. London : J.M. Dent, 1916, pp. 183-204.

0647. GRIGORESCU, Dan. Introduction to Misterle din Udolpho by Ann Radcliffe. Budapest, Hungary : Minerva, 1983.

0648. HAGSTRUM, Jean H. "Pictures to the Heart: The Psychological Picturesque in Ann Radcliffe's The Mysteries of Udolpho," in Centennial Studies: Essays Presented to Donald Greene in the Centennial Year of the University of Southern California, eds. Paul J. Korshin, Robert R. Allen. Charlottesville, VA : Virginia UP, 1984, pp.434-444.

0649. HAVENS, Raymond D. "Ann Radcliffe's Nature Descriptions," Modern, Language Notes, 66 (1951): 251-255.

0650. HELLER, Lynne Epstein. Ann Radcliffe's Gothic Landscape of Fiction and the Various Influences Upon It. New York : Arno Press, 1980.

0651. HUKE, I.R. "The Gothic Novels of the Radcliffe School: A Study of the Novels Written Between 1788 and 1800 by Mrs. Ann Radcliffe and Her Imitators, With Special Attention to the Relationship Between these Novels and the Theories of the Sublime Evolved by Edmund Burke and Others," Master of Philosophy Thesis, University of East Anglia, 1977.

0652. JEUNE, Simon. "Autour de L'Abbesse de Castro," Travaux de Linguistique et de Littérature (Université de Strasbourg), 20 (1972): 99-111.

0653. JONES, Lilla Maria Crisafulli. "Parodia e Satanismo nel Romanzo 'Italiano' di Ann Radcliffe," Spicilegio Moderno, 9 (1978): 136-145.

0654. KAHANE, Claire. "Gothic Mirrors and Feminine Identity," Centennial Review, 24 (1980): 43-64.

0655. KEEBLER, Lee E. "Ann Radcliffe: A Study in Achievement," Dissertation Abstracts, 28 (1968): 3145A (University of Wisconsin).

0656. KELLY, Gary. "'A Constant Vicissitude of Interesting Passions': Ann Radcliffe's Perplexed Narratives," Ariel: A Review of International English Literature, 10, number 2 (1979): 45-64.

0657. KOENIG, Linda Ruth. "Ann Radcliffe and Gothic Fiction," Dissertation Abstracts International, 39 (1978): 297A-298A (University of Iowa).

0658. KOOIMAN-VAN MIDDENDORP, Gerarda M. "Ann Radcliffe," in The Hero in the Feminine Novel. New York : Haskell House, 1966, pp.35-38.

0659. KORNIGER, Siegfried. "Radcliffe: The Mysteries of Udolpho," in Der Englische Roman: Vom Mittelalter zur Moderne. Düsseldorf, West Germany : Basel, 1969, I, pp.312-337.

0660. KOSTELNICK, Charles. "From Picturesque View to Picturesque Vision: William Gilpin and Ann Radcliffe," Mosaic, 18, number 3 (1985): 31-48.

0661. LANG, Andrew. "Mrs. Radcliffe's Novels," Cornhill Magazine, 9, number 49 (1900): 23-34.

0662. _______. "Mrs. Radcliffe's Novels," in Adventures Among Books. London : Longman's, 1905, pp.119-138.

0663. LÉVY, Maurice. "Une Nouvelle Source d'Ann Radcliffe: Les Memoires du Comte de Comminge," CALIBAN, 1 (1964): 149-156.

0664. MAGNIER, Mireille. "Le Fantastique Selon Mrs. Radcliffe," Mythes, Croyances et Religions de la Monde Anglo-Saxon, 3 (1985): 104-111.

0665. MAYO, Robert D. "And Radcliffe and Ducray-Duminil," Modern Language Review, 36 (1941): 501-505.

0666. MC CULLOUGH, Bruce. "The Gothic Romance, Mrs. Ann Radcliffe; The Mysteries of Udolpho," in Representative English Novelists: Defoe to Conrad. New York : Harper's, 1946, pp.84-96.

0667. MC INTYRE, Clara F. Ann Radcliffe in Relation to Her Time. New Haven, CT : Yale UP; Yale Studies in English Number 62, 1920; Rpt. Hamden, CT : Archon, 1970.

0668. MC KILLOP, A.D. "Mrs. Radcliffe on the Supernatural in Poetry," Journal of English and Germanic Philology, 31 (1932): 352-359.

0669. MESSAC, Régis. "Les Mystères du Château d'Udolphe," in Le Detective Novel et l'Influence de la Pensée Scientifique. Paris : Edouard Champion, 1929, pp.158-177.

0670. MEYER, Georges. "Les Romans de Mrs. Radcliffe," Revue Germanique, 5 (1909): 509-550.

0671. MOESCH, Vasil. Naturschau und Naturgefühl im dem Romanen der Mrs. Radcliffe und in der Zeitgenössischen Englischen Reiseliteratur. Freiburg, Germany : Caritas, 1924.

0672. MURRAH, Charles C. "Mrs. Radcliffe's Landscapes: The Eye and the Fancy," University of Windsor Review, 18 (1984): 7-23.

0673. MURRAY, E.B. Ann Radcliffe. New York : Twayne; Twayne English Authors Series Number 149, 1972.

0674. NICHOLS, Nina da Vinci. "Place and Eros in Radcliffe, Lewis, and Bronte," in The Female Gothic, ed. Juliann E. Fleenor. Montreal, Canada: Eden Press, 1983, pp.187-206

0675. NOLLEN, Elizabeth. "Ann Radcliffe's A Sicilian Romance: A New Source of Jane Austen's Sense and Sensibility," English Language Notes, 22 (1984): 30-37.

0676. PAPPAGEORGE, Julia di Stefano. "Coleridge's 'Mad Lutanist': A Romantic Response to Ann Radcliffe," Bulletin of Research in the Humanities, 82 (1979): 222-235.

0677. PECK, W.E. "Keats, Shelley, and Mrs. Radcliffe," Modern Language Notes, 39 (1924): 251-252.

0678. PLATT, Constance Mc Cormick. "Patrimony as Power in Four Eighteenth-

Century Women's Novels: Charlotte Lennox, Henrietta (1758); Fanny Burney, Evelina (1778); Charlotte Smith, Emmeline (1788); Ann Radcliffe, The Mysteries of Udolpho (1794)," Dissertation Abstracts International, 41 (1981): 3595A (University of Denver).

0679. POENICKE, Klaus. "'Schönheit im Schosse des Schreckens': Raumgefüge und Menschenbild im Englischen Schauerroman," Archiv für das Studium der Neueren Sprachen und Literaturen, 207 (1970): 1-19.

0680. POOVEY, Mary. "Ideology and The Mysteries of Udolpho," Criticism, 21 (1979): 307-330.

0681. POUND, Edward Fox. "The Influence of Burke and the Psychological Critics on the Novels of Ann Radcliffe," Dissertation Abstracts, 25 (1964): 1198 (University of Washington).

0682. PRICE, F.W. "Ann Radcliffe, Mrs. Siddons, and the Character of Hamlet," Notes & Queries, 23 (1976): 164-167.

0683. RENO, Robert Princeton. "The Gothic Visions of Ann Radcliffe and Matthew Gregory Lewis," Dissertation Abstracts International, 37 (1977): 7767A (Michigan State University).

0684. _______. The Gothic Visions of Ann Radcliffe and Matthew G. Lewis. New York : Arno Press, 1980.

0685. RONALD, Ann. "Terror-Gothic: Nightmare and Dream in Ann Radcliffe and Charlotte Bronte," in The Female Gothic, ed. Juliann E. Fleenor. Montreal, Canada : Eden Press, 1983, pp.176-186.

0686. ROPER, Derek. "Coleridge, Dyer and The Mysteries of Udolpho," Notes & Queries, 19 (1972): 287-289.

0687. RUFF, William. "Ann Radcliffe, or, The Hand of Taste," in The Age of Johnson, Essays Presented to Chauncey Brewster Tinker. New Haven : Yale UP, 1949, pp.183-193.

0688. SADLEIR, Michael. "Poems by Ann Radcliffe," Times Literary Supplement, March 29, 1928, p.242.

0689. SANNA, Vittoria. "La Datazione del Libro di Viaggi di Ann Radcliffe," in Critical Dimensions: English, German, and Comparative Literature Essays in Honor of Aurelio Zanco. Cuneo, Italy : SASTE, 1978, pp. 291-312.

0690. SCHROEDER, Natalie. "The Mysteries of Udolpho and Clermont: The Radcliffean Encroachment on the Art of Regina Maria Roche," Studies in the Novel, 12 (1980): 131-143.

0691. SEDGWICK, Eve Kosofsky. "The Character in the Veil: Imagery of the Surface in the Gothic Novel," Publications of the Modern Language Association, 96 (1981): 255-270.

0692. SHACKFORD, Martha Hale. "The Eve of St. Agnes and The Mysteries of Udolpho," Publications of the Modern Language Association, 36 (19-

21): 104-118.

0693. SHERMAN, Leona F. "Ann Radcliffe and the Gothic Romance: A Psychoanalytic Approach," Dissertation Abstracts International, 36 (1975): 1536A (SUNY at Buffalo).

0694. ______. Ann Radcliffe and the Gothic Romance. New York : Arno Press, 1980.

0695. SHROYER, Frederick. Introduction to The Castles of Athlin and Dunbayne; A Highland Story by Ann Radcliffe. New York : Arno Press, 1972.

0696. SMITH, Nelson C. "The Art of the Gothic: Ann Radcliffe's Major Novels," Dissertation Abstracts, 29 (1968): 240A-241A (Washington State University).

0697. ______. "Sense, Sensibility and Ann Radcliffe," Studies in English Literature, 1500-1900, 13 (1973): 577-590.

0698. ______. The Art of the Gothic: Ann Radcliffe's Major Novels. New York : Arno Press, 1980.

0699. SPECTOR, Robert D. and Martin Tucker. Introduction to A Sicilian Romance by Ann Radcliffe. New York : Johnson Reprint, 1971.

0700. SPINA, Georgio. L'Epoca d'Oro dei "Tales of Terror": Ann Radcliffe. Genova, Italy : Bozzi, 1970.

0701. STEEVES, Harrison R. Introduction to The Romance of the Forest by Ann Radcliffe in Three Eighteenth-Century Romances. New York : Charles Scribner's Sons, 1971.

0702. STOLER, John A. "Ann Radcliffe: The Novel of Suspense and Terror," Dissertation Abstracts International, 32 (1972): 5203A (University of Arizona).

0703. ______. Ann Radcliffe: The Novel of Suspense and Terror. New York : Arno Press, 1980.

0704. SUMMERS, Montague. "A Great Mistress of Romance: Ann Radcliffe, 1764-1823," Transactions of the Royal Society of Literature, 35 (1917): 39-78; Rpt. Essays in Petto by Montague Summers. Freeport, NY : Books for Libraries Press, 1967, pp.3-29.

0705. SWIGART, Ford H. Jr. "A Study of the Imagery in the Gothic Romances of Ann Radcliffe," Dissertation Abstracts, 27 (1967): 2509A-2510A (University of Pittsburgh).

0706. ______. "Ann Radcliffe's Veil Imagery," in Studies in the Humanities. Indiana, PA : Indiana of Pennsylvania UP, 1969, pp.55-59.

0707. ______. A Study of the Imagery in the Gothic Romances of Ann Radcliffe. New York : Arno Press, 1980.

0708. SYPHER, Wylie. "Social Ambiguity in the Gothic Novel," Partisan Review, 12 (1945): 50-60.

0709. TAMKIN, Linda Ellen. "Heroines in Italy: Studies in the Novels of Ann Radcliffe, George Eliot, Henry James, E.M. Forster, and D.H. Lawrence," Dissertation Abstracts International, 45 (1985): 2536A (University of California at Los Angeles).

0710. TATU, Chantal. "Cris et Chuchotements dans Les Mystères d'Udolphe d'Anne Radcliffe: Mais à Quoi Sert le Fantastique?" Caliban, 16 (1979): 87-97.

0711. _______. "L'Histoire des Mystères d'Udolphe en France, ou les Péripéties 'Populaires' d'un Imaginaire Conservateur," Europe, 659 (1984): 38-53.

0712. THOMAS, Donald. "The First Poetess of Romantic Fiction: Ann Radcliffe, 1764-1823," English, 15 (1964): 91-95.

0713. THOMPSON, L.F. "Ann Radcliffe's Knowledge of German," Modern Language Review, 20 (1925): 190-191.

0714. THOMSON, John. "The Novels of Ann Radcliffe," Unpublished Doctoral Dissertation, University of Otago, 1975.

0715. _______. "Ann Radcliffe's Use of Philippus Van Limborch's The History of the Inquisition," English Language Notes, 18 (1980): 31-33.

0716. _______. "Seasonal and Lighting Effects in Ann Radcliffe's Fiction," Journal of the Australasian Language and Literature Association: A Journal of Literary Criticism, Philology, and Linguistics, 56 (1981): 191-200.

0717. THORLEV, Peter Jr. The Byronic Hero: Types and Prototypes. Minneapolis, MN : Minnesota UP, 1962.

0718. TODD, Janet. "Posture and Imposture: The Gothic Manservant in Ann Radcliffe's The Italian," Women & Literature, 2 (1982): 25-38.

0719. TOMPKINS, J.M.S. "The Work of Mrs. Radcliffe and Its Influence on Lat-Later Writers," Doctoral Dissertation, Bedford College of the University of London, 1921.

0720. _______. "Raymond de Carbonnières, Grosley, and Mrs. Radcliffe," Review of English Studies, 5 (1929): 294-301.

0721. _______. Ann Radcliffe and Her Influence on Later Writers. New York : Arno Press, 1980.

0722. VARMA, Devendra P. Introduction to The Italian; or, The Confessional of the Black Penitents by Ann Radcliffe. New York : Russell & Russell, 1968.

0723. _______. Introduction to A Sicilian Romance by Ann Radcliffe, foreword by Howard Mumford Jones. New York : Arno Press, 1972.

0724. _______. Introduction to Gaston De Blondville; or, The Court of Henry III Keeping Festival in Ardenne by Ann Radcliffe. New York : Arno Press, 1972.

0725. _______. Introduction to The Romance of the Forest by Ann Radcliffe, foreword by Frederick Garber. New York : Arno Press, 1980.

0726. _______. "Ann Radcliffe," in Supernatural Fiction Writers, ed. E.F. Bleiler. New York : Charles Scribner's Sons, 1985, I, pp.145-151.

0727. WARE, Malcolm. "Mrs. Radcliffe's 'Picturesque Embellishment,'" Tennessee Studies in Literature, 5 (1960): 67-71.

0728. _______. Sublimity in the Novels of Ann Radcliffe: A Study of the Influence Upon Her Craft of Edmund Burke's Enquiry into the Origin of Our Ideas of the Sublime and Beautiful, English Institute of the University of Uppsala: Essays and Studies on English Language and Literature. Uppsala, Sweden: Lindequist, 1963; Rpt. Copenhagen, Den-Denmark : Ejnar Munksgaard, 1973.

0729. _______. "The Telescope Reversed: Ann Radcliffe and Natural Scenery," in A Provision of Human Nature: Essays on Fielding and Others in Honor of Miriam Austin Locke. University, AL : Alabama UP, 1977, pp. 169-189.

0730. WEISSMAN, Alan. "Thoughts in Things: Ann Radcliffe as a Psychological Novelist," Dissertation Abstracts International, 42 (1982): 4013A (City University of New York).

0731. WHITT, Celia. "Poe and The Mysteries of Udolpho," University of Texas Studies in English, 17 (1937): 124-131.

0732. WIETEN, Alida Albertine Sibbellina. Mrs. Radcliffe. Her Relation Towards Romanticism; With an Appendix on the Novels Falsely Ascribed to Her. Amsterdam, Netherlands : H.J. Paris, 1926.

0733. WOLFF, Cynthia G. "The Radcliffean Gothic Model: A Form for Feminine Sexuality," Modern Language Studies, 9, number 3 (1979): 98-113.

0734. WRIGHT, Andrew. Introduction to The Castle of Otranto, The Mysteries of Udolpho, Northanger Abbey. New York : Holt, Rinehart, Winston, 1963, pp.vii-xxi.

0735. WRIGHT, Eugene P. "A Divine Analysis of The Romance of the Forest," Discourse, 13 (1970): 379-387.

Clara Reeve
(1729-1807)

0736. EHLERS, Leigh A. "A Striking Lesson to Posterity: Providence and Character in Clara Reeve's The Old English Baron," Enlightenment Essays, 9 (1978): 62-76.

0737. REEVES, John K. "The Mother of Fatherless Fanny," Journal of English Literary History, 9 (1942): 224-233.

0738. ROBERTS, W. "Fatherless Fanny," Times Literary Supplement, January 17, 1935, p.33.

0739. SPECTOR, Robert D. Introduction to The Old English Baron by Clara Reeve, in Seven Masterpieces of Gothic Horror. New York : Bantam Books, 1963, pp.1-11.

0740. SPENCER, J. "Minor Women Novelists and Their Presentation of a Feminine Ideal, 1744-1800, With Special Reference to Sarah Fielding, Charlotte Lennox, Frances Brooke, Elizabeth Griffin, Harriet Lee, Clara Reeve, Charlotte Smith, Mary Wolstonecraft, and Jane West," Unpublished Doctoral Dissertation, Oxford University, 1982.

0741. TRAINER, James. Introduction to The Old English Baron by Clara Reeve. London : Oxford UP, 1967.

Mary Shelley
(1797-1851)

0742. ALDISS, Brian W. "Mary Wollstonecraft Shelley, 1797-1851," in Science Fiction Writers: Critical Studies of the Major Authors from the Early Nineteenth Century to the Present Day, ed. E.F. Bleiler. New York : Charles Scribner's Sons, 1982, pp.3-9.

0743. ARNOLD, Donna. "Frankenstein's Monster: Paragon or Paranoic?" Trace, 54 (Autumn, 1964): 385-387.

0744. AWAD, Louis. "The Alchemist in English Literature: Frankenstein," Bulletin of the Faculty of Arts (Fuad I University, Cairo), 13, part I (May, 1951): 33-82.

0745. BAUM, Joan. "The Lessons of Frankenstein," Rendezvous, 12, number 2 (1977): 5-8.

0746. BEAUCHAMP, Gorman. "The Frankenstein Complex and Asimov's Robots," Mosaic, 13, numbers 3-4 (1980): 83-94.

0747. BIGLAND, Eileen. Mary Shelley. London : Cassell, 1959; New York : Appleton-Century-Crofts, 1959.

0748. BLOOM, Harold. "Frankenstein, or, The New Prometheus," Partisan Review, 32 (1965): 611-618; Rpt. in Ringers in the Tower: Studies in the Romantic Tradition. Chicago : Chicago UP, 1971, pp.119-129.

0749. BOUJUT, Michel. "Preface and Filmography" to Frankenstein by Mary Shelley. Levallois-Perret (Hauts-de-Seine), France : Cercle du Bibliophile, 1969.

0750. BOUSQUET, Gilles. "Figures du Monstrueux et Récit Fantastique au XIXe Siècle," in Monstrueux dans la Littérature et la Pensée Anglaises, ed. Nadia J. Rigaud. Aix-le-Provence, France : U de Provence, 1985, pp.117-131.

0751. BOWERBANK, Sylvia. "The Social Order vs. the Wretch: Mary Shelley's Contradictory-Mindedness in *Frankenstein*," *Journal of English Literary History*, 46 (1979): 418-431.

0752. BROOKS, Anita. "Frankenstein's Lonely Monster," in *Practical English Handbook*, eds. Floyd Watkins, William Dillingham, Edwin Martin. Boston : Houghton, Mifflin, 1974, pp.287-308.

0753. BROOKS, Peter. "Godlike Science/Unhallowed Arts: Language and Monstrosity in *Frankenstein*," *New Literary History*, 9 (1978): 591-605.

0754. BUCHEN, Irving H. "*Frankenstein* and the Alchemy of Creation and Evolution," *Wordsworth Circle*, 8 (1977): 103-112.

0755. CALLAGHAN, Cecily. "Mary Shelley's *Frankenstein*: A Compendium of Romanticism," Unpublished Doctoral Dissertation, Leland Stanford Junior University, 1936.

0756. CALLAHAN, Patrick J. "*Frankenstein*, Bacon and the 'Two Truths,'" *Extrapolation*, 14 (1972): 39-48.

0757. CHURCH, Richard. *Mary Shelley (1797-1851)*. London : Gerald Howe, 1928; New York : Viking Press, 1928.

0758. CLARIDGE, Laura P. "Parent-Child Tensions in *Frankenstein*: The Search for Communion," *Studies in the Novel*, 17 (1985): 14-26.

0759. CLUBBE, John. "Mary Shelley as Autobiographer: The Evidence of the 1831 Introduction to *Frankenstein*," *Wordsworth Circle*, 12 (1981): 102-106.

0760. CONGER, Lesley. "Mary's Monster," *The Writer*, 89 (October, 1976): 8-10.

0761. CONGER, Syndy M. "A German Ancestor for Mary Shelley's Monster: Kahlert, Schiller, and the Buried Treasure of *Northanger Abbey*," *Philological Quarterly*, 59 (1980): 216-232.

0762. COTTOM, Daniel. "*Frankenstein* and the Monster of Representation," *Substance*, 28 (1980): 60-71.

0763. CRAFTS, Stephen. "*Frankenstein*: Camp Curiosity or Premonition?" *Cata-Catalyst*, 3 (1968): 96-103.

0764. CROUCH, Laura Ernestine. "The Scientist in English Literature: Domingo Gonsales (1638) to Victor Frankenstein (1817)," *Dissertation Abstracts International*, 36 (1975): 2181A (University of Oklahoma).

0765. ______. "Davy's A Discourse, Introductory to a Course of Lectures on Chemistry: A Possible Scientific Source of *Frankenstein*," *Keats-Shelley Journal*, 27 (1978): 35-44.

0766. CRUZALEGUI, Patricia. "Shelley: Observaciones Sobre una Estética del

Terror," Quimera: Revista de Literature, 31 (1983): 23-27.

0767. CUDE, Wilfred. "Mary Shelley's Modern Prometheus: A Study in the Ethics of Scientific Creativity," Dalhousie Review, 52 (1972): 212-225.

0768. DOWSE, Robert E. and D.J. Palmer. Introduction to Frankenstein; or, The Modern Prometheus by Mary Shelley. New York : E.P. Dutton, 1963.

0769. DUNN, Jane. Moon in Eclipse: A Life of Mary Shelley. New York : St. Martin's Press, 1978.

0770. DUNN, Richard J. "Narrative Distance in Frankenstein," Studies in the Novel, 6 (1974): 408-417.

0771. DUSSINGER, John A. "Kinship and Guilt in Mary Shelley's Frankenstein," Studies in the Novel, 8 (1976): 38-55.

0772. EBELING, Hermann. "Die Stunde Frankensteins," Der Monat, 19 (1967): 30-41.

0773. ELLIS, Kate. "Monsters in the Garden: Mary Shelley and the Bourgeois Family," in The Endurance of Frankenstein: Essays on Mary Shelley's Novel. Berkeley, CA : California UP, 1979, pp.123-142.

0774. EL-SHATER, Safaa. The Novels of Mary Shelley. Salzburg, Austria : Institut für Englische Sprache und Literatur, Universität Salzburg, 1977.

0775. FAIRCLOUGH, Peter and Mario Praz. Introduction to Frankenstein; or, The Modern Prometheus by Mary Shelley in Three Gothic Novels. Baltimore, MD : Penguin Books, 1968, pp.7-34.

0776. FLECK, P.D. "Mary Shelley's Notes to Shelley's Poems and Frankenstein," Studies in Romanticism, 6 (1967): 226-254.

0777. FLORESCU, Radu. "Mary Shelley and the Gothic Novel," in In Search of Frankenstein. New York : New York Graphic Society, 1975, pp.173-187.

0778. FOUST, R.E. "Monstrous Image: Theory of Fantasy Antagonists," Genre, 13 (1980): 441-453.

0779. FRANK, Frederick S. "Mary Shelley's Frankenstein: A Register of Research," Bulletin of Bibliography, 40 (1983): 163-187.

0780. GARDNER, Joseph H. "Mary Shelley's Divine Tragedy," Essays in Literature, 4 (1977): 182-197.

0781. GAYLIN, Willard. "The Frankenstein Myth Becomes a Reality--We Have the Awful Knowledge to Make Exact Copies of Human Beings," New York Times Magazine, March 5, 1972, pp.12-13, 41, 43-44, 48-49.

0782. GERARD, Albert. "Prométhée à l'Envers, ou le Mythe de Frankenstein,"

Synthèses, Revue Mensuelle Internationale, 7 (1953): 353-360.

0783. GERSON, Noel B. Daughter of Earth and Water. New York : William Morrow, 1973.

0784. GILBERT, Sandra. "Horror's Twin: Mary Shelley's Monstrous Eve," Feminist Studies, 4, number 2 (1978): 48-73.

0785. GILBERT, Sandra and Susan Gubar. "Horror's Twin: Mary Shelley's Monstrous Eve," in The Madwoman in the Attic: The Woman Writer and the Nineteenth-Century Literary Imagination. New Haven, CT : Yale UP, 1979, pp.213-247.

0786. GOLDBERG, M.A. "Moral and Myth in Mrs. Shelley's Frankenstein," Keats-Shelley Journal, 8 (1959): 27-38.

0787. GOSHKO, John M. "Frankenstein's Castle is no Horror Show," Boston Globe, November 19, 1972, p.B-38.

0788. GRAY, Douglas Kevin. "Frankenstein and the Development of the English Novel," Dissertation Abstracts International, 43 (1983): 2678A (University of Dallas).

0789. GRIFFIN, Andrew. "Fire and Ice in Frankenstein," in The Endurance of Frankenstein: Essays on Mary Shelley's Novel. Berkeley, CA : California UP, 1979, pp.49-73.

0790. GROSS, D. and M.J.H. Gross. "Joseph Grimaldi: An Influence on Frankenstein," Notes & Queries, 28 (1981): 403-404.

0791. GRYLLS, R. Glynn. Mary Shelley: A Biography. London : Oxford UP, 1938.

0792. HAINING, Peter. The Man Who Was Frankenstein. Chicago : Muller, 1979.

0793. HARRIS, Janet. The Woman Who Created Frankenstein: A Portrait of Mary Shelley. New York : Harper & Row, 1979.

0794. HARVEY, A.D. "Frankenstein and Caleb Williams," Keats-Shelley Journal, 29 (1980): 21-27.

0795. HILL, J.M. "Frankenstein and the Physiognomy of Desire," American Imago, 32 (1975): 335-358.

0796. HIRSCH, Gordon D. "The Monster Was a Lady: On the Psychology of Mary Shelley's Frankenstein," Hartford Studies in Literature, 7 (1975): 116-153.

0797. HITCHENS, Gordon. "'A Breathless Eagerness in the Audience': Historical Notes on Dr. Frankenstein and His Monster," Film Comment, 6 (1970): 49-51.

0798. HODGES, Devon. "Frankenstein and the Feminine Subversion of the Novel," Tulsa Studies in Women's Literature, 2 (1983): 155-164.

0799. HÖHNE, Horst. "Mary Shelley's *Frankenstein*: Komplexität eines Poetischen Bildes und das Ideologische Dilemma Romantischer Dichtung," *Zeitschrift für Anglistik und Amerikanistik (Leipzig)*, 22 (1974): 266-289.

0800. HOUGH, Jo, Brenda Hallenbeck, Francis Simson. "Creator, Created, Creature: A View of Mary Shelley's *Frankenstein*," in *Women Writers and the Literary Tradition*. Adelaide, Australia : Salisbury College of Advanced Education; SCAE Occasional Papers, 1978, pp.22-27.

0801. JACKSON, Donald George. "The Changing Myth of *Frankenstein*: A Historical Analysis of Interactions of a Myth, Technology, and Society," *Dissertation Abstracts International*, 37 (1977): 4664A (University of Texas at Austin).

0802. JOHNSON, Barbara. "My Monster/My Self," *Diacritics*, 12 (1982): 2-10.

0803. JOSEPH, Gerhard. "Frankenstein's Dream: The Child as Father of the Monster," *Hartford Studies in Literature*, 7 (1975): 97-115.

0804. JOSEPH, M.K. Introduction to *Frankenstein*; *or, The Modern Prometheus* by Mary Shelley. London : Oxford UP, 1969.

0805. KAPLAN, Morton and Robert Kloss. "Fantasy of Paternity and the Doppelgänger: Mary Shelley's *Frankenstein*," in *The Unspoken Motive: A Guide to Psychoanalytic Literary Criticism*. New York : Free Press, 1973, pp.119-145.

0806. KESTNER, Joseph. "Narcissism as Symbol and Structure: The Case of Mary Shelley's *Frankenstein*," in *The Nature of Identity*: *Essays Presented to Donald E. Haydon by the Graduate Faculty of Modern Letters, The University of Tulsa*, ed. William Weathers. Tulsa, OK : Tulsa UP, 1981, pp.15-25.

0807. KETTERER, David. "Mary Shelley and Science Fiction: A Select Bibliography Selectively Annotated," *Science-Fiction Studies*, 5 (1978): 172-178.

0808. ________. *Frankenstein's Creation*: *The Book, the Monster, and the Human Reality*. Victoria, BC : Victoria UP; English Literature Studies Number 16, 1979.

0809. ________. "Metaphoric Matrix: Magnetism in *Frankenstein*," in *Selected Proceedings of the 1978 Science Fiction Research Association National Conference*. Cedar Falls, IA : Northern Iowa UP, 1979, pp.55-67.

0810. KMETZ, Gail. "Mary Shelley: In the Shadow of *Frankenstein*," *Ms. Magazine*, February 15, 1975, pp.12-16.

0811. KNOEPFLMACHER, U.C. "Thoughts on the Aggression of Daughters," in *The Endurance of Frankenstein*: *Essays on Mary Shelley's Novel*. Berkeley, CA : California UP, 1979, pp.88-119.

0812. ________. "'Face to Face': Of Man-Apes, Monsters, and Readers," in *The Endurance of Frankenstein*: *Essays on Mary Shelley's Novel*. Berkeley,

CA : California UP, 1979, pp.317-324.

0813. LASZLO, Pierre. "Extase Sublime et Déclin de la Nature: Note sur le Frankenstein de Mary Shelley," Revue des Sciences Humaines, 4 (1982): 89-92.

0814. LAVALLEY, Albert J. "The Stage and Film Children of Frankenstein: A Survey," in The Endurance of Frankenstein: Essays on Mary Shelley's Novel. Berkeley, CA : California UP, 1979, pp.243-289.

0815. LEIGHTON, Margaret. Shelley's Mary: A Life of Mary Wollstonecraft Shelley. New York : Farrar, Straus, Giroux, 1973.

0816. LEVINE, George. "Frankenstein and the Tradition of Realism," Studies in the Novel, 7 (1973): 14-30.

0817. LEVINE, George and U.C. Knoepflmacher, eds. The Endurance of Frankenstein: Essays on Mary Shelley's Novel. Berkeley, CA : California UP, 1979.

0818. LEVINE, George. "The Ambiguous Heritage of Frankenstein," in The Endurance of Frankenstein: Essays on Mary Shelley's Novel. Berkeley, CA : California UP, 1979, pp.3-30.

0819. ______. The Realistic Imagination: English Fiction from Frankenstein to Lady Chatterley. Chicago : Chicago UP, 1981.

0820. LEWIS, Paul. "Victor Frankenstein and Owen Warland: The Artist as Satan and as God," Studies in Short Fiction, 14 (1977): 279-282.

0821. LUND, Mary Graham. "Mary Godwin Shelley and the Monster," University of Kansas City Review, 28 (1962): 253-258.

0822. ______. "Shelley as Frankenstein," Forum, 4, number 2 (1963): 28-31.

0823. ______. "The Faustian Theme in Mary Shelley's Frankenstein," Western World Review, 2 (Fall, 1967): 6-10.

0824. LYLES, William H. "Mary Shelley and Frankenstein," Times Literary Supplement, August 2, 1974, pp.834-835.

0825. ______. Mary Shelley: An Annotated Bibliography. New York : Garland Publishing, 1975.

0826. MARKUS, Manfred. "Erscheinungsformen des Feminismus in Mary Shelleys Frankenstein," Literatur in Wissenschaft und Unterricht, 16 (1983): 1-17.

0827. MAROWITZ, Harold J. "Frankenstein and the Recombinant DNA," in The Wine of Life and Other Essays on Societies, Energy, and Living Things. London : St. Martin's Press, 1979, pp.187-191.

0828. "Mary Shelley," Times Literary Supplement, February 2, 1951, p.69.

0829. MASSEY, Irving. "Singles and Doubles: Frankenstein," in The Gaping Pig: Literature and Metamorphoses. Berkeley, CA : California UP, 1976.

0830. MAYS, Milton A. "Frankenstein, Mary Shelley's Black Theodicy," Southern Humanities Review, 3 (1969): 146-153.

0831. MC CLOSKEY, F.H. "Mary Shelley's Frankenstein," in The Humanities in the Age of Science; In Honor of Peter Sammartino, ed. Charles Angoff. Rutherford, NJ : Fairleigh Dickinson UP, 1968, pp.116-138.

0832. MC GUIRE, Karen Elizabeth. "Pastoralism in the Novels of Mary Shelley," Dissertation Abstracts International, 38 (1978): 6145A-6146A (University of Southern California).

0833. ______. "The Artist as Demon in Mary Shelley, Stevenson, Walpole, Stoker, and King," Gothic, new series 1 (1986): 1-5.

0834. MC INERNEY, Peter. "Satanic Conceits in Frankenstein and Wuthering Heights," Milton and the Romantics, 4 (1980): 1-15.

0835. ______. "Frankenstein and the Godlike Science of Letters," Genre, 13 (1980): 455-475.

0836. MC KENNEY, John. "Nietzsche and the Frankenstein Creature," Dalhousie Review, 41 (1961): 40-48.

0837. MC LEOD, Patrick G. "Frankenstein: Unbound and Otherwise," Extrapolation, 21 (1980): 158-166.

0838. MC LOUGHLIN, Maryanne Thomasine. "Frankenstein's Rib," Dissertation Abstracts International, 45 (1984): 530A (Temple University).

0839. MILLHAUSER, Milton. "The Noble Savage in Mary Shelley's Frankenstein," Notes & Queries, 190 (1946): 248-250.

0840. MOECKLI, Gustave. "Un Genevois Méconnu: Frankenstein," Musées de Genève, 3 (November-December, 1962): 10-13.

0841. MOERS, Ellen. "Female Gothic: The Monster's Mother," New York Review of Books, March 21, 1974, pp.24-28.

0842. MONK, Patricia. "Frankenstein's Daughters: The Problems of the Feminine Image in Science Fiction," Mosaic, 13, numbers 3-4 (1980): 15-27.

0843. MOSKOWITZ, Sam. "The Sons of Frankenstein," in Explorers of the Infinite: Shapers of Science Fiction. Cleveland, OH : World Publishing, 1963, pp.33-45.

0844. MULLALY, Edward. "Frankenstein: The Novel," Fiddlehead, 113 (Spring, 1977): 150-152.

0845. MURRAY, E.B. "Shelley's Contribution to Mary's Frankenstein," Keats-Shelley Memorial Bulletin, 29 (1978): 50-68.

0846. _______. "Changes in the 1823 Edition of Frankenstein," Library, 6th series, 3 (1981): 320-327.

0847. NESTRICK, William. "Coming to Life: Frankenstein and the Nature of Film Narrative," in The Endurance of Frankenstein: Essays on Mary Shelley's Novel. Berkeley, CA : California UP, 1979, pp.290-315.

0848. NEUMANN, Bonnie R. "Mary Shelley," Dissertation Abstracts International, 33 (1973): 5689A (University of New Mexico).

0849. _______. Lonely Muse: A Critical Biography of Mary Wollstonecraft Shelley. Salzburg, Austria : Institut für Anglistik und Amerikanistik, Salzburg University; Romantic Reassessment Number 85, 1981.

0850. NITCHIE, Elizabeth. "The Stage History of Frankenstein," South Atlantic Quarterly, 41 (1942): 384-398.

0851. _______. Mary Shelley: Author of Frankenstein. New Brunswick, NJ : Rutgers UP, 1953; Rpt. Westport, CT : Greenwood Press, 1970.

0852. NOCHIMSON, Martha. "Mary Shelley," in Critical Survey of Long Fiction, ed. Frank Magill. Englewood Cliffs, NJ : Salem Press, 1983, VI, 2385-2395.

0853. NORMAN, Sylva. "Mary Shelley: Novelist and Dramatist," in On Shelley. London : Oxford UP, 1938.

0854. _______. "Mary Wollstonecraft Shelley," in Shelley and His Circle, ed. Kenneth Neill Cameron. Cambridge, MA : Harvard UP, 1970, pp.397-422.

0855. OATES, Joyce Carol. "Frankenstein's Fallen Angel," Critical Inquiry, 10 (1984): 543-554.

0856. _______. Afterword to Frankenstein; or, The Modern Prometheus by Mary Shelley, illustrated by Barry Moser. Berkeley, CA : California UP, 1984.

0857. OCASIO, Blanca. "Mary Shelley's Frankenstein: SF Paradigm," in Science Fiction Miscellany: Approaches to the Study of Science Fiction, ed. Madeleine F. Marshall. Mayaguez, PR : Puerto Rico UP, 1979, pp.19-pp.19-27.

0858. O'FLINN, Paul. "Production and Reproduction: The Case of Frankenstein," Literature & History: A New Journal for the Humanities, 9 (1983): 194-213.

0859. OZOLINS, Aija. "The Novels of Mary Shelley: From Frankenstein to Falkner," Dissertation Abstracts International, 33 (1972): 2389A (University of Maryland).

0860. _______. "Dreams and Doctrines: Dual Strands in Frankenstein," Science-Fiction Studies, 2 (1975): 103-112.

0861. ______. "Recent Work on Mary Shelley's *Frankenstein*," *Science-Fiction Studies*, 3 (1976): 187-202.

0862. PALACIO, Jean de. *Mary Shelley dans son Oeuvre: Contribution aux Etudes Shelleyennes*. Paris : Klincksieck, 1969.

0863. PALMER, D.J. and R.E. Dowse. "*Frankenstein*: A Moral Fable," *The Listener*, 68 (August 23, 1962): 281-284.

0864. PARRINDER, Patrick. "Frankenstein's Mother," *Science-Fiction Studies*, 6 (1979): 117.

0865. PATTERSON, Mary Katherine. "*Frankenstein* by Mary Shelley: Notes on a Divided Myth," *Dissertation Abstracts International*, 45 (1985): 23-53A (Ball State University).

0866. PAYOT, Roger. "Note sur Rousseau et *Frankenstein*," *Annales de la Société Jean-Jacques Rousseau*, 38 (1969-1971): 277-281.

0867. PEARSON, Edmund Lester. Introduction to *Frankenstein; or, The Modern Prometheus* by Mary Shelley. New York : Limited Editions Club, 1934; New York : Heritage Press, 1934.

0868. PECK, Walter E. "The Biographical Element in the Novels of Mary Wollstonecraft Shelley," *Publications of the Modern Language Association*, 38 (1923): 196-219.

0869. PITCHER, Edward W.R. "*Frankenstein* as Short Fiction: A Unique Adaptation of Mary Shelley's Novel," *Studies in Short Fiction*, 20 (1983): 49-52.

0870. POLLIN, Burton R. "Philosophical and Literary Sources of *Frankenstein*," *Comparative Literature*, 17 (1965): 97-108.

0871. POOVEY, Mary. "My Hideous Progeny: Mary Shelley and the Feminization of Romanticism," *Publications of the Modern Language Association*, 95 (1980): 332-347.

0872. ______. *The Proper Lady and the Woman Writer: Ideology as Style in the Works of Mary Wollstonecraft, Mary Shelley, and Jane Austen.* Chicago : Chicago UP, 1984.

0873. POWERS, Katherine Richardson. "The Influence of William Godwin on the Novels of Mary Shelley," *Dissertation Abstracts International*, 33 (1973): 4359A (University of Tennessee).

0874. ______. *The Influence of William Godwin on the Novels of Mary Shelley*. New York : Arno Press, 1980.

0875. PRESCOTT, F.C. "*Wieland* and *Frankenstein*," *American Literature*, 2 (1930): 172-173.

0876. RANDEL, Fred V. "*Frankenstein*, Feminism, and the Intertextuality of Mountains," *Studies in Romanticism*, 23 (1984): 515-532.

0877. RAO, E. Nageswara. "The Significance of Frankenstein," Triveni: A Cultural Journal, 37, number 3 (1968): 20-26.

0878. REED, John R. "Will and Fate in Frankenstein," Bulletin of Research in the Humanities, 83 (1980): 319-338.

0879. RIEGER, James. Introduction to Frankenstein; or, The Modern Prometheus by Mary Shelley. Indianapolis, MN : Bobbs-Merrill, 1974, pp.xi-xxxvii; Rpt. Chicago : Chicago UP, 1981.

0880. ROSENBERG, Samuel. "Happy Sesquicentennial, Dear Monster,--The Horrible Truth About Frankenstein," Life Magazine, March 15, 1968, pp. 74D-84; Rpt. as "Frankenstein, or Daddy's Little Monster," in Confessions of a Trivialist. Baltimore, MD : Penguin Books, 1972.

0881. RUBENSTEIN, Marc A. "'My Accursed Origin': The Search for the Mother in Frankenstein," Studies in Romanticism, 15 (1976): 165-194.

0882. RUDOLF, G. "Zur Psychologie der Horrorliteratur. Schizoidess Körpererleben am Beispeil von Frankensteins Monster," Zeitschrift für Psychosomatische Medizin und Psychoanalyse (Göttingen), 18 (July-September, 1972): 205-219.

0883. SCHOPF, Sue Weaver. "Of What a Strange Nature is Knowledge! Hartleian Psychology and the Creature's Arrested Moral Sense in Mary Shelley's Frankenstein," Romanticism Past and Present, 5 (1981): 33-52.

0884. SCHUG, Charles. "The Romantic Form of Mary Shelley's Frankenstein," Studies in English Literature, 1500-1900, 17 (1977): 607-619.

0885. SCOTT, Peter Dale. "Mary Wollstonecraft Godwin Shelley and Frankenstein: A Chronology," in The Endurance of Frankenstein: Essays on Mary Shelley's Novel. Berkeley, CA : California UP, 1979, pp.xvii-xx.

0886. ______. "Vital Artifice: Mary, Percy, and the Psychopolitical Integrity of Frankenstein," in The Endurance of Frankenstein: Essays on Mary Shelley's Novel. Berkeley, CA : California UP, 1979, pp.172-202.

0887. SEED, David. "Frankenstein: Parable or Spectacle?" Criticism, 24 (1982): 327-340.

0888. SENCOURT, Robert. "Mary Wollstonecraft Shelley," Contemporary Review, Number 1102 (October, 1957): 215-218.

0889. SHERWIN, Paul. "Frankenstein: Creation as Catastrophe," Publications of the Modern Language Association, 96 (1981): 883-902.

0890. ______. "A Psychoaesthetic Reading of Mary Shelley's Frankenstein," in English Forum, eds. Saul N. Brody, Harold Schechter. New York : AMS Press, 1985, pp.199-210.

0891. SMALL, Christopher. Ariel Like a Harpy: Shelley, Mary, and Frankenstein. London : Victor Gollancz, 1972; Pittsburgh, PA : Pittsburgh

UP, 1973.

0892. SMITH, Susan Harris. "Frankenstein: Mary Shelley's Psychic Divisiveness," Women & Literature, 5, number 2 (1977): 42-53.

0893. SPARK, Muriel. "Mary Shelley, A Prophetic Novelist," The Listener, 45 (February 22, 1951): 305-306.

0894. ________. Child of Light: A Reassessment of Mary Wollstonecraft Shelley. Hadley, Essex, England : Tower Bridge Publications, 1951; Rpt. Folcroft, PA : Folcroft, 1976; Rpt. Philadelphia : West, 1978.

0895. SPATT, Hartley S. "Mary Shelley's Last Men: The Truth of Dreams," Studies in the Novel, 7 (1975): 526-537.

0896. SPEARS, Marthalee Atkinson. "The Sympathetic Imagination in the Fiction of Mary Wollstonecraft Shelley," Dissertation Abstracts International, 41 (1980): 2620A (University of Kentucky).

0897. SPECTOR, Judith A. "Science Fiction and the Sex War: A Womb of One's Own," Literature and Psychology, 31 (1981): 21-32.

0898. STABLEFORD, Brian. "Frankenstein; or, The Modern Prometheus," in Survey of Modern Fantasy Literature, ed. Frank Magill. Englewood Cliffs, NJ : Salem Press, 1983, II, pp.575-580.

0899. STERRENBERG, Lee. "Mary Shelley's Monster: Politics and Psyche in Frankenstein," in The Endurance of Frankenstein: Essays on Mary Shelley's Novel. Berkeley, CA : California UP, 1979, pp.143-171.

0900. STEVICK, Philip. "Frankenstein and Comedy," in The Endurance of Frankenstein: Essays on Mary Shelley's Novel. Berkeley, CA : California UP, 1979, pp.221-239.

0901. SWINGLE, L.J. "Frankenstein's Monster and its Romantic Relatives: Problems of Knowledge in English Romanticism," Texas Studies in Literature and Language, 15 (1973): 51-66.

0902. TANNENBAUM, Leslie. "From Filthy Type to Truth: Miltonic Myth in Frankenstein," Keats-Shelley Journal, 26 (1977): 101-113.

0903. THOMSEN, Christian W. "Die Verantwortung des Naturwissenschaftlers in Mary Shelleys Frankenstein und Heinar Kipphardts In der Sache J. Robert Oppenheimer: Zur Literarischen Gestaltung eines Problems," Literatur in Wissenschaft und Unterricht (Kiel), 4 (1971): 16-26.

0904. THUR, Robert. "Longing for Union: The Doppelgänger in Wuthering Heights and Frankenstein," Dissertation Abstracts International, 37 (1977): 1472B (California School of Professional Psychology, San Francisco).

0905. TILLOTSON, Marcia. "'A Forced Solitude': Mary Shelley and the Creation of Frankenstein's Monster," in The Female Gothic, ed. Juliann E. Fleenor. Montreal, Canada : Eden Press, 1983, pp.167-175.

0906. TODD, Janet M. "Frankenstein's Daughter: Mary Shelley and Mary Wollstonecraft," Women & Literature, 4, number 2 (1976): 18-27.

0907. TORRES, Augusto M. "Complejo de Frankenstein," Cuadernos Hispanoamericanos, 291 (September, 1974): 702-707.

0908. TROPP, Martin. "Mary Shelley's Monster: A Study of Frankenstein," Dissertation Abstracts International, 34 (1973): 1871A (Boston Univer-University).

0909. ______. Mary Shelley's Monster: The Story of Frankenstein. Boston : Houghton, Mifflin, 1976.

0910. TURELL, Dan. "Vor Tids Jesus Eller Min Brorder Frankenstein," Ekstrabladet, 23 (1974): 11f.

0911. TWITCHELL, James B. "Frankenstein and the Anatomy of Horror," Georgia Review, 37 (1983): 41-78.

0912. VASBINDER, Samuel Holmes. "Scientific Attitudes in Mary Shelley's Frankenstein: Newtonian Monism as a Base for the Novel," Dissertation Abstracts International, 37 (1976): 2842A (Kent State University).

0913. ______. "A Possible Source for the Term 'Vermicelli' in Mary Shelley's Frankenstein," Wordsworth Circle, 12 (1981): 116-117.

0914. ______. Scientific Attitudes in Mary Shelley's Frankenstein. Ann Arbor, MI : UMI Research Press, 1984.

0915. VEEDER, William. "The Negative Oedipus: Frankenstein and the Shelleys," Critical Inquiry, 12 (1986): 365-390.

0916. ______. Mary Shelley and Frankenstein: The Fate of Androgyny. Chicago : Chicago UP, 1986.

0917. VLASOPOLOS, Anca. "Frankenstein's Hidden Skeleton: The Psycho-Politics of Oppression," Science-Fiction Studies, 10 (1983): 125-136.

0918. VOHL, Maria. Die Erzählungen der Mary Shelley und Ihre Urbilder. Heidelberg, Germany : C. Winter, 1913.

0919. VON MAANEN, W. "Mary Shelley en Haar 'Thriller' Frankenstein (1818)," Gids, 4 (1949): 133-138.

0920. WADE, Phil. "On the Occasion of the One Hundred Fiftieth Birthday of Frankenstein's Monster: Some Thoughts on His Parentage," South Atlantic Bulletin, 34 (1969): 10.

0921. ______. "Shelley and the Miltonic Element in Mary Shelley's Frankenstein," Milton and the Romantics, 2 (1976): 23-35.

0922. WALLING, William A. Mary Shelley. New York : Twayne; Twayne English Authors Series Number 128, 1972.

0923. WEBER, Ingeborg. "Wie Schaurig ist Frankenstein?" Anglia: Zeitschrift für Englische Philologie, 95, numbers 3-4 (1977): 404-425.

0924. WEINKAUF, Mary S. "The Daughters of Frankenstein: Women and Science Fiction," Cthulhu Calls, 5, number 1 (1977): 22-26.

0925. WEISSMAN, Judith. "A Reading of Frankenstein as the Complaint of a Political Wife," Colby Library Quarterly, 12 (1976): 171-180.

0926. WEXELBLATT, Robert. "The Ambivalence of Frankenstein," Arizona Quarterly, 36 (1980): 101-117.

0927. WHEELER, Wayne Bruce. "The Horror of Science in Politics: Prophecy and the Crisis of Human Values in Mary Shelley's Frankenstein and Aldous Huxley's Brave New World," Dissertation Abstracts International, 40 (1979): 2246A (Claremont Graduate School).

0928. WILT, Judith. "Frankenstein as Mystery Play," in The Endurance of Frankenstein: Essays on Mary Shelley's Novel. Berkeley, CA : California UP, 1979, pp.31-48.

0929. WOLF, Leonard. The Annotated Frankenstein. New York : Potter, 1977.

0930. ZDANYS, Jonas. "Raskolnikov and Frankenstein: The Deadly Search for a Rational Paradise," Cithara, 16 (1976): 57-67.

0931. ZIOLKOWSKI, Theodore J. "Science, Frankenstein, and Myth," Sewanee Review, 89 (1981): 34-56.

Percy Bysshe Shelley
(1792-1822)

0932. ANTIPPAS, Andy P. "The Structure of Shelley's St. Irvyne: Parallelism and the Gothic Mode of Evil," Tulane Studies in English, 18 (1970): 59-71.

0933. CHESSER, Eustace. Shelley and Zastrozzi: Self-Revelation of a Neurotic. London : Gregg/Archive, 1965.

0934. COATS, Sandra W. "Gothic Elements in Shelley's Prometheus Unbound," Dissertation Abstracts International, 32 (1972): 5732A-5733A (Texas A&M University).

0935. ________. "Shelley and the Promethean Myth," CCTE Proceedings, 48 (1983): 40-47.

0936. COLLINS, Grace Calvert. "Shelley's Treatment of the Legend of the Wandering Jew," Unpublished Master's Thesis, University of North Carolina, 1961.

0937. FRANK, Frederick S. Introduction to St. Irvyne; or, The Rosicrucian and Zastrozzi; A Romance by Percy Bysshe Shelley, foreword by A.J. Hartley. New York : Arno Press, 1977, pp.ix-xxv.

0938. FRIGO, Gabriele. "St. Irvyne, or, The Rosicrucian: Shelley Davvero Rosacrociano ad Oxford--1810-11?" Quaderne di Lingue e Letterature, 9 (1984): 33-55.

0939. HALLIBURTON, David G. "Shelley's 'Gothic' Novels," Keats-Shelley Journal, 16 (1967): 39-49.

0940. HILDEBRAND, William H. "On Three Prometheuses: Shelley's Two and Mary's One," Serif, 11, number 2 (1974): 3-11.

0941. HOGLE, Jerrold E. "Shelley's Fiction: 'The Stream of Fate,'" Keats-Shelley Journal, 30 (1981): 78-99.

0942. HUGHES, A.M.D. "Shelley's Zastrozzi and St. Irvyne," Modern Language Review, 7 (1912): 54-63.

0943. JONES, Frederick L. "Alastor Foreshadowed in St. Irvyne," Publications of the Modern Language Association, 49 (1934): 969-971.

0944. KOSZUL, André. "Quelques Sources des Romans de Shelley," Revue Germanique, 1 (1905): 178-183.

0945. MC CURDY, Harold G. "Shelley The Assassin," Georgia Review, 27 (1973): 182-193.

0946. MURPHY, John V. "Gothic Elements in Shelley's Canon," Dissertation Abstracts, 30 (1970): 3913A-3914A (University of Michigan).

0947. ______. The Dark Angel: Gothic Elements in Shelley's Works. Lewisburg, PA : Bucknell UP, 1975.

0948. SEED, David. "Shelley's 'Gothick' in St. Irvyne and After," in Essays on Shelley, ed. Miriam Allott. Totowa, NJ : Barnes & Noble, 1982, pp.39-70.

0949. ______. "Mystery and Monodrama in Shelley's Zastrozzi," Dutch Quarterly Review, 14 (1984): 1-17.

0950. SICKELS, Eleanor. "Shelley and Charles Brockden Brown," Publications of the Modern Language Association, 45 (1930): 1116-1128.

0951. SOLVE, Melvin T. "Shelley and the Novels of Brown," in Fred Newton Scott Anniversary Papers. Chicago : Chicago UP, 1929, pp.141-156.

0952. STRONG, Archibald. "The Sinister in Shelley," in Three Studies in Shelley. London : Oxford UP, 1921, pp.113-143.

0953. TWITCHELL, James B. "Shelley's Use of Vampirism in The Cenci," Tennessee Studies in Literature, 24 (1979): 120-133.

0954. YOUNG, A.B. "Shelley and M.G. Lewis," Modern Language Review, 1 (1906): 322-324.

0955. ZIMANSKY, Curt R. "Shelley's Wandering Jew: Some Borrowings from Lewis and Radcliffe," Studies in English Literature, 1500-1900, 18 (1978):

0956. ______. "Zastrozzi and The Bravo of Venice: Another Shelley Borrowing," Keats-Shelley Journal, 30 (1981): 15-17.

Charlotte Smith
(1749-1806)

0957. BOWSTEAD, Diana. "Convention and Innovation in Charlotte Smith's Novels," Dissertation Abstracts International, 39 (1979): 4264A-4265A (City University of New York).

0958. BUSHNELL, Nelson S. "Artistic Economy in Jane Eyre: A Contrast with The Old Manor House," English Language Notes, 5 (1968): 197-202.

0959. EHRENPREIS, Anne Henry. Introduction to The Old Manor House by Charlotte Smith. London : Oxford UP, 1969.

0960. ______. Introduction to Emmeline; The Orphan of the Castle by Charlotte Smith. London : Oxford UP, 1971.

0961. ELLIS, Katherine. "Charlotte Smith's Subversive Gothic," Feminist Studies, 3 (1976): 51-55.

0962. FOSTER, James R. "Charlotte Smith: Pre-Romantic Novelist," Publications of the Modern Language Association, 48 (1928): 463-475.

0963. FRY, Carrol L. "Charlotte Smith, Popular Novelist," Dissertation Abstracts International, 31 (1970): 5360A (University of Nebraska).

0964. ______. Charlotte Smith, Popular Novelist. New York : Arno Press, 1980.

0965. HILBISH, Florence May Anna. Charlotte Smith, Poet and Novelist (1749-1806). Gettysburg, PA : Times and News Publishing, 1941.

0966. PIORKOWSKI, Joan Lucille. "'Revolutionary' Sentiment: A Reappraisal of the Fiction of Robert Bage, Charlotte Smith, and Thomas Holcroft," Dissertation Abstracts International, 41 (1980): 2127A (Temple University).

0967. POLLIN, Burton. "Keats, Charlotte Smith, and the Nightingale," Notes & Queries, 13 (1966): 180-181.

0968. ROGERS, Katherine M. "Inhibitions of Eighteenth-Century Women Novelists: Elizabeth Inchbald and Charlotte Smith," Eighteenth-Century Studies, 11 (1977): 63-78.

0969. STANTON, Judith P. "Charlotte Smith's Prose: A Stylistic Study of Four of Her Novels," Dissertation Abstracts International, 39 (1979): 67-83A (University of North Carolina).

0970. TURNER, Rufus Paul. "Charlotte Smith (1749-1806): Some New Light on Her Life and Literary Career," Dissertation Abstracts, 27 (1966): 189A (University of Southern California).

0971. WHITING, George W. "Charlotte Smith, Keats, and the Nightingale," Keats-Shelley Journal, 12 (1963): 4-8.

Horace Walpole
(1717-1797)

0972. BARRELL, R.A. "Horace Walpole and France," Humanities Association Bulletin, 23, number 2 (1972): 33-40.

0973. BLEILER, E.F. Introduction to The Castle of Otranto by Horace Walpole in Three Gothic Novels. New York : Dover Publications, 1966, pp.vii-xl.

0974. BRANDENBERG, Alice S. "The Theme of The Mysterious Mother," Modern Language Quarterly, 10 (1949): 464-474.

0975. BURNEY, E.L. "Shakespeare in Otranto," Manchester Review, 12 (1972): 61-64.

0976. "The Castle of Otranto," Literary Review, February 25, 1922, p.451.

0977. "The Castle of Otranto," Notes & Queries, 180 (1941): 209.

0978. CLARKE, A.H.T. "Strawberry Hill," Times Literary Supplement, May 25, 1940, p.255.

0979. CONANT, Kenneth J. "Horace Walpole and the Gothic Revival," Old Wedgwood, 12 (1945): 62-69.

0980. CONGER, Syndy M. "Faith and Doubt in The Castle of Otranto," Gothic: The Review of Supernatural Horror Fiction, 1 (1979): 51-59.

0981. DOBRÉE, Bonamy. "Horace Walpole," in Restoration and Eighteenth-Century Literature: Essays in Honor of Alan Dugald Mc Killop, ed. Carroll Camden. Chicago : Chicago UP, 1963.

0982. DOLAN, Janet A. "Horace Walpole's The Mysterious Mother: A Critical Edition," Dissertation Abstracts International, 31 (1970):: 4115A-4116A (University of Arizona).

0983. DOUGHTY, Oswald. Introduction to The Castle of Otranto by Horace Walpole. London : Scholastics, 1929.

0984. EASTWOOD, Sidney K. "Horace Walpole," Notes & Queries, 189 (1945): 265.

0985. EHLERS, Leigh A. "The Gothic World as Stage: Providence and Character in The Castle of Otranto," Wascana Review, 14, number 2 (1980): 17-30.

0986. ENGLISH, Sarah Warder. "The Hunger of Imagination: A Study of the Prose Style in Four Gothic Novels," Dissertation Abstracts International, 39 (1979): 6773A-6774A (University of North Carolina).

0987. FAIRCLOUGH, Peter and Mario Praz. Introduction to The Castle of Otranto by Horace Walpole in Three Gothic Novels. Baltimore, MD : Penguin Books, 1968, pp.7-34.

0988. FRANCI, Giovanna. La Messa in Scena del Terrore: Il Romanzo Gotico Inglese. Ravenna, Italy : Longo, 1982.

0989. FRANK, Frederick S. "Horace Walpole's The Castle of Otranto: A Gothic Story," in Survey of Modern Fantasy Literature, ed. Frank Magill. Englewood Cliffs, NJ : Salem Press, 1983, pp.211-216.

0990. ______. "Proto-Gothicism: The Infernal Iconography of Walpole's Castle of Otranto," Orbis Litterarum, 41 (1986): 199-212.

0991. FUJIMOTO, Yukio. "From Amusement to Quest--The Castle of Otranto and Edgar Huntly," Chu-Shikoku Studies in American Literature, 14 (1978): 61-70.

0992. HARFST, Betsy Perteit. "Horace Walpole and the Unconscious: An Experiment in Freudian Analysis," Dissertation Abstracts, 29 (1968): 1511A-1512A (Northern Illinois University).

0993. ______. Horace Walpole and the Unconscious: An Experiment in Freudian Analysis. New York : Arno Press, 1980.

0994. HAVENS, Munson A. Horace Walpole and the Strawberry Hill Press, 1757-1789. Canton, PA : Kirgate Press, 1901.

0995. HAZEN, Allen T. A Bibliography of Horace Walpole. New Haven, CT : Yale UP, 1948.

0996. HENDERSON, Philip. Introduction to The Castle of Otranto by Horace Walpole in Shorter Novels of the Eighteenth Century. New York : E.P. Dutton, 1971, pp.v-xi.

0997. HOLZKNECHT, Karl J. "Horace Walpole as Dramatist," South Atlantic Quarterly, 28 (1929): 174-189.

0998. KALLICH, Martin. Horace Walpole. New York : Twayne; Twayne English Authors Series, 1971.

0999. KETTON-CREMER, R.W. Horace Walpole: A Biography. London : Longmans, Green, 1940; Rpt. London : Methuen, 1964.

1000. KILBY, Clyde S. "Horace Walpole on Shakespeare," Studies in Philology, 38 (1941): 480-493.

1001. LÉVY, Maurice. "Lecture Plurielle du Château d'Otrante," in La Mort, le Fantastique, le Surnaturel du XVIe Siècle à l'Époque Romantique. Lille, France : U de Lille Centre de Recherches dur l'Angleterre des Tudors à la Regénce, 1980, pp.149-153.

1002. LEWIS, Paul. "The Atheist's Tragedy and The Castle of Otranto: Expressions of the Gothic Vision," Notes & Queries, 25 (1978): 52-54.

1003. LEWIS, Wilmarth S. "The Genesis of Strawberry Hill," *Metropolitan Museum Studies*, 5, part 1 (1934): 57-92.

1004. ———. "Horace Walpole Reread," *Atlantic Monthly*, 176 (July, 1945): 48-51.

1005. ———. Introduction to *The Castle of Otranto* by Horace Walpole, notes by Joseph Reed, Jr. London : Oxford UP, 1969.

1006. MAGNIER, M. "*Le Château d'Otrante*, Ébauche d'un Retour au Moyen Age des Merveilles," *Mythes, Croyances et Religions dans le Monde Anglo-Saxon*, 2 (1984): 55-65.

1007. MASSARA, Giuseppe. "G.B. Piranesi and the Novel," in *Studi Inglesi: Raccolta di Saggi e Ricerche*, ed. Agostino Lombardo. Bari, Italy : Adriatica, 1978, pp.77-92.

1008. ———. *Il Teatro della Mente*: *Horace Walpole*. Bari, Italy : Adriatica, 1984.

1009. MEHROTRA, Kevala-Krishna. *Horace Walpole and the English Novel: A Study of the Influence of "The Castle of Otranto", 1764-1820*. Oxford : Basil Blackwell, 1934; Rpt. New York : Russell & Russell, 1970.

1010. MENGELING, Marvin E. "Walpole's 'Otranto': The Gothic Thrust Toward Heaven," *Count Dracula Society Quarterly*, 1, number 9 (1974): unpaginated.

1011. MUDRICK, Marvin. Introduction to *The Castle of Otranto* by Horace Walpole. London : Collier-Macmillan, 1963.

1012. PATERNA, Wilhelm. *Das Übersinnliche im Englischen Roman (von Horace Walpole bis Walter Scott)*. Hamburg, Germany : Lückte & Wulff, 1915.

1013. RIELY, John. "*The Castle of Otranto* Revisited," *Yale University Library Gazette*, 53 (1978): 1-17.

1014. RIGGS, Blanche. "The Place of Horace Walpole in the Gothic Revival," Unpublished Doctoral Dissertation, University of Chicago, 1909.

1015. ROSE, Edward J. "'The Queenly Personality': Walpole, Melville, and Mother," *Literature and Psychology*, 15 (1965): 216-229.

1016. SMITH, Horatio E. "Horace Walpole Anticipates Victor Hugo," *Modern Language Notes*, 41 (1926): 458-461.

1017. SMITH, Warren Hunting. "Strawberry Hill and *Otranto*," *Times Literary Supplement*, May 23, 1936, p.440.

1018. SOLOMON, Stanley J. "Subverting Propriety as a Pattern of Irony in Three Eighteenth-Century Novels: *The Castle of Otranto*, *Vathek*, and *Fanny Hill*," *Erasmus Review*, 1 (1971): 107-116.

1019. SPECTOR, Robert D. Introduction to *The Castle of Otranto* by Horace Walpole in *Seven Masterpieces of Gothic Horror*. New York : Bantam

Books, 1963, pp.1-11.

1020. SPURGEON, Caroline F.E. Introduction to *The Castle of Otranto* by Horace Walpole. London : Chatto & Windus, 1907.

1021. STEIN, Jess M. "Horace Walpole and Shakespeare," *Studies in Philology*, 31 (1934): 51-68.

1022. SUMMERS, Montague. Introduction to *The Castle of Otranto* by Horace Walpole. London : Constable, 1924, pp.ix-lvii.

1023. THIERGARD, Ulrich. "Schiller und Walpole: Ein Beitrag zu Schillers Verhältnis zur Schauerliteratur," *Jahrbuch der Schiller-Gesellschaft*, 3 (1959): 102-117.

1024. VALENSISE, Rachele. "*The Castle of Otranto* e l'Incubo del Potere," *Siculorum Gymnasium*, 28 (1975): 391-410.

1025. VARMA, Devendra P. "Horace Walpole," in *Supernatural Fiction Writers*, ed. E.F. Bleiler. New York : Charles Scribner's Sons, 1985, I, 131-137.

1026. VERZEA, Ileana. Introduction to *Castelul din Otranto* by Horace Walpole. Bucharest, Hungary : Minerva, 1982.

1027. WELCHER, Jeanne K. "The Literary Opinions of Horace Walpole," Unpublished Doctoral Dissertation, Fordham University, 1954.

1028. WRIGHT, Andrew. Introduction to *The Castle of Otranto* by Horace Walpole. New York : Holt, Rinehart, Winston, 1963, pp.vii-xxi.

IV. ENGLISH GOTHIC FICTION
Special Subject Areas

Canadian and Dominion Gothic

1029. ATWOOD, Margaret. "Canadian Monsters: Some Aspects of the Supernatural in Canadian Fiction," in The Canadian Imagination: Dimensions of a Literary Culture. Cambridge, MA : Harvard UP, 1977, pp.1-21.

1030. DAVIDSON, Arnold E. "Canadian Gothic and Anne Hébert's Kamouraska," Modern Fiction Studies, 27 (1981): 243-254.

1031. DIMÍC, Milan V. "Aspects of American and Canadian Gothicism," in Proceedings of the 7th Congress of the International Comparative Literature Association: Literatures of America: Dependence, Independence, Interdependence. Stuttgart, West Germany : Bibber, 1979, pp.143-149.

1032. HURLEY, Michael. "Wacousta: The Borders of Nightmare," in Beginnings: A Critical Anthology, ed. John Moss. Toronto : NC Press, 1980, pp. 60-69.

1033. KIRTZ, Mary Krywokulsky. "Mapping the Territory: Figurative Modes of Didacticism in the Novels of Margaret Atwood," Dissertation Abstracts International, 45 (1985): 2531A (Case-Western Reserve University).

1034. LENNOX, John Watt. "The Castle's Art: Elements of the Gothic in Selected Fiction of French Canada and the American South," Dissertation Abstracts International, 37 (1976): 7123A-7124A (University of New Brunswick).

1035. LIDOFF, Joan. "Domestic Gothic: The Imagery of Anger, Christina Stead's Man Who Loved Children," Studies in the Novel, 11 (1979): 201-215.

1036. MANDEL, Eli. "Atwood Gothic," Malahat Review: An International Quarterly of Life and Letters, 41 (1977): 165-174.

1037. _______. "Atwood's Poetic Politics," in Margaret Atwood: Language,

Text, and System, eds. Sherrill E. Grace and Lorraine Weir. Vancouver, Canada : British Columbia UP, 1983, pp.53-66.

1038. MC LEAN, Ken. "The Dark Covert of the Mind: Wacousta," Studies in Canadian Literature, 3 (1978): 124-126.

1039. NORTHEY, Margot Elizabeth. "Gothic and Grotesque Elements in Canadian Fiction," Dissertation Abstracts International, 36 (1974): 6676A (York University).

1040. ______. The Haunted Wilderness: The Gothic and Grotesque in Canadian Fiction. Toronto : Toronto UP, 1976.

1041. PETRONIO, Vivetta Giovanna. "Julien Green and the Gothic Tradition," Dissertation Abstracts International, 35 (1974): 4545A (Yale University).

1042. ROSOWSKI, Susan J. "Margaret Atwood's Lady Oracle: Social Mythology and the Gothic Novel," Research Studies, 49 (1981): 87-98.

1043. SCHEICK, W.J. "Gothic Grace and the Rainbow Aesthetic of Patrick White's Fiction: An Introduction," Texas Studies in Literature and Language, 21 (1979): 131-146.

1044. VINCENT, Sybil Korff. "The Mirror and the Cameo: Margaret Atwood's Comic/Gothic Novel, Lady Oracle," in The Female Gothic, ed. Juliann E. Fleenor. Montreal, Canada : Eden Press, 1983, pp.153-163.

Gothic Drama and Dramatists

1045. ADELSPERGER, Walter Charles. "Aspects of Staging of Plays of the Gothic Revival in England," Dissertation Abstracts, 20 (1960): 4212-4213 (Ohio State University).

1046. CARPI, Daniela. "Il Soprannaturale nel Teatro Elisibettiano-Giacobiano e nel Romanzo Gotico: Tra Metafisico e Sociale," Quaderni di Filologia Germanica della Facoltà di Lettere e Folosofia dell'Università di Bologna, 1 (1980): 41-54.

1047. DOE, Donald Bartlett. "The Sublime as an Aesthetic Correlative: A Study of Late Eighteenth-Century English Aesthetic Theory, Landscape Painting and Gothic Drama," Dissertation Abstracts International, 39 (1978): 516A (Ohio State University).

1048. EVANS, Bertrand. Gothic Drama from Walpole to Shelley. Berkeley and Los Angeles : California UP, 1947.

1049. HANAWALT, Leslie L. "The Rise of Gothic Drama, 1765-1800," Unpublished Doctoral Dissertation, University of Michigan, 1929.

1050. HAYTER, Alethea. "Coleridge, Maturin's Bertram, and Drury Lane," in New Approaches to Coleridge: Biographical and Critical Essays, ed. Donald Sultana. New York : Barnes & Noble, 1981, pp.17-37.

1051. HOEHN, Douglas William. "The First Season of Presumption! or, The Fate of Frankenstein," Theatre Studies, 26-27 (1978-1979): 79-88.

1052. KAUFMAN, Pamela M. "Oedipus and the Gothic Drama: A Psychologic Study of the Gothic Drama in Eighteenth-Century England," Dissertation Abstracts, 31 (1970): 2348A (University of California at Los Angeles).

1053. KNIGHT, G. Wilson. The Golden Labyrinth: A Study of British Drama. London : Phoenix, 1962.

1054. LAVALLEY, Albert J. "The Stage and Film Children of Frankenstein: A Survey," in The Endurance of Frankenstein: Essays on Mary Shelley's Novel. Berkeley, CA : California UP, 1979, pp.243-289.

1055. LOOMIS, Emerson R. "Gothic Drama as a Source for Gothic Fiction in the Magazines," Notes & Queries, 15 (1968): 28-29.

1056. NEUFELD, Mary Diana. "The Adaptation of the Gothic Novel to the English Stage, 1765-1826," Dissertation Abstracts International, 38 (1978): 6407A (Cornell University).

1057. NICHOLS, Harold J. "The Acting of Thomas Potter Cooke," Nineteenth-Century Theatre Research, 5 (Autumn, 1977): 73-84.

1058. PARTIN, Bruce Lynn. "The Horror Play: Its Transition from the Epic to the Dramatic Mode," Dissertation Abstracts International, 37 (1977): 4714A (Ohio State University).

1059. PECK, Louis F. "M.G. Lewis and the Larpent Catalogue," Huntington Library Quarterly, 5 (1942): 382-384.

1060. ________. "Act III of Lewis's Venoni," Modern Language Notes, 58 (1943): 265-268.

1061. PINSON, Ernest R. "The Black Sun: A Re-evaluation of Gothic Drama and its Influence," Dissertation Abstracts International, 31 (1970): 4132A (Ohio University).

1062. SCHONE, Annemarie. "Das Spiel mit dem 'Horror' im Bereich der Englische Komik," Archiv für das Studium der Neureren Sprachen und Literaturen, 194 (1958): 291-307.

1063. THORPE, Willard. "The Stage Adventures of Some Gothic Novels," Publications of the Modern Language Association, 43 (1928): 476-486.

1064. WISCHHUSEN, Stephen, ed. The Hour of One: Six Gothic Melodramas. London : Gordon Fraser, 1975.

Gothic Parodies and Parodists

1065. CORDASCO, Francesco. "A Poetic Stricture on the Gothic Romance Craze," Notes & Queries, 196 (1951): 258.

1066. LÉVY, Maurice. "Il Castello di Grimgothico; or, The Sepulchral Summons," Caliban, 3 (1967): 60-72.

1067. ________. "A Gothic Tale, By Several Hands," Caliban, 4 (1967): 59-62.

1068. LEWIS, Paul. "Mysterious Laughter: Humor and Fear in Gothic Fiction," Genre, 14 (1981): 309-327.

1069. ________. "Gothic and Mock Gothic: The Repudiation of Fantasy in Barrett's Heroine," English Language Notes, 21 (1983): 44-52.

1070. LOOMIS, Emerson R. "The Anti-Gothic Novel," Unpublished Doctoral Dissertation, Florida State University, 1957.

1071. MAY, Leland C. "Parodies of the Gothic Novel," Dissertation Abstracts International, 31 (1970): 4128A (Oklahoma State University).

1072. ________. Parodies of the Gothic Novel. New York : Arno Press, 1980.

1073. RALEIGH, Walter. Introduction to The Heroine; or, The Adventures of a Fair Romance Reader by Eaton Stannard Barrett. London : Henry Froude, 1909.

1074. SADLEIR, Michael. Introduction to The Heroine; or, The Adventures of a Fair Romance Reader by Eaton Stannard Barrett. New York : Frederick A. Stokes, 1927; London : Mathews & Marrot, 1927.

1075. SHEPPERSON, Archibald B. "Gothic Nonsense," in The Novel in Motley: A History of the Burlesque Novel in English. Cambridge, MA : Harvard UP, 1936, pp.154-181.

1076. STÉPHANE, Nelly. "Une Parodie de Roman Noir: Northanger Abbey de Jane Austen," Europe, 659 (1984): 19-28.

1077. WEISS, Fredric Norman. "Satiric Elements in Early Gothic Novels," Dissertation Abstracts International, 36 (1975): 2860A-2861A (University of Pennsylvania).

1078. ________. The Antic Spectre: Satire in Early Gothic Novels. New York : Arno Press, 1980.

1079. ZIMMERMAN, Everett. "The Function of Parody in Northanger Abbey," Modern Language Quarterly, 30 (1968): 53-63.

Gothic Revival Architecture as Related to Gothic Fiction

1080. ADDISON, Agnes. Romanticism and the Gothic Revival. New York : R.R. Smith, 1938; New York : Gordian Press, 1967.

1081. AUBIN, Robert A. "Grottoes, Geology, and the Gothic Revival," Studies in Philology, 31 (1934): 408-416.

1082. BINI, Benedetta. "Dalla Parola all 'Oggetto,'" *Calibano*, 3 (1979): 141-165.

1083. CLARK, Kenneth. *The Gothic Revival: An Essay in the History of Taste.* London : Constable, 1928; Rpt. London : John Murray, 1962.

1084. CLARKE, George. "Grecian Taste and Gothic Virtue: Lord Cobham's Gardening Programme and Its Iconography," *Apollo*, June 1973, pp.566-571.

1085. COLVIN, H.M. "Gothic Survival and Gothick Revival," *Architectural Review*, 103 (1948): 91-98.

1086. DAVIS, Terence. *The Gothick Taste.* Rutherford, NJ : Fairleigh Dickinson UP, 1975; London : David & Charles, 1976.

1087. DE BEER, E.S. "Gothic: Origin and Diffusion of the Term; The Idea of Style in Architecture," *Journal of the Warburg and Courtauld Institute*, 11 (1948): 143-162.

1088. EASTLAKE, Charles L. *A History of the Gothic Revival.* London : Longmans, Green, 1872; Rpt. New York : Humanities Press, 1970.

1089. GERMANN, Georg. *Gothic Revival in Europe and Britain: Sources, Influences, and Ideas.* London : Lund Humphries, 1973.

1090. HAFERKORN, Reinhard. *Gotik und Ruine in Der Englischen Dichtung des Achtzehnten Jahrhunderts.* Leipzig, Germany : Tauchnitz, 1925.

1091. HEILMAN, Robert B. "Fielding and the 'First Gothic Revival,'" *Modern Language Notes*, 57 (1942): 671-673.

1092. KERR, Joann. "Early and High Victorian: The Gothic Revival Architecture of Edmund Thomas Blacket and John Horbury Hunt," in *Australian Art and Architecture: Essays Presented to Bernard Smith*, eds. Anthony Bradley and Terry Smith. New York : Oxford UP, 1980, pp.17-32.

1093. KLIGER, Samuel. "The Gothic Revival and the German Translatio," *Modern Philology*, 45 (1947): 73-103.

1094. LANG, S. "Principles of the Gothic Revival in England," *Society of Architectural Historians Journal*, 15 (1966): 240-267.

1095. LOVEJOY, A.O. "The First Gothic Revival and the Return to Nature," *Modern Language Notes*, 47 (1932): 419-446.

1096. MACAULAY, Rose. *Pleasure of Ruins.* London : Weidenfeld & Nicolson, 1953; Rpt. London : Thames & Hudson, 1966.

1097. PATRICK, James. "Newman, Pugin, and Gothic," *Victorian Studies*, 24 (1981): 185-207.

1098. RICHARDSON, A.E. "The Gothic Revival in the Early Eighteenth Century," *Journal of the Royal Institute of British Architects*, 45 (1937):

140-141.

1099. RICHARDSON, Douglas Scott. "Gothic Revival Architecture in Ireland," Dissertation Abstracts International, 35 (1975): 5241A (Yale University).

1100. ROBSON-SCOTT, W.D. The Literary Background of the Gothic Revival in Germany. London : Oxford UP, 1965.

1101. ROWAN, A.J. "Batty Langley's Gothic," in Studies in Memory of David Talbot Rice. Edinburgh, Scotland : Edinburgh UP, 1976, pp.197-215.

1102. SHEEHY, Jeanne. J.J. Mc Carthy and the Gothic Revival in Ireland. Ulster, Ireland : Architectural Heritage Society, 1977.

1103. SMITH, Warren H. Architecture in English Fiction. New Haven, CT : Yale UP; Yale Studies in English Number 83, 1934.

1104. SUMMERS, Montague. "Architecture and the Gothic Novel," Architectural Design and Construction, 2 (1931): 78-81.

1105. WIEBENSON, Dora. "Greek, Gothic, and Nature: 1750-1820," in Essays in Honor of Walter Friedlander, Marsyas Supplement, 2 (1965): 187-194.

1106. YVON, Paul. Le Gothique et la Renaissance Gothique en Angleterre (17-50-1880), Essai et Psychologie Littéraire, Artique et Sociale. Caen, France : Jouan & Bigot, 1931.

Later English Gothic, 1820-1985 (Including Scott, Dickens, the Brontes, Le Fanu, and Stoker)

1107. ASTLE, Richard S. "Dracula as Totemic Monster: Lacan, Freud, Oedipus and History," Sub-Stance, 25 (1980): 98-105.

1108. AYLES, Daphne. "The Two Worlds of Bram Stoker," Dublin Magazine, 9 (Winter-Spring, 1971-1972): 62-66.

1109. BATCHLOR, John. "Arthur Machen's The Hill of Dreams," Journal of the Eighteen Nineties Society, 8 (1978): 3-10.

1110. BEACH, Joseph Warren. "The Sources of Stevenson's 'Bottle Imp,'" Modern Language Notes, 25 (1910): 12-18.

1111. BEETZ, Kirk. Wilkie Collins: An Annotated Bibliography. Metuchen, NJ : Scarecrow Press, 1978.

1112. BEGNAL, Michael H. Joseph Sheridan Le Fanu. Lewisburg, PA : Bucknell UP, 1971.

1113. BENTLEY, C.F. "The Monster in the Bedroom: Sexual Symbolism in Bram Stoker's Dracula," Literature and Psychology, 22 (1972): 27-34.

1114. BIERMAN, Joseph S. "Dracula: Prolonged Childhood Illness and the Oral

Triad," American Imago, 29 (1972): 186-198.

1115. _______. "The Genesis and Dating of Dracula from Bram Stoker's Working Notes," Notes & Queries, 24 (1977): 39-41.

1116. BLEILER, E.F. Introduction to The Haunted Hotel by Wilkie Collins in Three Supernatural Novels of the Victorian Period. New York : Dover Publications, 1975.

1117. _______. Introduction to Ghost Stories of an Antiquary by Montague Rhodes James. New York : Dover Publications, 1971.

1118. _______. Introduction to Varney the Vampyre; or, The Feast of Blood by James Malcolm Rymer or Thomas Peckett Prest. New York : Dover Publications, 1972.

1119. BLINDERMAN, Charles S. "Vampurella: Darwin and Count Dracula," Massachusetts Review, 21 (1980): 411-428.

1120. BLOCK, Ed Jr. "James Sully, Evolutionist Psychology, and Late Victorian Gothic Fiction," Victorian Studies, 25 (1982): 443-467.

1121. BOATRIGHT, Mody C. "Scott's Theory and Practice Concerning the Use of the Supernatural in Prose Fiction in Relation to the Chronology of the Waverley Novels," Publications of the Modern Language Association, 50 (1935): 235-261.

1122. BOSWELL, George W. "Supernaturalism in Scott's Novels," Mississippi Folklore Register, 8, number 2 (1974): 187-199.

1123. BOWEN, Elizabeth. Introduction to Uncle Silas; A Tale of Bartram Haugh by Joseph Sheridan Le Fanu. London : Cresset Press, 1947.

1124. BRANTLINGER, Patrick. "Imperial Gothic: Atavism and the Occult in the British Adventure Novel, 1880-1914," English Literature in Transition (1880-1920), 28 (1985): 243-252.

1125. BRITTON, Terry D. "From Ambivalence to Acquiescence: Studies in Gothic Metaphor," Dissertation Abstracts International, 42 (1982): 4829A-4830A (University of Oklahoma).

1126. BROWNE, Joseph. "Ghosts and Ghouls and Le Fanu," Canadian Journal of Irish Studies, 8 (1982): 5-15.

1127. BROWNE, Nelson. Sheridan Le Fanu. London : Arthur Barker, 1951.

1128. BROWNELL, David. "Wicked Dreams: The World of Sheridan Le Fanu," Armchair Detective, 9 (1976): 191-197.

1129. BURT, Daniel S. "A Victorian Gothic: G.W.M. Reynolds' Mysteries of London," New York Literary Forum, 7 (1980): 141-158.

1130. _______. "Melodrama, Sensation, and Suspense in the Victorian Novel," Dissertation Abstracts International, 41 (1980): 2610A (New York University).

1131. BUSHNELL, Nelson S. "Artistic Economy in Jane Eyre: A Contrast with The Old Manor House," English Language Notes, 5 (1968): 197-202.

1132. BUTLER, Marilyn. Peacock Displayed: A Satirist in His Context. London: Routledge & Kegan Paul, 1979.

1133. BYERS, Thomas B. "Good Men and Monsters: The Defenses of Dracula," Literature and Psychology, 3, number 4 (1981): 24-31.

1134. CAMERON, Donald. "History, Religion, and the Supernatural: The Failure of The Monastery," Studies in Scottish Literature, 6 (1979): 76-90.

1135. CARLSEN, M.M. "What Stoker Saw: An Introduction to the Literary Vampire," Folklore Forum, number 2 (1977): 26-30.

1136. CARPI SERTORI, Daniela. "I Romanzi d'Occultisimo di Dennis Wheatley: Fra Letteratura d'Elite e Letteratura di Consumo," Quaderni di Filologia Germanica della Facoltà di Lettera e Filosofia dellà Università di Bologna, 2 (1982): 149-165.

1137. CASSASAZZA, Alice C. "Arthur Machen's Treatment of the Occult and a Consideration of Its Reception in England and America," Dissertation Abstracts International, 32 (1971): 2633A-2634A (University of Southern California).

1138. CLEMENTS, William M. "Formula as Genre in Popular Horror Literature," Research Studies, 49 (1981): 116-123.

1139. COATES, J.D. "Techniques of Terror in The Woman in White," Durham University Journal, 73 (1981): 177-189.

1140. COATS, Daryl R. "Bram Stoker and the Ambiguity of Identity," Publications of the Mississippi Philological Association, 1984, pp.88-105.

1141. CONGER, Syndy Mc Millen. "The Reconstruction of the Gothic Feminine Ideal in Emily Bronte's Wuthering Heights," in The Female Gothic, ed. Juliann E. Fleenor. Montreal, Canada : Eden Press, 1983, pp.91-106.

1142. COOLEY, Leo P. "Joseph Sheridan Le Fanu: The Struggle of an Irish Imagination," Dissertation Abstracts International, 30 (1970): 3453A-3454A (New York University).

1143. COOLIDGE, Archibald C. Jr. "Charles Dickens and Mrs. Radcliffe: A Farewell to Wilkie Collins," Dickensian, 58 (1962): 112-116.

1144. CORDERY, Gareth. "The Gothic and the Sentimental in Charles Dickens," Dissertation Abstracts International, 36 (1975): 6697A (University of Wisconsin).

1145. COX, J. Randolph. "Montague Rhodes James: An Annotated Bibliography of Writings About Him," English Literature in Transition (1880-1920), 12 (1969): 203-211.

1146. ______. "Ghostly Antiquary: The Stories of Montague Rhodes James," English Literature in Transition (1880-1920), 12 (1969): 197-202.

1147. CRAFT, Christopher. "Kiss Me With Those Red Lips: Gender and Inversion in Bram Stoker's Dracula," Representations, 8 (1984): 107-133.

1148. CRAWFORD, Gary W. "Sheridan Le Fanu and In a Glass Darkly," Romantist, 4-5 (1980-1981): 25-27.

1149. DAHL, Curtis. "Bulwer-Lytton and the School of Catastrophe," Philological Quarterly, 32 (1953): 428-442.

1150. DANIELSON, Henry. Arthur Machen: A Bibliography, intro. Henry Savage. Ann Arbor, MI : Plutarch, 1971.

1151. DEMETRAKOPOULOS, Stephanie. "Feminism, Sex Role Exchanges, and Other Subliminal Fantasies in Bram Stoker's Dracula," Frontiers: Journal of Women's Studies, 2, number 3 (1977): 104-113.

1152. DENMAN, Peter. "Le Fanu and Stoker: A Probable Connection," Eire-Ireland, 9 (Autumn, 1974): 152-158.

1153. DODSON, Charles B. Introduction to Nightmare Abbey and Crotchet Castle by Thomas Love Peacock. New York : Holt, Rinehart, Winston, 1971.

1154. DUNAE, Patrick A. "Penny Dreadfuls: Late Nineteenth-Century Boys' Literature and Crime," Victorian Studies, 22 (1979): 133-150.

1155. DUNN, Richard J. "Aspects of a Novelist's Development: Dickens's Mastery of Horror and Terror," Unpublished Doctoral Dissertation, Case-Western Reserve University, 1964.

1156. ______. "Dickens's Mastery of the Macabre," Dickens Studies, 1 (1965): 33-39.

1157. EDENS, Walter Eugene. "Joseph Sheridan Le Fanu: A Minor Victorian and His Publisher," Dissertation Abstracts, 24 (1963): 725-726 (University of Illinois).

1158. EIGNER, Edwin Moss. "The Double in the Fiction of R.L. Stevenson," Dissertation Abstracts, 24 (1963): 741-742 (University of Iowa).

1159. ELLIS, Stewart Marsh. Wilkie Collins, Le Fanu, and Others. London : Constable, 1931.

1160. FAIG, Kenneth W. Jr. "About Bram," Romantist, 4-5 (1980-1981): 39-40.

1161. FARSON, Daniel. The Man Who Wrote Dracula: A Biography of Bram Stoker. London : Joseph, 1974; New York : St. Martin's Press, 1976.

1162. FAUROT, Ruth M. "The Early Novels of William Harrison Ainsworth," Unpublished Doctoral Dissertation, University of North Carolina, 1953.

1163. FENTON, Edith M. "The Spirit of Wuthering Heights as Distinguished from That of Gothic Romance," Washington University Studies, 8, Humanistic Series Number 1 (1920): 103-122.

1164. FLORESCU, Radu and Raymond Mc Nally. In Search of Dracula: A True History of Dracula and the Vampire Legends. Greenwich, CT : New York Graphic Society, 1973.

1165. FLOWER, Timothy F. "Charles Dickens and Gothic Fiction," Dissertation Abstracts International, 32 (1972): 6927A (Rutgers University).

1166. FONTANA, Ernest. "Lombroso's Criminal Man and Stoker's Dracula," Victorian Newsletter, 66 (1984): 25-27.

1167. FRANZETTI, Jack P. "A Study of the Preternatural Fiction of Sheridan Le Fanu and Its Impact upon the Tales of Dr. Montague Rhodes James," Unpublished Doctoral Dissertation, St. John's University, 1956.

1168. FREYE, Walter. The Influence of "Gothic" Literature on Sir Walter Scott. Rostock, Germany : H. Winterberg, 1902.

1169. FRY, Carrol L. "Fictional Conventions and Sexuality in Dracula," Victorian Newsletter, 42 (1972): 20-22.

1170. GARNETT, David, ed. Introduction to Thomas Love Peacock: The Complete Novels. London : Rupert Hart-Davis, 1963.

1171. GARSIDE, Peter. "Headlong Hall Revisited," Trivium, 14 (1979): 107-126.

1172. GATES, David Phillip. "The Image of the Labyrinth in Selected Novels by Wilkie Collins, Charles Dickens, and Joseph Sheridan Le Fanu," Dissertation Abstracts International, 43 (1983): 2678A (University of Western Ontario).

1173. GATTEGNO, Jean. "Folie, Croyance et Fantastique dans Dracula," Littérature, 8 (1972): 72-83.

1174. GORDON, Jan B. "Narrative Enclosure as Textual Ruin: An Archeology of Gothic Consciousness," Dickens Studies Annual: Essays on Victorian Fiction, 11 (1983): 209-238.

1175. _______. "Gossip, Diary, Letter, Text: Anne Bronte's Narrative Tenant and the Problematic of the Gothic Sequel," Journal of English Literary History, 51 (1984): 719-745.

1176. GOSS, Michael. "A Sense of Wonder, a Sense of Fear: Aspects of the Supernatural in Victorian Life and Popular Literature, 1840-1900," Unpublished Master of Philosophy Dissertation, University of Nottingham, 1973.

1177. "The Gothic Romance: Thrillers of the Eighteenth Century," Times Literary Supplement, December 24, 1938, p.817.

1178. GRAY, Margaret K., ed. Margaret Oliphant: Selected Stories of the Supernatural. Edinburgh, Scotland : Scottish Academic Press, 1985.

1179. GRIFFIN, Gail B. "'"Your Girls That You All Love Are Mine"': Dracula and the Victorian Male Sexual Imagination," International Journal of Women's Studies, 3 (1980): 454-465.

1180. HAINING, Peter. Introduction to The Gentlewomen of Evil: An Anthology of Rare Supernatural Stories from the Pens of Victorian Ladies. New York : Taplinger, 1967.

1181. ______. Introduction to The Penny Dreadful: or, Strange, Horrid & Sensational Tales. London : Victor Gollancz, 1975.

1182. ______. The M.R. James Book of the Supernatural. London : Foulsham, 1979.

1183. HARRIS, Jean Ambuter. "The Gothic Side of Familiar Things: Conscious Gothicism in Dickens' Early Fiction," Dissertation Abstracts International, 44 (1984): 3694A-3695A (Rutgers University).

1184. HARTLAND, R.W. Walter Scott et le Roman "Frénétique": Contribution à l'Etude de Leur Fortune en France. Paris : Édouard Champion, 1928.

1185. HATLEN, Burton. "The Return of the Repressed/Oppressed in Bram Stoker's Dracula," Minnesota Review, 15 (1980): 80-97.

1186. HEILMAN, R.B. "Charlotte Bronte's 'New Gothic,'" in From Jane Austen to Joseph Conrad: Essays Collected in Memory of James T. Hillhouse, eds. Robert C. Rathburn, Martin Steinmann, Jr. Minneapolis, MN : Minnesota UP, 1958, pp.118-132; Rpt. in Victorian Literature: Modern Essays in Criticism, ed. Austin Wright. New York : Oxford UP, 1961, pp.71- 85.

1187. HEIM, William J. "Joseph Sheridan Le Fanu," in Critical Survey of Long Fiction, ed. Frank Magill. Englewood Cliffs, NJ : Salem Press, 1983, IV, pp.1620-1628.

1188. HELDMAN, James M. Jr. "Wilkie Collins and the Sensation Novel," Dissertation Abstracts, 28 (1968): 3637A-3638A (University of North Carolina).

1189. HENNELLY, Mark M. Jr. "Dracula: The Gnostic Quest and Victorian Wasteland," English Literature in Transition (1880-1920), 20 (1977): 13-25; Rpt. in Literature of the Occult: A Collection of Critical Essays, ed. Peter Messent. Englewood Cliffs, NJ : Prentice-Hall, 1981, pp.139-155.

1190. ______. "Stevenson's 'Silent Symbols' of the 'Fatal Crossroads' in Dr. Jekyll and Mr. Hyde," Gothic: The Review of Supernatural Horror Fiction, 1 (1979): 10-16.

1191. HOMANS, Margaret. "Dreaming of Children: Literalization in Jane Eyre and Wuthering Heights," in The Female Gothic, ed. Juliann E. Fleenor. Montreal, Canada : Eden Press, 1983, pp.257-279.

1192. HUGHES, Winifred. The Maniac in the Cellar: Sensation Novels of the

1860s. Princeton, NJ : Princeton UP, 1980.

1193. IRVIN, Eric. "Dracula's Friends and Forerunners," Quadrant, 135 (1978): 42-44.

1194. JACKSON, Rosemary. "Dickens and the Gothic Tradition," Dissertation Abstracts International, 40 (1979): 4/99C (York University).

1195. ________. "The Silenced Text: Shades of Gothic in Victorian Fiction," Minnesota Review, 13 (1979): 98-112.

1196. JARRETT, David. "The Fall of the House of Clennam: Gothic Conventions in Little Dorrit," Dickensian, 73 (1977): 155-161.

1197. JOHNSON, Alan P. "'Dual Life': The Status of Women in Stoker's Dracula," Tennessee Studies in Literature, 27 (1984): 20-39.

1198. JOHNSON, E.D.H. "'Daring the Dread Glance': Charlotte Bronte's Treatment of the Supernatural in Villette," Nineteenth-Century Fiction, 20 (1966): 325-336.

1199. JONES, Joseph. "Desperate Remedies and the Victorian Sensation Novel," Nineteenth-Century Fiction, 20 (1965): 35-50.

1200. JOSLIN, Michael Edward. "The Mariner Hath His Will: Joseph Conrad and Gothicism," Dissertation Abstracts International, 38 (1978): 5487A (University of South Carolina).

1201. KAPLAN, Morton N. "Iris Murdoch and the Gothic Tradition," Dissertation Abstracts International, 31 (1970): 1231A-1232A Columbia University).

1202. KELLY, Patrick J. "The Way of the Labyrinth: Mystery and Detection in the Novels of Charles Dickens," Dissertation Abstracts International, 41 (1980): 2613A-2614A (University of Toronto).

1203. KELLY, Richard. "The Haunted House of Bulwer-Lytton," Studies in Short Fiction, 8 (1971): 581-587.

1204. KENDRICK, Walter M. "The Sensationalism of The Woman in White," Nineteenth-Century Fiction, 32 (1977): 18-35.

1205. KENTON, Edna. "A Forgotten Creator of Ghosts," Bookman, 69 (1929): 528-534.

1206. KHATTAB, Ezzat A. "Equilibrium Disturbed: Hardy's Ghostly Poems," Journal of the College of Arts, King Saud University, 11 (1984): 83-96.

1207. KIRKPATRICK, Larry. "The Gothic Flame of Charles Dickens," Victorian Newsletter, 31 (1967): 20-24.

1208. KIRTLEY, Basil F. "Dracula, the Monastic Chronicles and Slavic Folklore," Midwest Folklore, 6 (1956): 133-139.

1209. KOSTELNICK, Charles. "Dickens's Quarrel with the Gothic: Ruskin, Durtles, and Edwin Drood," Dickens Studies Newsletter, 8 (1977): 104-108.

1210. LEATHERDALE, Clive. Dracula, the Novel and the Legend: A Study of Bram Stoker's Gothic Masterpiece. Wellingborough, England : Aquarian Press, 1985.

1211. LETSON, Russell Francis Jr. "The Approaches to Mystery: The Fantasies of Arthur Machen and Algernon Blackwood," Dissertation Abstracts International, 36 (1976): 8047A (Southern Illinois University).

1212. LIDSTON, Robert. "Dracula and Salem's Lot: Why Monsters Won't Die," West Virginia University Philological Papers, 28 (1982): 70-78.

1213. LOE, Thomas Benjamin. "The Gothic Strain in the Victorian Novel: Four Studies," Dissertation Abstracts International, 35 (1974): 2231A (University of Iowa).

1214. LOTTES, Wolfgang. "Dracula & Co.: Der Vampir in der Englischen Literatur," Archiv für das Studium der Neueren Sprachen und Literaturen, 220 (1983): 285-299.

1215. LOUGHEED, W.C. "An Addition to the Le Fanu Bibliography," Notes & Queries, 209 (1964): 224.

1216. LOZÈS, Jean. "Joseph Shéridan Le Fanu, Prince de l'Invisible au 'Grand Siècle' des Vampires," Caliban, 6 (1979): 53-63.

1217. ________. "Un Choix Raisonné: Le Mode Fantastique chez Joseph Sheridan Le Fanu," Etudes Irlandaises, 9 (1984): 57-66.

1218. LUBBOCK, Samuel Guerney. A Memoir of Montague Rhodes James (1862-1936), With a List of His Writings by A.L. Scholfield. Cambridge, England : Cambridge UP, 1939.

1219. LUDLAM, Harry. A Biography of Dracula: The Life Story of Bram Stoker. London : Fireside Press of W. Foulsham, 1962.

1220. MAC GILLIVRAY, Royce. "Dracula: Bram Stoker's Spoiled Masterpiece," Queen's Quarterly, 79 (1972): 518-527.

1221. MADDOX, James H. Jr. "The Survival of Gothic Romance in the Nineteenth Century Novel: A Study of Scott, Charlotte Bronte and Dickens," Dissertation Abstracts International, 32 (1971): 442A (Yale University).

1222. MAGNIER, Mireille. "L'Art du Conteur dans 'Carmilla,'" in Linguistique, Civilisation, Littérature, ed. André Bordeaux. Paris : Marcel Didier, 1980, pp.268-274.

1223. MANSFIELD, Joseph Gerard. "Another World Than This: The Gothic and the Catholic in the Novels of Muriel Spark," Dissertation Abstracts International, 34 (1973): 5980A (University of Iowa).

1224. MASON, Michael. "Ghostly Conventions," Times Literary Supplement, January 16, 1976, p.51.

1225. MAXWELL, Richard C. Jr. "G.W.M. Reynolds, Dickens, and The Mysteries of London," Nineteenth-Century Fiction, 32 (1977): 188-213.

1226. MAY, Charles E. "Hardy's Diabolical Dames: A Generic Consideration," Genre, 8 (1974): 307-321.

1227. MAYO, Robert Donald. "The Waverley Novels in Their Relations to Gothic Fiction," Unpublished Doctoral Dissertation, Princeton University, 1938.

1228. MC CORMACK, W.J. "Swedenborgianism as Structure in Le Fanu's Uncle Silas," Long Room, Bulletin of the Library of Trinity College, Dublin, 6 (Autumn, 1972): 23-29.

1229. ______. Sheridan Le Fanu and Victorian Ireland. London : Oxford UP, 1980.

1230. MC MASTER, R.D. "Dickens and the Horrific," Dalhousie Review, 38 (1958): 18-28.

1231. MC NALLY, Raymond. The Essential Dracula. New York : Mayflower Books, 1979.

1232. MENGEL, Ewald. "The Structure and Meaning of Dickens's 'The Signalman,'" Studies in Short Fiction, 20 (1983): 271-280.

1233. MERIELEES, Edith R. "The Contemporary Ghost," Bookman, 72 (1930): 280-283.

1234. MISNER, Lucienne. "Joseph Sheridan Le Fanu's Uncle Silas and the Tradition of Fantastic Literature," Unpublished Doctoral Dissertation, University of Strasbourg, 1969.

1235. "Miss Braddon: The Writer and Her Work," Bookman, 41 (April, 1915): 149-157.

1236. MITCHELL, Giles. "Incest, Demonism, and Death in Wuthering Heights," Literature and Psychology, 23 (1973): 27-36.

1237. MIYOSHI, Masao. "Dr. Jekyll and the Emergence of Mr. Hyde," College English, 27 (1966): 470-474, 479-480.

1238. MOERS, Ellen. "Female Gothic: Monsters, Goblins, Freaks," New York Review of Books, April 4, 1974, pp.35-39.

1239. MOORE, Kevin Z. "The Poet Within the Architect's Ring: Desperate Remedies, Hardy's Hybrid-Detective Gothic Narrative," Studies in the Novel, 14 (1982): 31-42.

1240. MORETTI, Franco. "The Dialectic of Fear: Dracula and Frankenstein," New Left Review, Number 136 (November-December, 1982): 67-85.

1241. MULLER, C.H. "Victorian Sensationalism: The Short Stories of Wilkie Collins," Unisa English Studies, 11, number 1 (1973): 12-24.

1242. MURPHY, Brian. "The Nightmare of the Dark: The Gothic Legacy of Count Dracula," Odyssey: A Journal of the Humanities, 1, number 2 (1976): 9-15.

1243. NALECZ-WOJTCZAK, Jolanta. "Uncle Silas: A Link Between the Gothic Romance and the Detective Novel in England," Studia Anglica Posnaniensia: An International Review of English Studies, 12 (1980): 157-167.

1244. NANDRIS, Grigore. "The Historical Dracula: The Theme of His Legend in the Western and in the Eastern Literatures of Europe," Comparative Literature Studies, 3 (1966): 367-396.

1245. NYBERG, Benjamin Matthew. "The Novels of Mary Elizabeth Braddon (1837-1915)," Dissertation Abstracts, 26 (1966): 6047-6048 (University of Colorado).

1246. OINAS, Felix J. "East European Vampires & Dracula," Journal of Popular Culture, 16, number 1 (1982): 108-116.

1247. OREL, Harold. "'Rigid Adherence to Facts': Le Fanu's In a Glass Darkly," Eire-Ireland: A Journal of Irish Studies, 20 (1985): 65-88.

1248. PARSONS, Coleman O. "The Interest of Scott's Public in the Supernatural," Notes & Queries, 185 (1943): 92-100.

1249. ______. "Scott's Fellow Demonologists," Modern Language Quarterly, 4 (1943): 473-493.

1250. ______. Witchcraft and Demonology in Scott's Fiction, With Chapters on the Supernatural in Scottish Literature. Edinburgh, Scotland : Oliver & Boyd, 1964.

1251. PATTERSON, Charles I. "Empathy and the Daemonic in Wuthering Heights," in The English Novel in the Nineteenth Century: Essays on the Literary Mediation of Human Values, ed. George Goodin. Urbana, IL : Illinois UP, 1972, pp.81-96.

1252. PERRY, Dennis R. "Whitman's Influence on Stoker's Dracula," Walt Whitman Review, 3, number 3 (1986): 29-35.

1253. PINKUS, Philip. "The Satiric Novels of Thomas Love Peacock," Kansas Quarterly, 1 (1969): 64-76.

1254. POTEET, Lewis J. "Dorian Gray and the Gothic Novel," Modern Fiction Studies, 17 (1971): 239-248.

1255. POWELL, Kerry. "Tom, Dick, and Dorian Gray: Magic-Picture Mania in Late Victorian Fiction," Philological Quarterly, 62 (1983): 147-170.

1256. READ, Bill. "The Critical Reputation of Thomas Love Peacock with an

Annotated Enumerative Bibliography of Works by and About Peacock from February, 1800, to June, 1958," Dissertation Abstracts, 20 (1959): 1355-1356 (Boston University).

1257. ______. "Thomas Love Peacock: An Enumerative Bibliography," Bulletin of Bibliography, 24 (1963-1964): 32-34, 70-72, 88-91.

1258. REDDY, Maureen T. "Female Sexuality in 'The Poor Clare': The Demon in the House," Studies in Short Fiction, 21 (1984): 259-265.

1259. REED, John R. "The Occult in Later Victorian Literature," in Victorian Conventions. Athens, OH : Ohio UP, 1975, pp.459-473.

1260. REIERSTAD, Keith Brown. "The Demon in the House; or, The Domestication of Gothic in the Novels of Wilkie Collins," Dissertation Abstracts International, 37 (1976): 2204A (University of Pennsylvania).

1261. RICKS, Beatrice. "Characteristics of the Gothic Historical Novel in the Works of William Harrison Ainsworth," Unpublished Doctoral Dissertation, University of Oklahoma, 1954.

1262. RILEY, Michael. "Gothic Melodrama and Spiritual Romance: Vision and Fidelilty in Two Versions of Jane Eyre," Literature/Film Quarterly, 3 (1975): 145-159.

1263. ROBERTSON, Linda K. "Irish Ghosts: The Haunting of William Butler Yeats," Publications of the Missouri Philological Association, 10 (1985): 44-49.

1264. ROME, Joy J. "Twentieth-Century Gothic: Peake's Gormenghast," Unisa English Studies, 12, number 3 (1974): 42-54.

1265. RONALD, Ann. "Dickens' Gloomiest Gothic Castle," Dickens Studies Newsletter, 6 (1975): 71-75.

1266. RONAY, Gabriel. The Dracula Myth: The Truth About Dracula. London : W. H. Allen, 1972; New York : Stein and Day, 1972.

1267. ROOP, Kel. "Making Light in the Shadow Box: The Artistry of Le Fanu," Papers on Language and Literature, 21 (1985): 359-369.

1268. ROTH, Phyllis A. "Suddenly Sexual Women in Bram Stoker's Dracula," Literature and Psychology, 27 (1977): 113-121.

1269. RUSSELL, Samuel D. "Irony and Horror: The Art of M.R. James," Haunted: Studies in Gothic Fiction, 1, number 3 (1969): 96-106.

1270. SAPOSNIK, Irving S. "Aspects of Evil in the Works of Robert Louis Stevenson," Dissertation Abstracts, 26 (1966): 3961A-3962A (University of California at Berkeley).

1271. ______. "The Anatomy of Dr. Jekyll and Mr. Hyde," Studies in English Literature, 1500-1900, 11 (1971): 715-731.

1272. SAUNDERS, Vanessa Dickerson. "Gentle Spirits: Female Writers of the

Supernatural," *Dissertation Abstracts International*, 42 (1982): 4462A (Princeton University).

1273. SCHOLER, William Charles. "Bulwer-Lytton and the Supernatural," *Dissertation Abstracts International*, 37 (1977): 6512A (University of Illinois at Urbana-Champaign).

1274. SCOTT, James Frazier. "The Gothic Element in the Fiction of Thomas Hardy," *Dissertation Abstracts*, 21 (1961): 1556 (University of Kansas).

1275. ———. "Thomas Hardy's Use of the Gothic: An Examination of Five Representative Works," *Nineteenth-Century Fiction*, 17 (1963): 363-380.

1276. SECOR, Marie and Robert Secor. "Violet Hunt's *Tales of the Uneasy*: Ghost Stories of a Worldly Woman," *Women & Literature*, 6, number 1 (1978): 16-27.

1277. SEED, David. "Mystery in Everyday Things: Charles Dickens' 'Signalman,'" *Criticism*, 23 (1981): 42-57.

1278. ———. "The Narrative Method of *Dracula*," *Nineteenth-Century Fiction*, 40 (1986): 61-75.

1279. SENF, Carol A. "*Dracula*: The Unseen Face in the Mirror," *Journal of Narrative Technique*, 9 (1979): 160-170.

1280. ———. "*Dracula*: Stoker's Response to the New Woman," *Victorian Studies*, 26 (1982): 33-49.

1281. ———. "Brides of Dracula: From Novel to Film," *Studies in Popular Culture*, 7 (1984): 64-71.

1282. SHERIDAN, Daniel P. "Later Victorian Ghosts: Supernatural Fiction and Social Attitudes, 1870-1900," *Dissertation Abstracts International*, 35 (1974): 3770A (Northwestern University).

1283. ———. "Later Victorian Ghost Stories: The Literature of Belief," *Gothic*: *The Review of Supernatural Horror Fiction*, 2 (1980): 33-39.

1284. SHROYER, Frederick B. "A Critical Survey of Representative Works by Joseph Sheridan Le Fanu and Critical Comments Upon His Works," Unpublished Doctoral Dissertation, University of Southern California, 1955.

1285. ———. Introduction to *Uncle Silas* by Joseph Sheridan Le Fanu. New York : Dover Publications, 1966, pp.v-xiii.

1286. SLATTERY, Eugene E.M. "The Brontes: Refined Gothic," *Unisa English Studies*, 12, number 3 (1974): 24-27.

1287. SOULA, Jean-Pierre. "Du Féerique au Fantastique chez Arthur Machen," *Caliban*, 16 (1979): 121-130.

1288. STAHL, John Daniel. "The Source and Significance of the Revenant in Dickens's 'The Signal Man,'" Dickens Studies Newsletter, 11 (1980): 98-101.

1289. STARRETT, Vincent. Arthur Machen, A Novelist of Ecstasy and Sin. Chicago : M. Hill, 1918.

1290. STEIN, Gérard. "Dracula, ou la Circulation du 'Sang,'" Littérature, 8 (1972): 84-99.

1291. STEIN, Karen F. "Monsters and Madwomen: Changing Female Gothic," in The Female Gothic, ed. Juliann E. Fleenor. Montreal, Canada : Eden Press, 1983, pp.123-137.

1292. STEINER, Joan E. "Joseph Conrad and the Tradition of the Gothic Romance," Dissertation Abstracts International, 32 (1972): 6456A (Uni-(University of Michigan).

1293. STERN, Philip Van Doren. Introduction to Tales of Horror and the Supernatural by Arthur Machen. New York : Alfred Knopf, 1964.

1294. STEWART-GORDON, James. "Durable Dracula--Beloved Fiend of the Horror Circuit," Reader's Digest, November, 1975, pp.49-56.

1295. STRAUSS, P. "Escape from Nightmare Abbey," Theoria, 30 (1968): 65-68.

1296. SUCKSMITH, Harvey P. "The Secret of Immediacy: Dickens's Debt to the Tale of Terror in Blackwood's," Nineteenth-Century Fiction, 26 (1971): 145-157.

1297. _______. "Mrs. Gaskell's Mary Barton and William Mudford's The Iron Shroud," Nineteenth-Century Fiction, 29 (1975): 460-463.

1298. SULLIVAN, Jack. "Le Fanu's Chilling Creations," New York Times Book Review, September 21, 1975, pp.39-40.

1299. _______. "The English Ghost Story from Le Fanu to Blackwood," Dissertation Abstracts International, 39 (1978): 2265A (Columbia University).

1300. _______. Elegant Nightmares: The English Ghost Story from Le Fanu to Blackwood. Athens, OH : Ohio UP, 1978.

1301. SULLIVAN, Zoreh T. "Enchantment and the Demonic in the Novels of Iris Murdoch," Dissertation Abstracts International, 32 (1971): 458A (University of Illinois).

1302. _______. "Enchantment and the Demonic in Iris Murdoch: The Flight from the Enchanter," Midwest Quarterly, 16 (1975): 276-297.

1303. _______. "Iris Murdoch's Self-Conscious Gothicism: The Time of the Angels," Arizona Quarterly, 33 (1977): 47-60.

1304. _______. "The Contracting Universe of Iris Murdoch's Gothic Novels," Modern Fiction Studies, 23 (1977-78): 557-569.

1305. SUMMERS, Montague. Introduction to The Supernatural Omnibus. London : Doubleday, Doran, 1931.

1306. _______. "Miss Braddon," Times Literary Supplement, August 29, 1942, p.432.

1307. SWEETSER, Wesley D. "Arthur Machen: A Bibliography of Writings About Him," English Literature in Transition (1880-1920), 11 (1968): 1-1-33.

1308. _______. "Arthur Machen," English Literature in Transition (1880-1920), 18 (1975): 62-63.

1309. TEMPLE, Philip. "The Origins of 'Dracula,'" Times Literary Supplement, November 4, 1983, p.1216.

1310. THOMAS, Ronald Robert. "Dream, Power, and Authority in Nineteenth-Century British Fiction," Dissertation Abstracts International, 44 (1983): 179A (Brandeis University).

1311. TOMKINS, A.R. Introduction to Nightmare Abbey by Thomas Love Peacock. London : Blackie, 1966.

1312. TRANSUE, Harriet. "The Sensation Years: The Literary Character of England in the 1860's," Dissertation Abstracts International, 34 (1973): 2582A-2583A (Ohio State University).

1313. TWITCHELL, James B. "Heathcliff as Vampire," Southern Humanities Review, 11 (1977): 355-362.

1314. VANN, Joretta Joyce. "Ghosts Upon the Daylight: Fantasy and Realism in Nineteenth-Century Britain," Dissertation Abstracts International, 43 (1983): 2685A (University of Massachusetts).

1315. VAN THAL, Herbert. Introduction to Tales of Terror and the Supernatural by Wilkie Collins. New York : Dover Publications, 1970.

1316. VARMA, Devendra P. Introduction to Varney the Vampyre; or, The Feast of Blood by Thomas Preskett Prest, foreword by Robert Bloch. New York : Arno Press, 1972.

1317. VEEDER, William. "'Carmilla': The Arts of Repression," Texas Studies in Literature and Language, 22 (1980): 197-223.

1318. WAGENKNECHT, Edward. Introduction to Six Novels of the Supernatural. New York : Viking Press, 1948.

1319. WALL, Geoffrey. "'Different from Writing': Dracula in 1897," Literature and History, 10, number 1 (1984): 15-23.

1320. WALSH, Thomas P. "Dracula: Logos and Myth," Research Studies, 47 (1979): 229-237.

1321. WASSON, Richard. "The Politics of Dracula," English Literature in

Transition (1880-1920), 9 (1966): 24-27.

1322. WEBER, Carl J. "Ainsworth and Thomas Hardy," Review of English Studies, 17 (1941): 193-200.

1323. WEISSMAN, Judith. "Women and Vampires: Dracula as a Victorian Novel," Midwest Quarterly, 18 (1977): 392-405.

1324. WILSON, A.N. Introduction to Dracula by Bram Stoker. Oxford, England : Oxford UP, 1983.

1325. WINSOR, Dorothy A. "The Continuity of the Gothic: The Gothic Novels of Charlotte Bronte, Emily Bronte, and Iris Murdoch," Dissertation Abstracts International, 40 (1980): 5882A (Wayne State University).

1326. ______. "Iris Murdoch and the Uncanny: Supernatural Events in The Bell," Literature and Psychology, 30 (1980): 147-154.

1327. ______. "Solipsistic Sexuality in Iris Murdoch's Gothic Novels," Renascence, 34 (1981): 52-63.

1328. WOLF, Leonard. "The Gothic Novel and the Sleep of Reason," in A Dream of Dracula: In Search of the Living Dead. Boston : Little, Brown, 1972, pp.135-170.

1329. WOOD, Robin. "Burying the Undead: The Use and Obsolescence of Count Dracula," Mosaic: A Journal for the Interdisciplinary Study of Literature, 16, numbers 1-2 (1983): 175-187.

1330. ZAIC, Franz. "Robert Louis Stevenson: Strange Case of Dr. Jekyll and Mr. Hyde," in Der Englische Roman in 19. Jahrhundert: Interpretationen, eds. Paul Goetsch, Heinz Kosok, Kurt Otten. Berlin, East Germany : E. Schmidt, 1973, pp.243-252.

1331. ZEENDER, Marie-Noelle. "Miroir de l'Âme Irlandaise: Aspects du Fantastique chez Le Fanu, chez Wilde, et chez Stoker," Etudes Irlandaises, 9 (1984): 67-80.

Minor English Gothic Novelists and the Northanger Novels of Jane Austen (1764-1820)

1332. ADAMS, Donald K. "The Second Mrs. Radcliffe," Mystery and Detection Annual, 1 (1972): 48-64.

1333. ATKINSON, F.G. Introduction to Nocturnal Visit. A Tale by Regina Maria Roche, foreword by Robert D. Mayo. New York : Arno Press, 1977.

1334. AUERBACH, Nina. "Jane Austen and Romantic Imprisonment," in Jane Austen in a Social Context, ed. David Monaghan. Totowa, NJ : Barnes & Noble, 1981, pp.9-27.

1335. BROPHY, Brigid. Introduction to The Wild Irish Girl by Lady Morgan (Sydney Owenson). New York : Methuen, 1986.

1336. BUTLER, Marilyn. "The Woman at the Window: Ann Radcliffe in the Novels of Mary Wollstonecraft and Jane Austen," Women & Literature, 1 (1980): 128-148.

1337. CLUBBE, John. "Glenarvon Revised--and Revisited," Wordsworth Circle, 10 (1979): 205-217.

1338. COLEMAN, William E. Introduction to The Priory of St. Bernard; An Old English Tale by Mrs. M. Harley. New York : Arno Press, 1977.

1339. DAVIE, John. Introduction to Northanger Abbey and Persuasion by Jane Austen. London : Oxford UP, 1971.

1340. EHRENPREIS, Anne H. "Northanger Abbey: Jane Austen and Charlotte Smith," Nineteenth-Century Fiction, 25 (1970): 343-348.

1341. _______. Introduction to Northanger Abbey by Jane Austen. Harmondsworth, England : Penguin Books, 1972, pp.7-24.

1342. EMDEN, Cecil S. "The Composition of Northanger Abbey," Review of English Studies, 19, new series (1968): 279-287.

1343. FISHER, Benjamin Franklin IV. Introduction to The Abbess, A Romance by William Henry Ireland, foreword by Devendra P. Varma. New York : Arno Press, 1974.

1344. FREMANTLE, Anne. Afterword to Glenarvon by Lady Caroline Lamb. New York : Curtis Books, 1973, pp.251-254.

1345. GARRETT, John. Introduction to Count St. Blanchard; or, The Prejudiced Judge by Mrs. Mary Meeke, foreword by Devendra P. Varma. New York : Arno Press, 1977.

1346. GARVER, Joseph. "Gothic Ireland: Lady Caroline Lamb's Glenarvon," Irish University Review: A Journal of Irish Studies, 10 (1980): 213-228.

1347. GLOCK, Waldo. "Catherine Morland's Gothic Delusions: A Defense of Northanger Abbey," Rocky Mountain Review of Language and Literature, 32 (1978): 33-46.

1348. HOPKINS, Robert. "General Tilney and Affairs of State: The Political Gothic of Northanger Abbey," Philological Quarterly, 57 (1978): 213-224.

1349. HOWELLS, Coral Ann. Introduction to Manfroné; or, The One-Handed Monk by Mary Anne Radcliffe, foreword by Devendra P. Varma. New York : Arno Press, 1972.

1350. KELSALL, Malcolm. "The Byronic Hero and Revolution in Ireland: The Politics of Glenarvon," Byron Journal, 9 (1981): 4-19.

1351. LE TELLIER, Robert Ignatius. Kindred Spirits: Interrelations and Affinities Between the Romantic Novels of England and Germany (1790-1820) With Special Reference to the Work of Carl Grosse (1768-1847),

Forgotten Gothic Novelist and Theorist of the Sublime. Salzburg, Austria : Institut für Anglistik & Amerikanistik, 1982.

1352. LEVINE, George. "Translating the Monstrous: *Northanger Abbey*," *Nineteenth-Century Fiction*, 30 (1975): 335-350.

1353. _______. "*Northanger Abbey*: From Parody to Novel and Translated Monster," in *The Realistic Imagination: English Fiction from Frankenstein to Lady Chatterley*. Chicago : Chicago UP, 1981, pp.61-80.

1354. LOOMIS, Emerson R. "The Problem of the Gothic Novel in Wales," *National Library of Wales Journal*, 13 (1963): 67-69.

1355. MAGNIER, Mireille. "*Zofloya* et *Le Moine*," in *Autour de l'Idée de Nature; Histoire des Idées et Civilisation*: *Pédagogie et Divers*. Paris : Marcel Didier, 1977, pp.227-231.

1356. MAYO, Robert D. Introduction to *Grasville Abbey*; *A Romance* by George Moore, foreword by Devendra P. Varma. New York : Arno Press, 1974.

1357. MC CONNOCHIE, Arthur. "Francis Lathom, Forgotten Goth," Unpublished Doctoral Dissertation, University of Virginia, 1949.

1358. MC KILLOP, Alan D. "Jane Austen's Gothic Titles," *Notes & Queries*, 9, new series (1921): 361-362.

1359. NOEL-BENTLEY, E.R. "Jane Austen and Regina Maria Roche," *Notes & Queries*, 22 (1975): 390-391.

1360. ROBERTS, Bette B. "Marital Fears and Polygamous Fantasies in Eliza Parsons' *Mysterious Warning*," *Journal of Popular Culture*, 12 (1978): 42-51.

1361. RUFF, James L. Introduction to *Glenarvon* by Lady Caroline Lamb. Delmar, NY : SF&R, 1972.

1362. SADLEIR, Michael. *The Northanger Novels: A Footnote to Jane Austen*, English Association Pamphlet Number 68, November, 1927, 23 pp.

1363. _______. "'All Horrid?' Jane Austen and the Gothic Romance," in *Things Past*. London : Constable, 1944, pp.167-200.

1364. SCHROEDER, Natalie E. "Regina Maria Roche: Popular Novelist, 1789-1834," *Dissertation Abstracts International*, 39 (1979): 4962A-4963A (Northwestern University).

1365. _______. "Regina Maria Roche, Popular Novelist, 1789-1834: The Rochean Canon," *Papers of the Bibliographical Society of America*, 73 (1979): 462-468.

1366. _______. "*The Nun's Picture*: Religion and the Sensibility Romance of the 1830's," *South Central Bulletin*, 40 (1980): 163-165.

1367. _______. "The Anti-Feminist Reception of Regina Maria Roche," *Essays in Literature*, 9 (1982): 55-65.

1368. _______. "Regina Maria Roche and the Early Nineteenth-Century Irish Novel," Eire-Ireland: A Journal of Irish Studies, 19, number 2 (1984): 116-130.

1369. SHROYER, Frederick. Introduction to The Abbot of Montserrat; or, The Pool of Blood by William Child Green. New York : Arno Press, 1977.

1370. STÉPHANE, Nelly. "Une Parodie de Roman Noir: Northanger Abbey," Europe, 659 (1984): 19-28.

1371. SUMMERS, Montague. Introduction to The Necromancer; or, The Tale of the Black Forest by Karl Friedrich Kahlert or Lawrence Flammenberg. London : Robert Holden, 1927.

1372. _______. Introduction to Horrid Mysteries by the Marquis of Grosse. London : Robert Holden, 1927.

1373. _______. Introduction to Zofloya; or, The Moor by Charlotte Dacre (Rosa Matilda). London : Fortune Press, 1928.

1374. _______. "Byron's 'Lovely Rosa,'" in Essays in Petto. London : Fortune Press, 1928; Rpt. Freeport, NY : Books for Libraries, 1967.

1375. TANDRUP, Birthe. "Free Indirect Style and the Critique of the Gothic in Northanger Abbey," in The Romantic Heritage: A Collection of Critical Essays, ed. Kartsten Engelberg. Copenhagen, Denmark : Copenhagen UP, 1983, pp.81-92.

1376. TARR, Sister Mary Muriel. Introduction to The Monk of Udolpho; A Romance by T.J. Horsley Curties, foreword by Devendra P. Varma. New York : Arno Press, 1977.

1377. VARMA, Devendra P. Introduction to Horrid Mysteries by the Marquis of Grosse. London : Folio Press, 1968.

1378. _______. Introduction to The Midnight Bell by Francis Lathom. London: Folio Press, 1968.

1379. _______. Introduction to The Mysterious Warning; A German Tale by Eliza Parsons. London : Folio Press, 1968.

1380. _______. Introduction to The Castle of Wolfenbach by Eliza Parsons. London : Folio Press, 1968.

1381. _______. Introduction to Clermont by Regina Maria Roche. London : Folio Press, 1968.

1382. _______. Introduction to The Orphan of the Rhine by Eleanor Sleath. London : Folio Press, 1968.

1383. _______. Introduction to The Necromancer; or, The Tale of the Black Forest by Karl Friedrich Kahlert (Lawrence Flammenberg). London : Folio Press, 1968.

1384. ______. Introduction to The Confessions of the Nun of St. Omer by Charlotte Dacre. New York : Arno Press, 1972.

1385. ______. Introduction to The Nocturnal Minstrel; or, The Spirit of the Wood by Eleanor Sleath. New York : Arno Press, 1972.

1386. ______. Introduction to Netley Abbey; A Gothic Story by Richard Warner. New York : Arno Press, 1974.

1387. ______. Introduction to The Libertine by Charlotte Dacre, foreword by John Garrett. New York : Arno Press, 1974.

1388. ______. Introduction to The Passions by Charlotte Dacre, foreword by Sandra Knight-Roth. New York : Arno Press, 1974.

1389. ______. Introduction to Zofloya, or The Moor; A Romance of the Fifteenth Century, foreword by G. Wilson Knight. New York : Arno Press, 1974.

1390. ______. Introduction to Barozzi, or The Venetian Sorceress; A Romance of the Sixteenth Century by Mrs. Catherine Smith. New York : Arno Press, 1977.

1391. ______. Introduction to The Abbey of St. Asaph. A Novel by Isabella Kelly. New York : Arno Press, 1977.

1392. ______. Introduction to St. Margaret's Cave; or, The Nun's Story by Elizabeth Helme, foreword by Frederick Garber. New York : Arno Press, 1977.

1393. ZIMMERMAN, Everett. "The Function of Parody in Northanger Abbey," Modern Language Quarterly, 30 (1968): 53-63.

Pre-Gothic Tendencies and Graveyard Verse

1394. ALMIRALL, Catherine L. "Smollett's 'Gothic': An Illustration," Modern Language Notes, 68 (1953): 408-410.

1395. AUBIN, Robert A. "Three Notes on Graveyard Poetry," Studies in Philology, 32 (1935): 103-109.

1396. ______. "Some Augustan Gothicists," Harvard Studies and Notes in Philology and Literature, 17 (1935): 15-25.

1397. BAINE, Rodney. Daniel Defoe and the Supernatural. Athens, GA : Georgia UP, 1968.

1398. BEER, Gillian. "'Our Unnatural No-Voice': The Heroic Epistle, Pope, and Women's Gothic," Yearbook of English Studies, 12 (1982): 125-151.

1399. BROWNELL, M.R. "Pope and the Vampires in Germany," Eighteenth-Century Life, 2 (1976): 96-97.

1400. BRUCKMANN, Patricia C. "The Settings in Pamela," Transactions of the Samuel Johnson Society of the Northwest, 6 (1973): 1-10.

1401. CONANT, Martha Pike. The Oriental Tale in England in the Eighteenth Century. New York : Columbia UP, 1908; Columbia University Studies in Comparative Literature Number 9; Rpt. New York : Octagon Books, 1966.

1402. DENNIS, L.A. "The Attitude of the Eighteenth Century Towards the Medieval Romances," Unpublished Doctoral Dissertation, Stanford University, 1929.

1403. DRAPER, John W. The Funeral Elegy and the Rise of English Romanticism. New York : New York UP, 1929; Rpt. New York : Octagon Books, 1967.

1404. DUTT, Sukumar. The Supernatural in English Romantic Poetry. Being a Critical Survey of Supernaturalism; Its Growth and Phases of Development in English Poetry During 1780-1830. Calcutta, India : Calcutta UP, 1938; Rpt. Folcroft, PA : Folcroft Library, 1972.

1405. ENG, Steve. "Supernatural Verse in English," in Horror Literature: A Core Collection and Reference Guide, ed. Marshall B. Tymn. New York: R.R. Bowker, 1981, pp.401-452.

1406. FRANK, Frederick S. "From Boudoir to Castle Crypt: Richardson and the Gothic Novel," Revue des Langues Vivantes, 41 (1975): 49-59.

1407. GRANT, Damian. Introduction to The Adventures of Ferdinand Count Fathom by Tobias Smollett. New York : Oxford UP, 1971.

1408. GUTHKE, Karl S. Der Deutsche Sturm und Drang und die Englische Vorromantik. Göttingen, West Germany : Vandenhoeck & Ruprecht, 1958.

1409. LÉVY, Maurice. "Shakespeare et le Roman 'Gothique,'" Caliban, 1 (1965): 47-63.

1410. MADOFF, Mark. "The Useful Myth of Gothic Ancestry," Studies in Eighteenth Century Culture, 8 (1979): 337-350.

1411. MC INTYRE, Clara F. "The Later Career of the Elizabethan Villain-Hero," Publications of the Modern Language Association, 40 (1925): 874-880.

1412. O'CONNOR, Robert Harold. "The Gothic Ballad in British Romantic Literature," Dissertation Abstracts International, 40 (1980): 5454A (Bowling Green University).

1413. PARSONS, Coleman O. "Ghost-Stories Before Defoe," Notes & Queries, 201 (1956): 293-298.

1414. PLAISANT, Michele. "Sentiment et Représentation de la Mort chez quelques Poètes Anglais du XVIIIe Siècle," in Le Mort, Le Fantastique, le Surnaturel du XVIe Siècle à l'Époque Romantique. Villeneuve d'Ascq, France : Centre de Recherches sur l'Angleterre des Tudors à la Régence, Université de Lille III, PU de Lille, 1981, pp.67-76.

1415. SAMOORIAN, Vahe. "The Way to Otranto: Gothic Elements in Eighteenth-Century English Poetry, 1717-1762," Dissertation Abstracts International, 31 (1970): 6631A (Bowling Green University).

1416. SPACKS, Patricia A. The Insistence of Horror: Aspects of the Supernatural in Eighteenth-Century Poetry. Cambridge, MA : Harvard UP, 19-1962.

1417. ______. "Horror-Personification in Late Eighteenth-Century Poetry," Studies in Philology, 59 (1962): 560-578.

1418. THACKER, Christopher. "'Wish'd, Wint'ry, Horror': The Storm in the Eighteenth Century," Comparative Literature, 19 (1967): 36-57.

1419. THÜRNAU, C. Geister in Englischen Litteratur des 18. Jahrhunderts. Berlin : Palestra, Band 60, 1906.

The Romantic Poets and Gothicism

1420. BINDMAN, David. "Blake's 'Gothicised Imagination' and the History of England," in William Blake: Essays in Honour of Sir Geoffrey Keynes. Oxford, England : Clarendon Press, 1973, pp.29-49.

1421. BOGAN, James. "Vampire Bats & Blake's Spectre," Blake Newsletter, 10 (1976): 32-33.

1422. BRISMAN, Leslie. "Coleridge and the Supernatural," Studies in Romanticism, 21 (1982): 123-159.

1423. BUCHEN, Irving H. "Wordsworth's Gothic Ballads," Genre, 3 (1970): 85-96.

1424. CHATHA, Diljit Kaur. "The Supernatural as a Rhetorical Focus in the Three Major Poems of Samuel Taylor Coleridge," Dissertation Abstracts International, 46 (1985): 704A (Texas Woman's University).

1425. CHRISTENSEN, Merton A. "Udolpho, Horrid Mysteries, and Coleridge's Machinery of the Imagination," Wordsworth Circle, 2 (1971): 153-159.

1426. CLAPP, Edwin R. "La Belle Dame as Vampire," Philological Quarterly, 27 (1948): 89-92.

1427. COBURN, Kathleen. "Coleridge and Wordsworth on 'the Supernatural,'" University of Toronto Quarterly, 25 (1956): 121-130.

1428. DÉDÉYAN, Charles. "Le Thème de Faust: Byron, Mrs. Shelley, C.R. Maturin," Revue des Lettres Modernes, 3 (1956): 49-96.

1429. DINGLEY, R.J. "Coleridge and the 'Frightful Fiend,'" Notes & Queries, 226 (1981): 313-314.

1430. DOUGHTY, Oswald. "Coleridge and the 'Gothic Novel' or 'Tales of Terror,'" English Miscellany, 23 (1972): 125-148.

1431. EASSON, Roger R. "Blake and the Gothic," in Blake in His Time, eds. Robert N. Essick, Donald R. Pearce. Bloomington, IN : Indiana UP, 1978, pp.145-154.

1432. EHRSTINE, John W. "Byron and the Metaphysic of Self-Destruction," in The Gothic Imagination: Essays in Dark Romanticism, ed. G.R. Thompson. Pullman, WA : Washington State UP, 1974, pp.94-108.

1433. ELKINS, Aubrey C. Jr. "Wordsworth and Gothicism," Dissertation Abstracts, 29 (1969): 4454A (Cornell University).

1434. FAIRCHILD, Hoxie N. "Byron and Monk Lewis," Times Literary Supplement, May 11, 1946, p.223.

1435. FARRAND, Margaret L. "Udolpho and Childe Harold," Modern Language Notes, 45 (1930): 220-221.

1436. FRANKE, Wolfgang. "Don Juan and the Black Friar: A Byronic Variant of the Ghost Story," in The Constance Byron Symposium. Salzburg, Austria : Institut für Anglistik und Amerikanstik, 1978, pp.21-7.

1437. GARBER, Frederick. "Byron's Giaour and the Mark of Cain," Etudes Anglaises, 26 (1973): 150-159.

1438. GILPATRIC, Mary Ellen. "Gothic Elements in English Romantic Poetry," Dissertation Abstracts, 27 (1966): 179A (Kent State University).

1439. GORDON, Jan B. "De Quincey as Gothic Parasite: The Dynamic of Supplementarity," in Thomas De Quincey: Bicentenary Studies, ed. Robert Lance Snyder. Norman, OK : Oklahoma UP, 1985, pp.239-262.

1440. GREGORY, Horace. "On the Gothic Imagination and the Survival of Beddoes," in The Shield of Achilles: Essays on Beliefs in Poetry. New New York : Harcourt, Brace, 1944, pp.45-61; Rpt. Greenwood, CT : Greenwood Press, 1970.

1441. HAYTER, Alethea. "Coleridge, Maturin's Bertram, and Drury Lane," in New Approaches to Coleridge: Biographical and Critical Essays, ed. Donald Sultana. New York : Barnes & Noble, 1981, pp.17-37.

1442. HUME, Robert D. "Exuberant Gloom, Existential Agony, and Heroic Despair: Three Varieties of Negative Romanticism," in The Gothic Imagination: Essays in Dark Romanticism, ed. G.R. Thompson. Pullman, WA : Washington State UP, 1974, pp.109-127.

1443. JARRETT, David. "The Source for Keats's Magic Casements," Notes & Queries, 26 (1979): 232-235.

1444. KETCHIN, Samuel Cathcart. "Byron's Use of Gothicism," Dissertation Abstracts, 19 (1959): 2614-2615 (Emory University).

1445. LAU, Beth. "Madeline at Northanger Abbey: Keats's Anti-Romances and Gothic Satire," Journal of English and Germanic Philology, 84 (19-

85): 30-50.

1446. LEVER, K.M. "De Quincey as Gothic Hero: A Perspective on Confessions of an English Opium Eater and Suspiria De Profundis," Texas Studies in Literature and Language, 21 (1979): 332-346.

1447. LONGUEIL, A.E. "Gothic Romance, Its Influence on the Romantic Poets Wordsworth, Keats, Coleridge, Byron, and Shelley," Unpublished Doctoral Dissertation, Harvard University, 1920.

1448. LOVELL, Ernest J. Jr. "Byron's 'The Island' and Maturin's Melmoth the Wanderer," Notes & Queries, 194 (1949): 497-499.

1449. O'CONNOR, Robert H. "Keats' 'The Eve of St. Agnes' and Ballad Gothicism," Lamar Journal of the Humanities, 9 (1983): 17-27.

1450. ________. "The Rime of the Ancient Mariner and Tales of the Devil: A Note," Wordsworth Circle, 15 (1984): 81-82.

1451. PAPPAGEORGE, Julia di Stephano. "Coleridge's 'Mad Lutanist': A Romantic Response to Ann Radcliffe," Bulletin of Research in the Humanities, 82 (1979): 222-235.

1452. PATTERSON, Charles I. "The Authenticity of Coleridge's Reviews of Gothic Romances," Journal of English and Germanic Philology, 50 (1951): 517-521.

1453. PECK, W.E. "Keats, Shelley, and Mrs. Radcliffe," Modern Language Notes, 39 (1924): 251-252.

1454. PETERFREUND, Stuart. "Keats's Debt to Maturin," Wordsworth Circle, 13 (1982): 45-49.

1455. POLLIN, Burton R. "Keats, Charlotte Smith, and the Nightingale," Notes & Queries, 13, new series (1966): 180-181.

1456. ________. "Byron, Poe, and Miss Matilda," Names, 16 (1968): 390-414.

1457. PRICE, James L. "The Turn Towards the Supernatural in Keats, Goethe, and Nerval," Dissertation Abstracts International, 34 (1974): 7201A (Yale University).

1458. PRICKETT, Stephen. "Romantic Literature," in The Romantics. New York : Holmes & Meier, 1981.

1459. ROPER, Derek. "Coleridge, Dyer, and The Mysteries of Udolpho," Notes & Queries, 19, new series (1972): 287-289.

1460. ROSE, Edward J. "The 'Gothicized Imagination' or 'Michelangelo Blake,'" in Blake in His Time, eds. Robert N. Essick, Donald R. Pearce. Bloomington, IN : Indiana UP, 1978, pp.155-169.

1461. SCHEPER, Astrid J. "Glorious Gothic Scenes," Byron Society Newsletter, 7 (1980-82): 15-16.

1462. SHACKFORD, Martha Hale. "The Eve of St. Agnes and The Mysteries of Udolpho," Publications of the Modern Language Association, 36 (1921): 104-118.

1463. SISKIN, Clifford. "Wordsworth's Gothic Endeavor: From Esthwaite to the Great Decade," Wordsworth Circle, 10 (1979): 161-173.

1464. SNYDER, Robert Lance. "Klosterheim: De Quincey's Gothic Masque," Research Studies, 49 (1981): 129-142.

1465. TETREAULT, Ronald. "Shelley and Byron Encounter the Sublime: Switzerland, 1816," Revue des Langues Vivantes, 41 (1975): 145-155.

1466. THORSLEV, Peter Jr. The Byronic Hero: Types and Prototypes. Minneapolis, MN : Minnesota UP, 1962.

1467. TUTTLE, Donald R. "Christabel Sources in Percy's Reliques and the Gothic Romances," Publications of the Modern Language Association, 53 (1938): 445-474.

1468. TWITCHELL, James B. "La Belle Dame as Vampire," College English Association Critic, 37 (1975): 31-33.

1469. ______. "The Supernatural Structure of Byron's Manfred," Studies in English Literature, 1500-1900, 15 (1975): 601-614.

1470. ______. "The Rime of the Ancient Mariner as Vampire Poem," College Literature, 4 (1977): 21-37.

Shilling Shockers, Gothic Chapbooks,
Short Tales of Terror, Periodical Gothicism,
Anti-Catholicism, and Revolutionary Themes

1471. BERMAN, Ruth. "Critical Reactions to Fantasy in Four Nineteenth Century Periodicals: Edinburgh Review, Blackwood's, Fraser's Magazine, The Cornhill Magazine," The Sphinx: A Magazine of Literature and Society, 4, number 1 (1981): 1-37.

1472. BOSTROM, Irene. "The Novel and Catholic Emancipation," Studies in Romanticism, 2 (1963): 155-176.

1473. BRIGGS, Julia. Night Visitors: The Rise and Fall of the English Ghost Story. London : Faber, 1977.

1474. FERGUSON, Mary Louise Dechert. "My Spectre Around Me: The Reluctant Rebellion of the Gothic Novelists," Dissertation Abstracts International, 42 (1982): 4457A (Vanderbilt University).

1475. HAINING, Peter. Introduction to Gothic Tales of Terror: Classic Horror Stories from Great Britain, Europe, and the United States, 1765-1840. New York : Taplinger, 1972, pp.1-7.

1476. ______. Introduction to Great British Tales of Terror: Gothic Stories of Horror and Romance. London : Victor Gollancz, 1972.

1477. ________. Introduction to *The Shilling Shockers: Stories of Terror from the Gothic Bluebooks*. New York : St. Martin's Press, 1979.

1478. KIEVITT, Frank David. "Attitudes Toward Roman Catholicism in the Later Eighteenth-Century Novel," *Dissertation Abstracts International*, 36 (1975): 1481A-1482A (Columbia University).

1479. MAYO, Robert D. "The Gothic Story in the Magazines," *Modern Language Review*, 37 (1942): 448-454.

1480. ________. "Gothic Romance in the Magazines," *Publications of the Modern Language Association*, 65 (1950): 762-789.

1481. PAULSON, Ronald. "Gothic Fiction and the French Revolution," *Journal of English Literary History*, 48 (1981): 532-554.

1482. PITCHER, E.W. "Changes in Short Fiction in Britain 1785-1810: Philosophic Tales, Gothic Tales, and Fragments and Visions," *Studies in Short Fiction*, 13 (1976): 331-354.

1483. PORTE, Joel. "In the Hands of an Angry God: Religious Terror in Gothic Fiction," in *The Gothic Imagination: Essays in Dark Romanticism*, ed. G.R. Thompson. Pullman, WA : Washington State UP, 1974, pp.42-64.

1484. ROGERS, Katherine M. "Fantasy and Reality in the Fictional Convents of the Eighteenth Century," *Comparative Literature Studies*, 22 (1985): 297-316.

1485. SEARCH, Pamela. *The Supernatural in the English Short Story*. London : B. Harrison, 1959.

1486. SEON, Manley and Gogo Lewis. *Ladies of the Gothic: Tales of Romance and Terror Told by the Gentle Sex*. New York : Lothrop, Lee, and Shephard, 1975.

1487. SHELDEN, Pamela J. and Kurt Paul. "Daylight Nightmares," *Gothic: The Review of Supernatural Horror Fiction*, 1 (1979): 1-6.

1488. SKARDA, Patricia L. and Nora Crow Jaffe. "General Introduction," to *The Evil Image: Two Centuries of Gothic Short Fiction and Poetry*. New York : New American Library, 1981, pp.xi-xxix.

1489. SONNENFIELD, Albert. "Twentieth Century Gothic: Reflections on the Catholic Novel," *Southern Review*, 1 (1965): 388-405.

1490. SPECTOR, Robert D. Introduction to *Seven Masterpieces of Gothic Horror*. New York : Bantam Books, 1963, pp.1-11.

1491. ________. Introduction to *The Candle and the Tower*. New York : Warner Paperback Library, 1974, pp.7-12.

1492. SULLIVAN, Jack. Introduction to *Lost Souls: A Collection of English Ghost Stories*. Athens, OH : Ohio UP, 1983, pp.1-12.

1493. TARR, Sister Mary Muriel. Catholicism in Gothic Fiction: A Study of the Nature and Function of Catholic Materials in Gothic Fiction in England (1762-1820). Washington, DC : Catholic University of America UP, 1946; Rpt. Ann Arbor, MI : University Microfilm International, 1980.

1494. WAMELING, Grete. Geisterhaftes und Okkultistisches in der Englischen Erzählerkunst von 1880-1890. Emstetten, Germany : Heinrich & J. Lechte, 1931.

1495. WATT, William Whyte. Shilling Shockers of the Gothic School: A Study of Chapbook Gothic Romances. Cambridge, MA : Harvard UP, 1932; Rpt. New York : Russell & Russell, 1967.

1496. WISE, Herbert A. and Phyllis Fraser. Introduction to Great Tales of Terror and the Supernatural. New York : Random House; Modern Library Giant Number 72, 1944, pp.xi-xvii.

1497. WOLF, Jack C. and Barbara H. Wolf. Introduction to Ghosts, Castles, and Victims: Studies in Gothic Terror. Greenwich, CT : Fawcett Books, 1976.

V. AMERICAN GOTHIC FICTION

General Histories, Critical Surveys, Definitions of Genre

1498. ACCETTA, Michael Angelo. "Gothic Elements in the Early American Novel, 1775-1825," Dissertation Abstracts, 14 (1954): 1394 (University of Pittsburgh).

1499. BANTA, Martha. "American Apocalypses: Excrement and Ennui," Studies in the Literary Imagination, 7 (1974): 1-30.

1500. BENTON, Richard P. "The Problems of Literary Gothicism," ESQ: A Journal of the American Renaissance, 18 (1972): 5-9.

1501. BETTS, William. "The Faust Tradition in American Literature," Unpublished Doctoral Dissertation, Pennsylvania State University, 1954.

1502. BRADBURY, Malcolm. "American Gothic," The Listener, November 7, 1963, p.763.

1503. BROWN, Herbert Ross. The Sentimental Novel in America, 1789-1860. Durham, NC : Duke UP, 1940; Rpt. New York : Octagon Books, 1975.

1504. COAD, Oral S. "The Gothic Element in American Literature Before 1835," Journal of English and Germanic Philology, 24 (1925): 72-93.

1505. ______. "Jersey Gothic," Proceedings of the New Jersey Historical Society," 84 (1966): 89-112.

1506. DAHL, Curtis. "The American School of Catastrophe," American Quarterly, 11 (1959): 380-390.

1507. DAVIS, David Brion. Homicide in American Fiction, 1798-1860: A Study in Social Values. Ithaca, NY : Cornell UP, 1957.

1508. DIMAGGIO, Richard S. "The Tradition of the American Gothic Novel," Dissertation Abstracts International, 37 (1976): 307A (University of Arizona).

1509. DIMIĆ, Milan V. "Aspects of American and Canadian Gothicism," in Proceedings of the 7th Congress of the International Comparative Literature Association: Literatures of America: Dependence, Independence, Interdependence. Stuttgart, West Germany : Bieber, 1979, pp.143-149.

1510. EGAN, Kenneth. "Apocalypse Against Progress: Gothic and Pastoral Modes in the American Romance," Dissertation Abstracts International, 45 (1985): 2526A-2527A (University of Wisconsin).

1511. EMMONS, Winfred S. Jr. "The Materials and Methods of American Horror Fiction in the Nineteenth Century," Unpublished Doctoral Dissertation, Louisiana State University, 1952.

1512. FIEDLER, Leslie. Love and Death in the American Novel. New York : Criterion, 1960; Rpt. New York : Dell, 1966.

1513. ______. "Second Thoughts on Love and Death in the American Novel: My First Gothic Novel," Novel, I (1967): 1-19.

1514. GILLESPIE, Gerald. "Rogues, Fools, and Satyrs: Ironic Ghosts in American Fiction," in Modern American Fiction: Insights and Foreign Lights, ed. Wolodymyr T. Zyla, Wendell M. Aycocks. Lubbock, TX : Texas Technological UP, 1972, pp.89-106.

1515. GREEN, Gary Lee. "The Language of Nightmare: A Theory of American Gothic Fiction," Dissertation Abstracts International, 46 (1985): 1279A (University of Oklahoma).

1516. GROSS, Louis S. "The Transformed Land: Studies in American Gothic Narrative," Dissertation Abstracts International, 47 (1986): 1323A (University of Pennsylvania).

1517. HARDMAN, Marion P. "Terror in American Prose Fiction," Unpublished Doctoral Dissertation, University of Minnesota, 1939.

1518. ISANI, Mukhtar. "The Oriental Tale in America Through 1865: A Study in American Fiction," Dissertation Abstracts, 24 (1963): 297-298 (Princeton University).

1519. JUSTUS, James. "Beyond Gothicism: Wuthering Heights and an American Tradition," Tennessee Studies in Literature, 5 (1960): 25-33.

1520. KERR, Howard, John W. Crowley and Charles L. Crow, eds. The Haunted Dusk: American Supernatural Fiction, 1820-1920. Athens, GA : Georgia UP, 1983.

1521. LOSHE, Lillie Deming. "The Gothic and the Revolutionary," in The Early American Novel. New York : Columbia UP; Columbia University Studies in English and Comparative Literature, 1907; Rpt. New York : Frederick Ungar, 1966.

1522. MALIN, Irving. New American Gothic. Carbondale, IL : Southern Illinois UP, 1962.

1523. ______. "American Gothic Images," Mosaic: A Journal for the Interdisciplinary Study of Literature, 6 (1973): 145-171.

1524. MOGEN, David. "Frontier Myth and American Gothic," Genre, 14 (1981): 329-346.

1525. PAYNE, Ladell. Black Novelists and the Southern Literary Tradition. Athens, GA : Georgia UP, 1981.

1526. PETTER, Henri. The Early American Novel. Columbus, OH : Ohio State UP, 1971.

1527. PHILLIPS, George L. "The Gothic Element in the American Novel Before 1830," West Virginia University Bulletin: Philological Studies, 3 (1939): 37-45.

1528. QUINN, Arthur Hobson. "Some Phases of the Supernatural in American Literature," Publications of the Modern Language Association, 25 (1910): 114-133.

1529. RANIERI, Marietta R. "The Self Behind the Self: The Americanization of the Gothic," Dissertation Abstracts International, 34 (1973): 5200A-5201A (Pennsylvania State University).

1530. REDDEN, Sister Mary Maurita. The Gothic Fiction in the American Magazines (1765-1800). Washington, DC : Catholic University of America UP, 1939.

1531. RINGE, Donald A. American Gothic: Imagination and Reason in Nineteenth-Century Fiction. Lexington, KY : Kentucky UP, 1982.

1532. ROWE, Anne E. "Honor, Chivalry, and the Gothic in the Southern Imagination," Mississippi Quarterly, 37 (1984): 109-114.

1533. SEIDNAR-KEDAR, Eva Helen. "'Ghosts in the Air of America': Transformation as Theme and Technique in North American Dark Romance," Dissertation Abstracts International, 44 (1984): 3074A (University of Toronto).

1534. SEROVA, V.N. "Traditsii Goticheskogo Romano v Americanskom Romantizme," Nauchnye Trudy Kubanskogo Universiteta, Krasnodar, 155 (1972): 27-39.

1535. SHELDEN, Pamela J. "American Gothicism: The Evolution of a Mode," Dissertation Abstracts International, 35 (1974): 1634A-1635A (Kent State University).

1536. SLOAN, De Villo. "Influences of Industrialization on the Origins and Development of American Gothic Fiction," Dissertation Abstracts International, 43 (1982): 1548A (SUNY at Buffalo).

1537. STEWART, Susan. "The Epistemology of the Horror Story," Journal of American Folklore, 95 (1982): 33-50.

1538. TEN BROEKE, Patricia A.M. "The Shadow of Satan: A Study of the Devil Archetype in Selected American Novels from Hawthorne to the Present Day," Dissertation Abstracts International, 32 (1972): 6457A-6458A

(University of Texas at Austin).

1539. THOMPSON, G.R. "The Apparition of This World: Transcendentalism and the American 'Ghost Story,'" in Bridges to Fantasy, eds. George Slusser, Eric S. Rabkin, Robert E. Scholes. Carbondale, Il : Southern Illinois UP, 1982, pp.90-107.

1540. TUCKER, Amy. "America's Gothic Landscape," Dissertation Abstracts International, 40 (1980): 5868A (New York University).

1541. YAGI, Toshio. "Amerikan Goshikku no Tanjo," in Shiro to Memai: Goshikku o Yomu, eds. Masao Shimura, Takao Tomiyama. Tokyo, Japan : Kokusho Kankokai, 1982, pp.139-173.

1542. YATES, Jo Anne. "American Gothic: Sources of Terror in American Fiction Before the Civil War," Dissertation Abstracts International, 41 (1980): 1602A (University of North Carolina).

VI. AMERICAN GOTHIC FICTION
Individual Author Studies

Charles Brockden Brown
(1771-1810)

1543. ALDERSON, Evan. "To Reconcile With Common Maxims: Edgar Huntly's Ruses," Pacific Coast Philology, 10 (1975): 5-9.

1544. AXELROD, Alan David. "Charles Brockden Brown: An American Tale," Dissertation Abstracts International, 40 (1980): 4033A (University of Iowa).

1545. _______. Charles Brockden Brown: An American Tale. Austin, TX : Texas UP, 1983.

1546. BAYM, Nina. "A Minority Reading of Wieland," in Critical Essays on Charles Brockden Brown, ed. Bernard Rosenthal. Boston : G.K. Hall, 1981, pp.87-103.

1547. BEAVER, Harold. "The Heart's Extremes," Times Literary Supplement, May 1, 1981, p.490.

1548. BELL, Michael. "'The Double-Tongued Deceiver': Sincerity and Duplicity in the Novels of Charles Brockden Brown," Early American Literature, 9 (1974): 143-163.

1549. BENNETT, Charles E. "Charles Brockden Brown's 'Portrait of an Emigrant,'" College Language Association Journal, 14 (1970): 87-90.

1550. _______. "The Charles Brockden Brown Canon," Dissertation Abstracts International, 35 (1974): 3670A (University of North Carolina).

1551. _______. "Charles Brockden Brown and the International Novel," Studies in the Novel, 12 (1980): 62-64.

1552. _______. "Charles Brockden Brown: Man of Letters," in Critical Essays on Charles Brockden Brown, ed. Bernard Rosenthal. Boston : G.K. Hall, 1981, pp.212-223.

1553. BENNETT, Maurice J. "Charles Brockden Brown's Ambivalence Toward Art and Imagination," Essays in Literature, 10 (1983): 55-69.

1554. BERANGER, Jean F. "A Psychoanalytic Approach to Structure," in Proceedings of a Symposium on American Literature, ed. Marta Sienicka. Poznan, Poland : Adama Mickiewicza, 1979, pp.7-19.

1555. BERNARD, Kenneth. "The Novels of Charles Brockden Brown: Studies in Meaning," Dissertation Abstracts, 23 (1962): 1008 (Columbia University).

1556. ______. "Charles Brockden Brown and the Sublime," Personalist, 45 (1964): 235-249.

1557. ______. "Arthur Mervyn: The Ordeal of Innocence," Texas Studies in Language and Literature, 6 (1965): 441-459.

1558. ______. "Edgar Huntly: Charles Brockden Brown's Unsolved Murder," Library Chronicle, 33 (1967): 30-53.

1559. ______. "Charles Brockden Brown," in Minor American Novelists, ed. Charles A. Hoyt. Carbondale, IL : Southern Illinois UP, 1971, pp.1-9.

1560. BERTHOFF, Warner B. "The Literary Career of Charles Brockden Brown," Unpublished Doctoral Dissertation, Harvard University, 1954.

1561. ______. "Adventures of the Young Man: An Approach to Charles Brockden Brown," American Quarterly, 9 (1957): 421-434.

1562. ______. "'A Lesson on Concealment': Brockden Brown's Method of Fiction," Philological Quarterly, 37 (1958): 45-57.

1563. ______. Introduction to Arthur Mervyn; or, Memoirs of the Year 1793 by Charles Brockden Brown. New York : Holt, Rinehart, and Winston, 1962, pp.vii-xviii.

1564. BERTHOLD, Dennis. "Charles Brockden Brown, Edgar Huntly, and the Origins of the American Picturesque," William and Mary Quarterly, 41, number 1 (1984): 62-84.

1565. ______. "Desacralizing the American Gothic: An Iconographic Approach to Edgar Huntly," Studies in American Fiction, 14 (1986): 127-138.

1566. BLAKE, Warren Barton. "Brockden Brown and the Novel," Sewanee Review, 18 (1910): 431-443.

1567. BONNEY, Agnes M. "Artistic Uses of Supernaturalism in the Fiction of Brown, Irving, and Hawthorne," Dissertation Abstracts International, 39 (1979): 4945A (Washington University).

1568. BRANCACCIO, Patrick. "Studied Ambiguities: Arthur Mervyn and the Problem of the Unreliable Narrator," American Literature, 42 (1970): 18-27.

1569. BREDAHL, A. Carl Jr. "Transformations in Wieland," Early American Literature, 12 (1977): 177-192.

1570. ______. "The Two Portraits in Wieland," Early American Literature, 16 (1981): 54-59.

1571. BROWN, Susan Marie Williams. "Villainy in Brockden Brown's Wieland and Arthur Mervyn: Structural Unity Through the Development of Characters and Universal Themes," Dissertation Abstracts International, 43 (1982): 1146A (Texas Woman's University).

1572. BULGHERONI, Marisa. "Charles Brockden Brown tra il Romanzo e la Storia," Studi Americani, 10 (1964): 57-69.

1573. ______. La Tentazione della Chimera: Charles Brockden Brown e le Origini del Romanzo Americano. Rome, Italy : Storia e Letteratura, 1965.

1574. BUTLER, David L. "A Study of the Literary Style of the Novels of Charles Brockden Brown," Dissertation Abstracts International, 34 (1974): 5093A (St. Louis University).

1575. ______. Dissecting a Human Heart: A Study of Style in the Novels of Charles Brockden Brown. Washington, DC : University Press of America, 1978.

1576. BUTLER, Michael D. "Charles Brockden Brown's Wieland: Method and Meaning," Studies in American Fiction, 4 (1976): 127-142.

1577. CARPENTER, Charles A. "Selective Bibliography of Writings About Charles Brockden Brown," in Critical Essays on Charles Brockden Brown, ed. Bernard Rosenthal. Boston : G.K. Hall, 1981, pp.224-239.

1578. CHRISTENSEN, Peter J. "The First Locked-Room Mystery? Charles Brockden Brown's Wieland," Armchair Detective, 10 (1977): 368-369.

1579. CHRISTOPHERSEN, Bill. "Charles Brockden Brown's Ormond: The Secret Witness as Ironic Motif," Modern Language Studies, 10, number 2 (1980): 37-41.

1580. ______. "The Witch in the Churn: Depravity and Self-Discovery in Charles Brockden Brown's Gothic Romances," Dissertation Abstracts International, 43 (1982): 1542A-1543A (Columbia University).

1581. ______. "Father of the American Novel: Brockden Brown in the 80's," Western Humanities Review, 39 (1985): 77-85.

1582. CLARK, Beverly Lyon. "Charles Brockden Brown's Contagious Unreliability," International Fiction Review, 8 (1981): 91-97.

1583. CLARK, David Lee. "Introduction to Edgar Huntly; or, The Memoirs of a Sleep-Walker by Charles Brockden Brown. New York : Macmillan, 1928.

1584. ______. Charles Brockden Brown: Pioneer Voice of America. Durham: Duke UP, 1952.

1585. CLEMAN, John. "Ambiguous Evil: A Study of Villains and Heroes in Charles Brockden Brown's Major Novels," Early American Literature, 10 (1975): 190-219.

1586. COYLE, James John. "The Problem of Evil in the Major Novels of Charles Brockden Brown," Dissertation Abstracts, 21 (1961): 3780 (University of Michigan).

1587. CRAFT, Commodore Jr. "A Study of the Interaction of Good and Evil in the Four Major Novels of Charles Brockden Brown," Dissertation Abstracts International, 37 (1977): 6483A (Ball State University).

1588. CREE, Charles George. "The Pastoral and the Theme of the Validity of Authorship in American Fiction," Dissertation Abstracts International, 41 (1981): 4032A (University of Indiana).

1589. DAVIDSON, Kathy N. "The Matter and Manner of Charles Brockden Brown's Alcuin," in Critical Essays on Charles Brockden Brown, ed. Bernard Rosenthal. Boston : G.K. Hall, 1981, pp.71-86.

1590. DAVIES, Rosemary Reeves. "Charles Brockden Brown's Ormond: A Possible Influence Upon Shelley's Conduct," Philological Quarterly, 43 (1964): 133-137.

1591. ELLIOTT, Emory. "Narrative Unity and Moral Resolution in Arthur Mervyn," in Critical Essays on Charles Brockden Brown, ed. Bernard Rosenthal. Boston : G.K. Hall, 1981, pp.142-163.

1592. FEENEY, Joseph. "Modernized by 1800: The Portrait of Urban America, Especially Philadelphia, in the Novels of Charles Brockden Brown," American Studies, 23 (1982): 25-38.

1593. FERGUSON, Robert A. "Yellow Fever and Charles Brockden Brown: Context of the Emerging Novelist," Early American Literature, 14 (1979-80): 293-305.

1594. ______. "Literature and the Vocation in the Early Republic: The Example of Charles Brockden Brown," Modern Philology, 78 (1980): 139-152.

1595. FLANDERS, Jane T. "Charles Brockden Brown and William Godwin: Parallels and Divergences," Dissertation Abstracts, 26 (1965): 3334-3335 (University of Wisconsin).

1596. FLECK, Richard F. "Symbolic Landscapes in Edgar Huntly," Research Studies, 39 (1971): 229-232.

1597. FRANK, Frederick Stilson. "Perverse Pilgrimage: The Role of the Gothic in the Works of Charles Brockden Brown, Edgar Allan Poe, and Nathaniel Hawthorne," Dissertation Abstracts, 29 (1968): 1866A-1867A (Rutgers University).

1598. ______. "Wieland; or, The Transformation," in Survey of Modern Fantasy Literature, ed. Keith Neilson. Englewood Cliffs, NJ : Salem

Press, 1983, pp.2126-2131.

1599. FRANK, J.G. "The Wieland Family in Charles Brockden Brown," Monatshefte, 42 (1950): 347-353.

1600. FRANKLIN, Wayne. "Tragedy and Comedy in Brown's Wieland," Novel, 8 (1975): 147-163.

1601. FRICKE, Max. Charles Brockden Browns Leben und Werke. Hamburg, Germany : Meissner, 1911.

1602. FUJIMOTO, Yukio. "On C.B. Brown's Narrative Technique," Hiroshima Studies in English Language and Literature, 24 (1979): 43-52.

1603. FUSSELL, Edwin Sill. "Wieland: A Literary and Historical Reading," Early American Literature, 18 (1983): 171-186.

1604. GARROW, Scott. "Character Transformation in Wieland," Southern Quarterly, 4 (1966): 308-318.

1605. GILMORE, Michael T. "Calvinism and Gothicism: The Example of Brown's Wieland," Studies in the Novel, 9 (1977): 107-118.

1606. GRABO, Norman S. The Coincidental Art of Charles Brockden Brown. Chapel Hill, NC : North Carolina UP, 1981.

1607. GREINER, Donald J. "Brown's Use of the Narrator in Wieland: An Indirect Plea for the Acceptance of Fiction," College Language Association Journal, 13 (1969): 131-136.

1608. HARDT, John Stephen. "The Darkening Garden: Paradisal Skepticism in American Fiction, Brown through Melville," Dissertation Abstracts International, 45 (1984): 521A (University of Missouri at Columbia).

1609. HARE, Robert Rigby. "Ormond: The Influence of Rousseau, Godwin, and Mary Wollstonecraft," Dissertation Abstracts, 28 (1968): 4599A (University of Maryland).

1610. HAYNE, Barrie Stewart. "The Divided Self: The Alter Ego as Theme and Device in Brockden Brown, Hawthorne, and James," Unpublished Doctoral Dissertation, Harvard University, 1964.

1611. HEDGES, William. "Charles Brockden Brown and the Culture of Contradictions," Early American Literature, 9 (1974): 107-142.

1612. HELLER, Terry. "Charles Brockden Brown," in Critical Survey of Long Fiction, ed. Frank Magill. Englewood Cliffs, NJ : Salem Press, I, 312-324.

1613. HEMENWAY, Robert E. "The Novels of Charles Brockden Brown: A Critical Study," Dissertation Abstracts, 28 (1966): 676A (Kent State University).

1614. HEMENWAY, Robert E. and Dean H. Keller. "Charles Brockden Brown: America's First Important Novelist: A Check List of Biography and Criticism," Papers of the Bibliographical Society of America, 60 (1966): 349-362.

1615. HEMENWAY, Robert E. "Brockden Brown's Twice Told Insanity Tale," American Literature, 40 (1968): 211-215.

1616. HENDRICKSON, James C. "A Note on Wieland," American Literature, 8 (1936): 305-306.

1617. HESFORF, Walter. "Do You Know the Author? The Question of Authorship in Wieland," Early American Literature, 17 (1982): 239-248.

1618. HIRSH, David H. "Charles Brockden Brown as Novelist of Ideas," Books at Brown, 20 (1965): 165-184.

1619. HOBSON, Robert W. "Voices of Carwin and Other Mysteries in Charles Brockden Brown's Wieland," Early American Literature, 10 (1975): 307-309.

1620. HOEKSTRA, Ellen Louise Jarvis. "The Characterization of Women in the Novels of Charles Brockden Brown," Dissertation Abstracts International, 36 (1976): 8059A (Michigan State University).

1621. HUGHES, Philip Russell. "Archetypal Patterns in Edgar Huntly," Studies in the Novel, 5 (1973): 176-190.

1622. HUME, Robert D. "Charles Brockden Brown and the Uses of Gothicism: A Reassessment," ESQ: A Journal of the American Renaissance, 18 (1972): 10-18.

1623. JENKINS, R.B. "Invulnerable Virtue in Wieland and 'Comus,'" South Atlantic Bulletin, 38 (1973): 72-75.

1624. JORDAN, Cynthia S. "On Rereading Wieland: The Folly of Precipitate Conclusions," Early American Literature, 16 (1981): 154-174.

1625. JUSTUS, James H. "Arthur Mervyn, American," American Literature, 42 (1970): 304-324.

1626. KESHIAN, Charles G. "The Political Character of the Novels of Charles Brockden Brown," Unpublished Doctoral Dissertation, University of California at Berkeley, 1973.

1627. KIMBALL, Arthur G. "Savages and Savagism: Brockden Brown's Dramatic Irony," Studies in Romanticism, 6 (1967): 214-225.

1628. ______. Rational Fictions: A Study of Charles Brockden Brown. Mc Minnville, OR : Linfield Research Institute, 1968.

1629. KINSLOW, Kenneth Joseph. "Quaker Doctrines and Ideas in the Novels of Charles Brockden Brown," Dissertation Abstracts International, 39 (1978): 2938A-2939A (University of Notre Dame).

1630. KIRKHAM, E. Bruce. "A Note on Wieland," American Notes & Queries, 5

(1967): 86-87.

1631. KRAUSE, Sydney J. and Janet Nieset. "A Census of the Works of Charles Brockden Brown," Serif, 3, number 4 (1966): 27-55.

1632. KRAUSE, Sydney J. "Ormond: Seduction in a New Key," American Literature, 44 (1973): 570-584.

1633. ______. "Romanticism in Wieland: Brown and the Reconciliation of Opposites," in Artful Thunder: Versions of the Romantic Tradition in American Literature in Honor of Howard P. Vincent. Kent, OH : Kent State UP, 1975, pp.13-24.

1634. KRAUSE, Sydney J., S.W. Reid, and Alexander Cowie, eds. Wieland; or, The Transformation by Charles Brockden Brown. Kent, OH : Kent State UP, 1977.

1635. KRAUSE, Sydney J. "Ormond: How Rapidly and How Well 'Composed, Arranged, and Delivered,'" Early American Literature, 13 (1978): 238-249.

1636. ______. "Clara Howard and Jane Talbot: Godwin on Trial," in Critical Essays on Charles Brockden Brown, ed. Bernard Rosenthal. Boston : G. K. Hall, 1981, pp.184-211.

1637. ______. "Edgar Huntly and the American Nightmare," Studies in the Novel, 13 (1981): 294-302.

1638. KRAUSE, Sydney J. and S.W. Reid, eds. Ormond; or, The Secret Witness by Charles Brockden Brown. Kent, OH : Kent State UP, 1982.

1639. ______. "Historical Essay and Textual Essay," for Edgar Huntly; or, The Memoirs of a Sleep-Walker by Charles Brockden Brown. Kent, OH : Kent State UP, 1984.

1640. KREYLING, Michael. "Construing Brown's Wieland: Ambiguity and Derridean 'Freeplay,'" Studies in the Novel, 14 (1982): 43-54.

1641. KRIEG, Joann Peck. "Charles Brockden Brown and the Empire of Romance," Dissertation Abstracts International, 40 (1979): 2682A (City University of New York).

1642. LEVINE, Paul. "The American Novel Begins," American Scholar, 35 (1966): 134-148.

1643. LEVINE, Robert S. "Villainy and the Fear of Conspiracy in Charles Brockden Brown's Ormond," Early American Literature, 15 (1980): 124-140.

1644. ______. "Conspiracy Fears and the American Romance, 1789-1860," Dissertation Abstracts International, 41 (1981): 4713A-4714A (Stanford University).

1645. ______. "Arthur Mervyn's Revolutions," Studies in American Fiction, 12 (1984): 145-160.

1646. LIMPRECHT, Nancy Silverman. "Repudiating the Self-Justifying Fiction: C.B. Brown, N. Hawthorne, and H. Melville as Anti-Romancers," Dissertation Abstracts International, 39 (1978): 886A (University of California at Berkeley).

1647. LYTTLE, David. "The Case Against Carwin," Nineteenth-Century Fiction, 26 (1971): 257-269.

1648. MANLY, William M. "The Importance of Point of View in Brockden Brown's Wieland," American Literature, 35 (1964): 311-321.

1649. MARCHAND, Ernest. "The Literary Opinions of Charles Brockden Brown," Studies in Philology, 31 (1934): 541-566.

1650. _______. Introduction to Ormond; or, The Secret Witness by Charles Brockden Brown. New York : Hafner, 1962, pp.ix-xliv.

1651. MARTINEZ, Inez A. "Charles Brockden Brown: Fictitious Historian," Dissertation Abstracts International, 40 (1979): 3302A (University of Wisconsin).

1652. MC ALEXANDER, Patricia J. "Sexual Morality in the Fiction of Charles Brockden Brown: Index to a Personal and Cultural Debate Regarding Passion and Reason," Dissertation Abstracts International, 34 (1974): 6597A (University of Wisconsin).

1653. _______. "Arthur Mervyn and the Sentimental Love Tradition," Studies in the Literary Imagination, 9 (1976): 31-41.

1654. MC CAY, Mary Ann D. "Women in the Novels of Charles Brockden Brown: A Study," Dissertation Abstracts International, 35 (1974): 3692A (Tufts University).

1655. MICKLUS, Robert. "Charles Brockden Brown's Curiosity Shop," Early American Literature, 15 (1980): 172-187.

1656. MONAHAN, Kathleen Nolan. "The Relationship Between Character and Idea in the Novels of Charles Brockden Brown," Dissertation Abstracts International, 42 (1982): 3159A (New York University).

1657. MYERS, Anne Caldwell. "The Novels of Charles Brockden Brown: A Rejection of Utopia," Dissertation Abstracts International, 42 (1981): 704A-705A (Arizona State University).

1658. NELSON, Carl W. Jr. "The Novels of Charles Brockden Brown: Irony and Illusion," Dissertation Abstracts International, 32 (1971): 392A (SUNY at Binghamton).

1659. _______. "Brown's Manichean Mock-Heroic: The Ironic Self in a Hyperbolic World," West Virginia University Philological Papers, 20 (1973): 26-42.

1660. _______. "A Just Reading of Charles Brockden Brown's Ormond," Early American Literature, 8 (1973): 163-178.

1661. ________. "A Method for Madness: The Symbolic Patterns in Arthur Mervyn," West Virginia University Philological Papers, 22 (1975): 29-50.

1662. NEWMAN, Robert D. "Brown's Edgar Huntly," Explicator, 40, number 4 (1982): 25-26.

1663. NYE, Russel B. "The Early Novel: Charles Brockden Brown's American Gothic," in American Literary History; 1607-1830. New York : Alfred A. Knopf, 1970, pp.241-244.

1664. OLIVER, Lawrence James Jr. "Kinesthetic Imagery and the Nightmare of Falling in the Fiction of Brown, Cooper, Poe, and Melville," Dissertation Abstracts International, 42 (1981): 216A (Pennsylvania State University).

1665. PARKER, Patricia. Charles Brockden Brown: A Reference Guide. Boston : G.K. Hall, 1980.

1666. PATRICK, Marietta Stafford. "Romantic Iconography in Charles Brockden Brown," Dissertation Abstracts International, 41 (1980): 675A (University of Kentucky).

1667. ________. "Charles Brockden Brown's Ormond: A Psychological Portrait of Constantia Dudley," Journal of Evolutionary Psychology, 5, numbers 1-2 (1984): 112-128.

1668. ________. "Romantic Iconography in Wieland," South Atlantic Review, 49, number 4 (1984): 65-74.

1669. PATTEE, Fred Lewis. Introduction to Wieland; or, The Transformation by Charles Brockden Brown. New York : Hafner, 1960, pp.ix-xlvi.

1670. PEASE, Marilyn Theresa. "The Novels of Charles Brockden Brown: Studies in the Rise of Consciousness," Dissertation Abstracts, 28 (1968): 4140A (Fordham University).

1671. PERSON, Leland S. Jr. "'My Good Mama': Women in Edgar Huntly and Arthur Mervyn," Studies in American Fiction, 9 (1981): 33-46.

1672. PRESCOTT, F.C. "Wieland and Frankenstein," American Literature, 2 (1930): 172-173.

1673. PRIBEK, Thomas. "A Note on Depravity in Wieland," Philological Quarterly, 64 (1985): 273-278.

1674. PRIDGEON, Charles T. Jr. "Insanity in American Fiction from Charles Brockden Brown to Oliver Wendell Holmes," Dissertation Abstracts, 31 (1970): 1766A-1767A (Duke University).

1675. REID, S.W. "Brockden Brown in England: Notes on Henry Colburn's 1822 Editions of His Novels," Early American Literature, 9 (1974): 188-195.

1676. REID, S.W. and James F. Caccamo. "The States and Issues of Brown's Edgar Huntly," Papers of the Bibliographical Society of America, 75 (1981): 326-339.

1677. RICKS, Christopher. "Chamber of Horrors," New Statesman, March 11, 1966, pp.339-340.

1678. RIDGELY, J.V. "The Empty World of Wieland," in Individual and Community: Variations on a Theme in American Fiction. Durham, NC : Duke UP, 1975, pp.3-16.

1679. RINGE, Donald A. Charles Brockden Brown. New York : Twayne; Twayne United States Authors Series Number 98, 1966.

1680. _______. "Charles Brockden Brown," in Major Writers of Early American Literature. Madison, WI : Wisconsin UP, 1972, pp.273-294.

1681. _______. "Early American Gothic: Brown, Dana and Allston," American Transcendental Quarterly, 19 (1973): 3-8.

1682. RODGERS, Paul C. Jr. "Brown's Ormond: The Fruits of Improvisation," American Quarterly, 26 (1974): 4-22.

1683. ROSE, Harriet. "The First-Person Narrator as Artist in the Works of Charles Brockden Brown, Nathaniel Hawthorne, and Henry James," Dissertation Abstracts International, 33 (1973): 6373A (Indiana University).

1684. ROSENTHAL, Bernard. "Introduction," to Critical Essays on Charles Brockden Brown, ed. Bernard Rosenthal. Boston : G.K. Hall, 1981, pp. 1-21.

1685. _______. "The Voices of Wieland," in Critical Essays on Charles Brockden Brown, ed. Bernard Rosenthal. Boston : G.K. Hall, 1981, pp. 104-125.

1686. RUSSO, James R. "The Tangled Web of Deception and Imposture in Charles Brockden Brown's Ormond," Early American Literature, 14 (1979): 205-227.

1687. _______. "The Chameleon of Convenient Vice: A Study of the Narrative of Arthur Mervyn," Studies in the Novel, 11 (1979): 381-405.

1688. _______. "The Craft of Charles Brockden Brown's Fiction," Dissertation Abstracts International, 40 (1980): 5058A-5059A (University of Arizona).

1689. _______. "'The Chimeras of the Brain': Clara's Narrative in Wieland," Early American Literature, 16 (1981): 60-88.

1690. SAMUELS, Shirley. "Plague and Politics in 1793: Arthur Mervyn," Criticism, 27 (1985): 225-246.

1691. SCHEICK, William J. "The Problem of Origination in Brown's Ormond," in Critical Essays on Charles Brockden Brown, ed. Bernard Rosenthal. Boston : G.K. Hall, 1981, pp.126-141.

1692. SCHNEIDER, Evelyn S. "The Changing Image of Charles Brockden Brown as Seen by American Critics from 1815 to the Present," Dissertation Abstracts International, 32 (1972): 6943A (Rutgers University).

1693. SCHULZ, Dieter. "Edgar Huntly as Quest Romance," American Literature, 43 (1971): 323-335.

1694. SCHULZ, Max F. "Brockden Brown: An Early Casualty of the American Experience," in Americana-Austriaca: Beiträge zur Amerikankunde, Band 2. Vienna, Austria : W. Braumüller, 1970, pp.81-90.

1695. SELTZER, Mark. "Saying Makes It So: Language and Event in Brown's Wieland," Early American Literature, 13 (1978): 81-91.

1696. SHELDEN, Pamela J. "The Shock of Ambiguity: Brockden Brown's Wieland and the Gothic Tradition," De Kalb Literary Arts Journal (Clarkston, GA), 10, number 4 (1977): 17-26.

1697. SLANINA, Ann Margaret. "The Development of Charles Brockden Brown's Literary Ideas: A Study of His Major Novels," Dissertation Abstracts International, 37 (1976): 2187A-2188A (University of New Mexico).

1698. _______. "Charles Brockden Brown's Wieland: A Story With a Moral," Re: Artes Liberales, 6, number 2 (1980): 11-22.

1699. SLATER, John F. "The Sleepwalker and the Great Awakening: Brown's Edgar Huntly and Jonathan Edwards," Papers on Language and Literature, 19 (1983): 199-217.

1700. SMITH, Allan Gardner. "Nineteenth-Century Psychology in the Fiction of Charles Brockden Brown, Edgar Allan Poe, and Nathaniel Hawthorne," Dissertation Abstracts International, 35 (1975): 7880A-7881A (Indiana University).

1701. SNELL, George. "Charles Brockden Brown: Apocalypticalist," University of Kansas City Review, 11 (1944): 131-138; Rpt. in The Shapers of American Fiction, 1798-1947. New York : Cooper Square, 1961, pp.32-45.

1702. SOLDATI, Joseph A. "Configurations of Faust: Three Studies in the Gothic (1798-1820)," Dissertation Abstracts International, 32 (1972): 6945A (Washington State University).

1703. _______. "The Americanization of Faust: A Study of Charles Brockden Brown's Wieland," ESQ: A Journal of the American Renaissance, 20 (1974): 1-14.

1704. _______. Configurations of Faust: Three Studies in the Gothic (1798-1820). New York : Arno Press, 1980.

1705. SPANGLER, George M. "C.B. Brown's Arthur Mervyn: A Portrait of the Young American Artist," American Literature, 52 (1981): 578-592.

1706. STEINBERG, Paul Scott. "On the Brink of the Precipice: Madness in the

Writings of Charles Brockden Brown," Dissertation Abstracts International, 43 (1983): 2671A (University of California at Berkeley).

1707. STINEBACK, David, ed. Edgar Huntly; or, The Memoirs of a Sleep-Walker by Charles Brockden Brown. New Haven, CT : College and University Press Services, 1974.

1708. STOUT, Janis P. "Urban Gothicists: Brown, Lippard, Poe," in Sodoms in Eden: The City in American Fiction Before 1860. Westport, CT : Greenwood Press, 1976.

1709. STROZIER, Robert. "Wieland and Other Romances: Horror in Parentheses," Emerson Society Quarterly, 50 (1968): 24-29.

1710. SULLIVAN, Michael Patrick. "Reconciliation and Subversion in the Novels of Charles Brockden Brown," Dissertation Abstracts International, 45 (1984): 1401A (University of Rhode Island).

1711. TILTON, Eleanor M. "In the Labyrinth of Charles Brockden Brown's Prose: The Bicentennial Edition," Early American Literature, 19 (1984): 191-208.

1712. TOLES, George. "Charting the Hidden Landscape: Edgar Huntly," Early American Literature, 16 (1981): 133-153.

1713. TOMLINSON, David Otis. "Women in the Writing of Charles Brockden Brown: A Study in the Development of an Author's Thought," Dissertation Abstracts International, 35 (1974): 5431A (University of North Carolina).

1714. TRICOMI, Elizabeth Taylor. "The Search for Knowledge in the Major Novels of Charles Brockden Brown," Dissertation Abstracts International, 31 (1971): 5430A (Northwestern University).

1715. TUTOR, Jonathan C. "Disappointed Expectations: Artistic Strategy in Ormond," Publications of the Mississippi Philological Association, (1985): 67-80.

1716. VAN DER BEETS, Richard and Paul Witherington. "My Kinsman, Brockden Brown: Robin Molineux and Arthur Mervyn," American Transcendental Quarterly, 1 (1969): 13-15.

1717. VILAS, Martin S. Charles Brockden Brown: A Study of Early American Fiction. Burlington, VT : Free Press Association, 1904; Rpt. Folcroft, PA : Folcroft Library Editions, 1973.

1718. VOLOSHIN, Beverly Rose. "The Lockean Tradition in the Gothic Fiction of Brown, Poe, and Melville," Dissertation Abstracts International, 40 (1980): 4047A (University of California at Berkeley).

1719. ______. "Wieland: 'Accounting for Appearances,'" New England Quarterly, 59 (1986): 341-357.

1720. WARCHOL, Tomasz Andrzej. "A Study of the Fiction of Charles Brockden Brown," Dissertation Abstracts International, 45 (1984): 1755A (University of Massachusetts).

1721. WARFEL, Harry R. "Charles Brockden Brown's German Sources," Modern Language Quarterly, 1 (1940): 357-363.

1722. ______. Charles Brockden Brown: American Gothic Novelist. Gainesville, FL : Florida UP, 1949.

1723. WEBER, Alfred. "Charles Brockden Browns Theorie der Geschichtsschreibung und des Romans," in Geschicte und Fiktion: Amerikanische Prosa im 19. Jahrhundert. Göttingen, West Germany : Vandenhoeck & Ruprecht, 1972, pp.15-41.

1724. WELDON, Roberta F. "Charles Brockden Brown's Wieland: A Family Tragedy," Studies in American Fiction, 12 (1984): 1-11.

1725. WILEY, Lulu Rumsey. Sources and Influence of the Novels of Charles Brockden Brown. New York : Vantage Press, 1950.

1726. WITHERINGTON, Paul. "Narrative Techniques in the Novels of Charles Brockden Brown," Dissertation Abstracts, 25 (1964): 2992 (University of Texas).

1727. ______. "Image and Idea in Wieland and Edgar Huntly," Serif, 3 (1966): 19-26.

1728. ______. "Benevolence and the 'Utmost Stretch': Charles Brockden Brown's Narrative Dilemma," Criticism, 14 (1972): 175-191.

1729. ______. "Charles Brockden Brown's Other Novels: Clara Howard and Jane Talbot," Nineteenth-Century Fiction, 29 (1974): 257-272.

1730. ______. "Charles Brockden Brown: A Bibliography Essay," Early American Literature, 9 (1974): 164-187.

1731. ______. "Charles Brockden Brown's Ormond: The American Artist and His Masquerades," Studies in American Fiction, 4 (1976): 111-119.

1732. ______. "'Not My Tongue Only': Form and Language in Brown's Edgar Huntly," in Critical Essays on Charles Brockden Brown, ed. Bernard Rosenthal. Boston : G.K. Hall, 1981, pp.164-183.

1733. WYSS, Hal H. "Involuntary Evil in the Fiction of Brown, Cooper, Poe, Hawthorne, and Melville," Dissertation Abstracts International, 32 (1971): 1489A (Ohio State University).

1734. YARBROUGH, Stephen R. "The Tragedy of Isolation: Fictional Technique and Environmentalism in Wieland," Studies in American Fiction, 8 (1980): 98-105.

1735. YOUNG, Philip. "Born Decadent: The American Novel and Charles Brockden Brown," Southern Review, 17 (1981): 501-519.

1736. ZIFF, Larzer. "A Reading of Wieland," Publications of the Modern Language Association," 77 (1962): 51-57.

Ambrose Bierce
(1842-1914?)

1737. BLEILER, E.F. Introduction to *Ghost and Horror Stories of Ambrose Bierce*. New York : Dover Publications, 1964, pp.v-xx.

1738. FORTENBERRY, George E. "Ambrose Bierce (1842-1914?): A Critical Bibliography of Secondary Comment," *American Literary Realism*, 4 (1971): 11-56.

1739. GRENANDER, M.E. "Bierce's Turn of the Screw: Tales of Ironical Terror," *Western Humanities Review*, 11 (1957): 257-264.

1740. MC LEAN, Robert C. "The Deaths in Ambrose Bierce's 'Halpin Frayser,'" *Papers on Language and Literature*, 10 (1974): 394-402.

1741. RUBENS, Philip M. "The Literary Gothic and the Fiction of Ambrose Gwinett Bierce," *Dissertation Abstracts International*, 37 (1976): 1555A (Northern Illinois University).

1742. ______. "The Gothic Foundations of Ambrose Bierce's Fiction," *Nyctalops*, 2, number 7 (1978): 29-31.

1743. STEIN, William Bysshe. "Bierce's 'The Death of Halpin Frayser': The Poetics of Gothic Consciousness," *ESQ*: *A Journal of the American Renaissance*, 18 (1972): 115-122.

1744. UCHIDA, Yoko. "A Study of Ambrose Bierce: The Unknown Realm of Mind," *Collected Essays by Members of the Faculty (Kyoritsu Women's Junior College)*, 28 (1985): 39-50.

Nathaniel Hawthorne
(1804-1864)

1745. ALLEN, M.L. "The Black Veil: Three Versions of a Symbol," *English Studies*, 47 (1966): 286-289.

1746. ANDOLA, John Anthony. "Nathaniel Hawthorne's Use of Mesmerism in Four Major Works," *Dissertation Abstracts International*, 42 (1981): 1631A-1632A (Ball State University).

1747. BARRY, Elaine. "Beyond the Veil: A Reading of Hawthorne's 'The Minister's Black Veil,'" *Studies in Short Fiction*, 17 (1980): 15-20.

1748. BAYM, Nina. "Hawthorne's Gothic Discards: *Fanshawe* and 'Alice Doane,'" *Nathaniel Hawthorne Journal*, (1974): 105-115.

1749. BEEBE, Maurice and Jack Hardie. "Criticism of Nathaniel Hawthorne: A Selected Checklist," *Studies in the Novel*, 2 (1970): 519-587.

1750. BERGMAN, Eugene. "The Divided Self in Hawthorne and Dostoevsky," *Dissertation Abstracts International*, 39 (1979): 4933A-4934A (George Washington University).

1751. BERTHOLD, Dennis. "Hawthorne, Ruskin, and the Gothic Revival: Transcendent Gothic in The Marble Faun," ESQ: A Journal of the American Renaissance, 20 (1974): 13-52.

1752. CALHOUN, Thomas O. "Hawthorne's Gothic: An Approach to the Last Four Fragments," Genre, 3 (1970): 229-241.

1753. CHARNEY, Maurice. "Hawthorne and the Gothic Style," New England Quarterly, 34 (1961): 36-49.

1754. CHISHOLM, Richard M. "The Use of Gothic Materials in Hawthorne's Mature Romances," Dissertation Abstracts International, 31 (1970): 382A (Columbia University).

1755. COHEN, Hubert I. "The Grotesque in the Fiction of Nathaniel Hawthorne," Dissertation Abstracts International, 31 (1970): 4153A (University of Michigan).

1756. CURRAN, Ronald T. "Hawthorne as Gothicist," Dissertation Abstracts, 30 (1970): 4404A-4405A (University of Pennsylvania).

1757. _______. "The Reluctant Yankee in Hawthorne's Abortive Gothic Romances," Nathaniel Hawthorne Journal, (1974): 179-194.

1758. _______. "'Yankee Gothic': Hawthorne's 'Castle of Pyncheon,'" Studies in the Novel, 8 (1976): 69-80.

1759. CURTSINGER, E.C. "The Byronic Hero and Nathaniel Hawthorne's Isolatoes: A Comparative Study," Unpublished Doctoral Dissertation, Notre Dame University, 1965.

1760. DOUBLEDAY, Neal Frank. "Hawthorne's Use of Three Gothic Patterns," College English, 7 (1946): 250-262.

1761. _______. "'That Tinge of the Marvelous': Hawthorne's Gothic Habit" and "The Gothic Naturalized: 'The Prophetic Pictures,'" in Hawthorne's Early Tales: A Critical Study. Durham, NC : Duke UP, 1972, pp.52-62; pp.109-117.

1762. ELDER, Marjorie. "Hawthorne's The Marble Faun: A Gothic Structure," Costerus: Essays in English and American Language and Literature, 1 (1972): 81-88.

1763. GOLDSTEIN, Jesse Sidney. "The Literary Source of Hawthorne's Fanshawe," Modern Language Notes, 60 (1945): 1-8.

1764. HAMADA, Masjiro. "The House of the Seven Gables: Ni Okeru Gothic Romance Teki Yoso," Studies in English Literature (Tokyo), 45 (1968): 49-61.

1765. HULL, Raymona E. "Hawthorne and the Magic Elixir of Life: The Failure of a Gothic Theme," ESQ: A Journal of the American Renaissance, 18 (1972): 97-107.

1766. JOHNSON, Evelyn C. "Nathaniel Hawthorne and the Supernatural," Unpublished Doctoral Dissertation, Stanford University, 1938.

1767. KAFTAN, Robert A. "A Study of the Gothic Techniques in the Novels of Nathaniel Hawthorne," Dissertation Abstracts, 29 (1968): 1899A (Michigan State University).

1768. LA REGINA, Gabriella. "'Rappaccini's Daughter': The Gothic as a Catalyst for Hawthorne's Imagination," Studi Americani, 17 (1971): 29-74.

1769. LEWIS, Paul. "Mournful Mysteries: Gothic Speculation in The Scarlet Letter," American Transcendental Quarterly, 44 (1979): 279-293.

1770. LUNDBLAD, Jane. Nathaniel Hawthorne and the European Literary Tradition. Cambridge, MA : Harvard UP, 1947; Rpt. as Nathaniel Hawthorne and the Tradition of the Gothic Romance. New York : Haskell House, 1964.

1771. MARKUS, Manfred. "Hawthorne's 'Alice Doane's Appeal': An Anti-Gothic Tale," Germanisch-Romanische Monatsschrift, 25 (1975): 338-349.

1772. NEWLIN, Paul A. "'Vague Shapes of the Borderland': The Place of the Uncanny in Hawthorne's Gothic Vision," ESQ: A Journal of the American Renaissance, 18 (1972): 83-96.

1773. POLLIN, Burton R. "'Rappaccini's Daughter,'--Sources and Names," Names, 14 (1966): 30-35.

1774. SOKOLOFF, B.A. "Ethan Brand's Twin," Modern Language Notes, 73 (1958): 413-414.

1775. ST. ARMAND, Barton Levi. "Hawthorne's 'Haunted Mind': A Subterranean Drama of the Self," Criticism, 13 (1971): 1-25.

1776. STAY, Byron L. "Nathaniel Hawthorne: A Study of the Divided Self," Dissertation Abstracts International, 41 (1980): 1059A (University of Delaware).

1777. STEIN, William B. "Faustian Symbolism in the Gothic Romance," in Hawthorne's Faust: A Study of the Devil Archetype. Gainesville, FL : Florida UP, 1953, pp.35-50.

1778. STOEHR, Taylor. "Hawthorne and Mesmerism," Huntington Library Quarterly, 33 (1969): 33-60.

1779. TURNER, H. Arlin. "Hawthorne's Literary Borrowings," Publications of the Modern Language Association, 51 (1936): 543-562.

1780. WALSH, Thomas F. "The Devils of Hawthorne and Flannery O'Connor," Xavier University Studies, 5 (1966): 117-122.

1781. WOODBRIDGE, Benjamin M. "Supernaturalism in Hawthorne and Poe," Colorado College Publications, 2 (1911): 135-154.

Washington Irving
(1783-1859)

1782. CLENDENNING, John. "Irving and the Gothic Tradition," Bucknell Review, 12, number 2 (1964): 90-98.

1783. DEVLIN, James E. "Irving's 'Adventure of the German Student,'" Studies in American Fiction, 7 (1980): 92-95.

1784. GETZ, John R. "Irving's 'Dolph Heyliger': Ghost Story or Tall Tale?" Studies in Short Fiction, 16 (1979): 67-68.

1785. LUPACK, Barbara Tepa. "Irving's German Student," Studies in Short Fiction, 21 (1984): 398-400.

1786. LYNCH, James J. "The Devil in the Writings of Irving, Hawthorne, and Poe," New York Folklore Quarterly, 8 (1952): 111-131.

1787. MASIELLO, Lea. "Speaking of Ghosts: Style in Washington Irving's Tales of the Supernatural," Dissertation Abstracts International, 44 (1983): 1792A (University of Cincinnati).

1788. REICHART, Walter A. Washington Irving and Germany. Ann Arbor, MI : Michigan UP, 1957.

1789. RINGE, Donald A. "Irving's Use of the Gothic Mode," Studies in the Literary Imagination, 7 (1974): 51-65.

1790. THOMPSON, G.R. "Washington Irving and the American Ghost Story," in The Haunted Dusk: American Supernatural Fiction, 1820-1920, eds. Howard Kerr, John W. Crowley, Charles L. Crow. Athens, GA : Georgia UP, 1983, pp.13-36.

1791. WAGENKNECHT, Edward. Introduction to Washington Irving's Tales of the Supernatural. Owings Mills, MD : Stemmer House, 1982.

Henry James
(1843-1916)

1792. AKIYAMA, Masayuki. "James and Nanboku: A Comparative Study of Supernatural Stories in the West and East," Comparative Literature Studies, 22 (1985): 43-52.

1793. ALLEN, John R. "The Governess and the Ghosts in The Turn of the Screw," Henry James Review, 1 (1980): 73-80.

1794. BANTA, Martha. "The Two Worlds of Henry James: A Study in the Fiction of the Supernatural," Dissertation Abstracts, 26 (1985): 1035-1036 (University of Indiana).

1795. _______. "The House of Seven Ushers and How They Grew: A Look at Jamesian Gothicism," Yale Review, 57 (1967): 56-85.

1796. _______. Henry James and the Occult: The Great Extension. Bloomington, IN : Indiana UP, 1972.

1797. DEFREN, Judith. "The Silent Scream: Patterns of Horror in the Works of Henry James," Dissertation Abstracts International, 46 (1985): 151A (University of Manitoba).

1798. DENNIS, Larry R. "Spectres and Spectators in The Turn of the Screw and The Innocents," in Purdue University Fifth Annual Conference on Film, ed. Maud Walther. Lafayette, IN : Purdue UP, 1980, pp.96-102.

1799. DUPERRAY, Max. "Possession et Exorcisme: Aspects du Fantasme Jamesien dans quelques Ghostly Tales," in Société des Anglicistes de l'Enseignment Supérieur (Echanges: Actes du Congrès de Strasbourg), ed. G. Laprevotte. Paris : Marcel Didier, 1982, pp.321-332.

1800. EDEL, Leon. Introduction to The Ghostly Tales of Henry James. New Brunswick, NJ : Rutgers UP, 1948, pp.v-xxxii.

1801. GRUNES, Dennis. "The Demonic Child in The Turn of the Screw," Psychocultural Review: Interpretations in the Psychology of Art, Literature and Society, 2 (1978): 221-239.

1802. MACKENZIE, Manfred. "The Turn of the Screw: Jamesian Gothic," Essays in Criticism, 12 (1962): 34-38.

1803. MARTIN, Jay. "Ghostly Rentals, Ghostly Purchases: Haunted Imaginations in James, Twain, and Bellamy," in The Haunted Dusk: American Supernatural Fiction, 1820-1920, eds. Howard Kerr, John W. Crowley, Charles L Crow. Athens, GA : Georgia UP, 1983, pp.123-131.

1804. MERIVALE, Patricia. "The Esthetics of Perversion: Gothic Artifice in Henry James and Witold Gombrowicz," Publications of the Modern Language Association, 93 (1978): 992-1002.

1805. NETTELS, Elsa. "The Portrait of a Lady and the Gothic Romance," South Atlantic Bulletin, 39 (1974): 73-82.

1806. PROBERT, K.G. "Christopher Newman and the Artistic American View of Life," Studies in American Fiction, 11 (1983): 203-215.

1807. ROVIT, Earl. "The Ghosts in Henry James's 'The Jolly Corner,'" Tennessee Studies in Literature, 10 (1965): 65-72.

1808. SCHLEIFER, Ronald. "Trap of the Imagination: The Gothic Tradition, Fiction, and The Turn of the Screw," Criticism, 22 (1980): 297-319.

1809. SCOTT, James B. "How the Screw is Turned: James's Amusette," University of Mississippi Studies in English, 4 (1983): 112-131.

1810. SHELDEN, Pamela Jacobs. "Jamesian Gothicism: The Haunted Castle of the Mind," Studies in the Literary Imagination, 7 (1974): 121-134.

1811. SKLEPOWICH, E.A. "Gossip and Gothicism in The Sacred Fount," Henry James Review, 2 (1981): 112-115.

1812. SMYTH, Paul Rockwood. "Gothic Influences in Henry James's Major Fiction," Dissertation Abstracts International, 41 (1981): 4063A (Michigan State University).

1813. THOMAS, Lloyd Spencer. "The Haunts of Language, Superstition and Subterfuge in Henry James's Stories of the Supernatural," Dissertation Abstracts International, 36 (1975): 1512A (SUNY at Binghamton).

1814. THORBERG, Raymond. "Terror Made Relevant: James's Ghost Stories," Dalhousie Review, 47 (1967): 185-191.

1815. UNRUE, Darlene H. Henry James and the Gothic Romance," Dissertation Abstracts International, 32 (1972): 4028A (Ohio State University).

1816. _______. "The Occult Metaphor as Technique in The Portrait of a Lady," Henry James Review, 2 (1981): 199-203.

1817. WEISSMAN, Judith. "Antique Secrets in Henry James," Sewanee Review, 93 (1985): 196-215.

1818. ZABLOTNY, Elaine. "Henry James and the Demonic Vampire and Madonna," Psychocultural Review: Interpretations in the Psychology of Art, Literature and Society, 3 (1980): 203-224.

Later American Gothic
(1820-1985)
Including Faulkner, Flannery O'Connor,
Stephen King and the Popular American Gothic

1819. ABARTIS, Caesarea. "Ugly-Pretty, Dull-Bright, Weak-Strong Girl in the Gothic Mansion," Journal of Popular Culture, 13 (1979): 257-263.

1820. ALLEN, Dennis W. "Horror and Perverse Delight: Faulkner's 'A Rose for Emily,'" Modern Fiction Studies, 30 (1984): 685-696.

1821. ANDREWS, William L. The Literary Career of Charles W. Chesnutt. Baton Rouge, LA : Louisiana State UP, 1980.

1822. BALDANZA, Frank. "Northern Gothic," Southern Review, 10 (1974): 566-582.

1823. BENDIXEN, Alfred, ed. Haunted Women: The Best Supernatural Tales by American Women Writers. New York : Frederick Ungar, 1985.

1824. BLAKE, Nancy. "Other Voices, Other Rooms: Southern Gothic or Medieval Quest?" Delta: Revue Centre d'Études et de Recherche sur les Ecrivains du Sud Etats-Unis, 11 (1980): 31-47.

1825. BLAU, H. "The American Dream in American Gothic: The Plays of Sam Shepard and Adrienne Kennedy," Modern Drama, 27 (1984): 520-539.

1826. BLEIKASTEN, André. "Terror and Nausea: Bodies in Sanctuary," Faulkner Journal, 1 (1985): 17-29.

1827. BLEILER, E.F. Introduction to *The King in Yellow and Other Horror Stories* by Robert W. Chambers. New York : Dover Publications, 1970, pp.vii-xiii.

1828. BLOOM, Kathleen Burke. "The Grotesque in the Fiction of Joyce Carol Oates," *Dissertation Abstracts International*, 40 (1979): 2059A (Loyola of Chicago).

1829. BOWEN, Robert O. "Hope vs. Despair in the New Gothic Novel," *Renascence*, 13 (1961): 147-152.

1830. BOWMAN, Barbara. "Victoria Holt's Gothic Romances: A Structuralist Inquiry," in *The Female Gothic*, ed. Juliann E. Fleenor. Montreal, Canada : Eden Press, 1983, pp.69-81.

1831. BRADY, Ruth A.H.H. "The Reality of Gothic Terror in Faulkner," *Dissertation Abstracts International*, 32 (1972): 5774A-5775A (University of Texas at Austin).

1832. BROWNING, Preston M. Jr. "Flannery O'Connor and the Demonic," *Modern Fiction Studies*, 19 (1973): 29-41.

1833. BRUMBAUGH, Thomas B. "The Facile Francis Marion Crawford," *Markham Review*, 4 (1974): 70-71.

1834. BURGESS, Anthony. "'Boo,'" *New York Times Book Review*, February 11, 1973, pp.2, 24, 26.

1835. CHELL, Cara. "Un-Tricking the Eye: Joyce Carol Oates and the Feminine Ghost Story," *Arizona Quarterly*, 41 (1985): 5-23.

1836. CHRISTOPHERSEN, Bill. "'Jean Ah-Pouquelin': Cable's Place in Southern Gothic," *South Dakota Review*, 20 (1982): 55-66.

1837. CHU, Li-Min. "The Ghostly Tales of Edith Wharton," *Bulletin of National Taiwan University*, 26 (1977): 417-448.

1838. CRAWFORD, Gary W. "Stephen King's American Gothic," in *Discovering Stephen King*, ed. Darrell Schweitzer. Mercer Island, WA : Starmont House, 1985, pp.41-45.

1839. CURRAN, Ronald. Introduction to *Witches, Wraiths, and Warlocks: Supernatural Tales of the American Renaissance*. Greenwich, CT : Fawcett-Crest, 1971.

1840. DENDINGER, Lloyd N. "The Ghoul-Haunted Woodland of Robert Frost," *South Atlantic Bulletin*, 38 (1973): 87-94.

1841. DERSNAH, James Louis. "The Gothic World of Tennessee Williams," *Dissertation Abstracts International*, 45 (1985): 3131A (University of Wisconsin).

1842. DICKINSON, Donald C. "Joyce Carol Oates: A Bibliographical Checklist," *American Book Collector*, 2, number 6 (1981): 26-39.

1843. DOUGLAS, Wallace W. "Drug Store Gothic: The Style of Robert Penn Warren," College English, 15 (1954): 265-272.

1844. DUFFY, Martha. "On the Road to Manderley," Time Magazine, April 12, 1971, pp.95-96.

1845. EGAN, James. "Antidetection: Gothic and Detective Conventions in the Fiction of Stephen King," Clues: A Journal of Detection, 5 (1984): 131-146.

1846. ________. "'A Single Powerful Spectacle': Stephen King's Gothic Melo-Melodrama," Extrapolation, 27 (1986): 62-75.

1847. EISINGER, Chester E. "The Gothic Spririt in the Forties," in Pastoral and Romance: Modern Essays in Criticism, ed. Eleanor Terry Lincoln. Englewood Cliffs, NJ : Prentice-Hall, 1969, pp.289-296.

1848. EWING, Emma Mai. "Gothic Mania: A Roundup Review," New York Times Book Review, May 11, 1975, pp.10, 12-13.

1849. FISHER, Benjamin Franklin IV. "George Washington Harris and Supernaturalism," Publications of the Mississippi Philological Association, 1 (1982): 18-23.

1850. FLEENOR, Juliann E. "The Gothic Prism: Charlotte Perkins Gilman's Gothic Stories and Her Autobiography," in The Female Gothic, ed. Juliann E. Fleenor. Montreal, Canada : Eden Press, 1983, pp.227-241.

1851. FRAZER, David. "Gothicism in Sanctuary: The Black Pall and the Crap Table," Modern Fiction Studies, 2 (1956): 114-124.

1852. GENG, Veronica. "A Gallery of Ghosts and Ghouls," New York Times Book Review, November 16, 1975, p.44.

1853. GIBBS, Kenneth. "Stephen King and the Tradition of American Gothic," Gothic, new series 1 (1986): 6-14.

1854. GREINER, Donald J. Comic Terror: The Novels of John Hawkes. Memphis, TN : Memphis State UP, 1973.

1855. GRELLA, George. "Thrillers, Chillers, and Killers," Rochester Review, 32 (1970): 11-15.

1856. GRIBBEN, Alan. "'When Other Amusements Fail': Mark Twain and the Occult," in The Haunted Dusk: American Supernatural Fiction, eds. Howard Kerr, John W. Crowley, Charles L. Crow. Athens, GA : Georgia UP, 1983, pp.171-189.

1857. HAWKES, John. "Flannery O'Connor's Devil," Sewanee Review, 70 (1962): 395-407.

1858. "Heathcliffs, Cliff-Hangers," Newsweek, April 4, 1966, pp.101-102.

1859. HEMENWAY, Robert. "Gothic Sociology: Charles Chesnutt and the Gothic Mode," Studies in the Literary Imagination, 7 (1974): 101-119.

1860. HERRON, Don. "Russell Kirk: Ghost Master of Macosta," in Discovering Modern Horror, ed. Darrell Schweitzer. Mercer Island, WA : Starmont House, 1985, pp.21-47.

1861. HILL, Cason Louis. "A Bibliographical Study of George Washington Cable and a Check List of Criticism, 1870-1970," Dissertation Abstracts International, 38 (1978): 4816A (University of Georgia).

1862. HODGE, Marion Cecil Jr. "What Moment is not Terrible? An Introduction to the Works of Joyce Carol Oates," Dissertation Abstracts International, 35 (1975): 5407A (University of Tennessee).

1863. HOLMAN, Harriet R. "F. Marion Crawford and the Evil Eye," American Notes & Queries, 9 (1971): 103-104.

1864. HUNTER, Doreen. "America's First Romantics: Richard Henry Dana, Sr. and Washington Allston," New England Quarterly, 45 (1972): 3-30.

1865. INDICK, Ben P. "King and the Literary Tradition of Horror and the Supernatural," in Fear Itself: The Horror Fiction of Stephen King, eds. Tim Underwood and Chuck Miller. San Francisco, CA : Underwood-Miller, 1982, pp.153-167.

1866. JEANNOTTE, M. Sharon. "The Horror Within: The Short Stories of Joyce Carol Oates," The Sphinx: A Magazine of Literature and Society, 2, number 4 (1977): 25-36.

1867. JENNINGS, Gary. "Heathcliff Doesn't Smoke L&M's," New York Times Book Review, July 27, 1969, pp.4-5, 24.

1868. JOHNSON, Thomas Slayton. "The Horror in the Mansion: Gothic Fiction in the Works of Truman Capote and Carson Mc Cullers," Dissertation Abstracts International, 34 (1973): 2630A (University of Texas at Austin).

1869. JONES, Robert. The Shudder Pulps. West Linn, OR : FAX Collector's Editions, 1975.

1870. KAHANE, Claire. "The Maternal Legacy: The Grotesque Tradition in Flannery O'Connor's Female Gothic," in The Female Gothic, ed. Juliann E. Fleenor. Montreal, Canada : Eden Press, 1983, pp.242-256.

1871. KENNARD, Jean E. Number and Nightmare: Forms of Fantasy in Contemporary Fiction. Hamden, CT : Shoestring/Archon Press, 1975.

1872. KERR, Elizabeth M. William Faulkner's Gothic Domain. Port Washington, NY : Kennikat Press, 1978.

1873. LEIBER, Fritz. "Marbles and Cadavers," Haunted: Studies in Gothic Fiction, 1 (1968): 66-71.

1874. LEVINE, Paul. "Flannery O'Connor: The Soul of the Grotesque," in Minor American Novelists, ed. Charles A. Hoyt. Carbondale, IL : Southern Illinois UP, 1971, pp.95-117.

1875. MAGISTRALE, Anthony. "Crumbling Castles of Sand: The Social Landscape of Stephen King's Gothic Vision," Journal of Popular Literature, Fall/Winter (1985): 45-59.

1876. MARTIN, Carter W. "The Gothic Impulse," in The True Country: Themes in the Fiction of Flannery O'Connor. Nashville, TN : Vanderbilt UP, 1968, pp.152-188.

1877. MC CANN, William. "The Fictional Writing of Russell Kirk," Society for the Study of Midwestern Literature Newsletter, 15 (1985): 1-5.

1878. MC CORMICK, Lucienne P. "A Bibliography of Works by and About Joyce Carol Oates," American Literature, 43 (1971): 124-132.

1879. MODLESKI, Tania. "Popular Feminine Narratives: A Study of Romances, Gothics, and Soap Operas," Dissertation Abstracts International, 41 (1980): 2104A (Stanford University).

1880. MORAN, John C. "Recent Interest in F. Marion Crawford: A Bibliographical Account," Romantist, 1 (1977): 53-56.

1881. MORAN, John C., Edward Wagenknecht, Russell Kirk, and Donald Sydney-Fryer. "Introductions," to An F. Marion Crawford Companion. Westport, CT : Greenwood Press, 1981.

1882. MORRIS, James Kelly. "Stephen Crane and the Gothic Tradition," Dissertation Abstracts International, 44 (1983): 1802A (University of Mississippi).

1883. MULLER, Gilbert H. Nightmares and Visions: Flannery O'Connor and the Catholic Grotesque. Athens, GA : Georgia UP, 1972.

1884. MUSSELL, Kay Johnson. "The World of Modern Gothic Fiction: American Women and Their Social Myths," Dissertation Abstracts International, 35 (1973): 411A (University of Iowa).

1885. _______. "The Beautiful and the Damned: The Sexual Women in Gothic Fiction," Journal of Popular Culture, 9 (1975): 84-89.

1886. _______. "'But Why Do They Read Those Things?': The Female Audience and the Gothic Novel," in The Female Gothic, ed. Juliann E. Fleenor. Montreal, Canada : Eden Press, 1983, pp.57-68.

1887. _______. Fantasy and Reconciliation: Contemporary Formulas of Women's Romance Fiction. Westport, CT : Greenwood Press, 1984.

1888. NICHOLS, Lewis. "The Gothic Story," New York Times Book Review, July 27, 1969, p.25.

1889. NISLY, Paul Wayne. "Flannery O'Connor and the Gothic Impulse," Dissertation Abstracts International, 36 (1974): 892A-893A (University of Kansas).

1890. _______. "Wart Hogs from Hell: The Demonic and the Holy in Flannery

O'Connor's Fiction," Ball State University Forum, 22 (1981): 45-50.

1891. OAKS, Susan. "The Haunting Will: The Ghost Stories of Mary Wilkins Freeman," Colby Library Quarterly, 21 (1985): 208-220.

1892. PACE, Eric. "Gothic Novels Prove Bonanza for Publishers," New York Times, June 18, 1973, pp.31-34.

1893. _______. "Pulp Feminists: Gothic Liberation," Human Behavior, 7 (February, 1978): 50.

1894. PALUMBO, Donald. "Coincidence in Crime and Punishment and Light in August: Evidence of Supernatural Agents at Work in the Novels of Dostoevsky and Faulkner," Lamar Journal of the Humanities, 7 (1981): 41-51.

1895. PARK, Martha M. "Archibald Malmaison: Julian Hawthorne's Contribution to Gothic Fiction," Extrapolation, 15 (1973): 103-116.

1896. PARKS, John G. "'The Possibility of Evil': A Key to Shirley Jackson's Fiction," Studies in Short Fiction, 15 (1978): 320-323.

1897. _______. "Chambers of Yearning: Shirley Jackson's Use of the Gothic," Twentieth-Century Literature, 30 (1984): 15-29.

1898. PAULSON, Suzanne Morrow. "Apocalypse of Self, Resurrection of the Double: Flannery O'Connor's The Violent Bear It Away," Literature and Psychology, 30 (1980): 100-111.

1899. PERRY, J. Douglas Jr. "Gothic as Vortex: The Form of Horror in Capote, Faulkner, and Styron," Modern Fiction Studies, 19 (1973): 153-167.

1900. PETERS, Elizabeth. "Modern Gothics . . . The Willing Suspension of Disbelief," Writer, 87 (February, 1974): 15-17.

1901. PHILLIPS, Robert S. "The Gothic Architecture of The Member of the Wedding," Renascence, 16 (1964): 59-72.

1902. PINSKER, Sanford. "Isaac Bashevis Singer and Joyce Carol Oates: Some Versions of Gothic," Southern Review, 9 (1973): 895-908.

1903. PITAVY, François L. "The Gothicism of Absalom, Absalom!: Rosa Coldfield Revisited," in "A Cosmos of My Own": Faulkner and Yoknapatawpha, 1980. Jackson, MI : Mississippi UP, 1981, pp.199-226.

1904. PUTZEL, Max. "What is Gothic About Absalom, Absalom!?" Southern Literary Journal, 4 (1971): 3-14.

1905. RADWAY, Jane. "The Utopian Impulse in Popular Literature: Gothic Romances and 'Feminist' Protest," American Quarterly, 33 (1981): 140-162.

1906. _______. "The Aesthetic in Mass Culture; Reading the 'Popular' Literary Text," in The Structure of the Literary Process: Studies Dedicated to the Memory of Felix Vodicka, eds. Ronald Vroon, F.W. Galan. Amsterdam, Netherlands : Benjamins, 1982.

1907. ROBERTS, Bette B. "Anne Rice's Interview with a Vampire," New Mexico Humanities Review, 2 (1979): 48-63.

1908. ROSOWSKI, Susan J. "Willa Cather's American Gothic: Sapphira and the Slave Girl," Great Plains Quarterly, 4 (1984): 220-230.

1909. RUDIN, Seymour. "The Urban Gothic: From Transylvania to the South Bronx," Extrapolation, 25 (1984): 115-126.

1910. RUSS, Joanna. "Somebody's Trying to Kill Me and I Think It's My Husband: The Modern Gothic," Journal of Popular Culture, 6 (1973): 666-691.

1911. RYAN, Steven Tom. "Chaotic Slumber: Picaresque and Gothic in Contemporary American Novels," Dissertation Abstracts International, 37 (1976): 2187A (University of Utah).

1912. SAYRE, Nora. "Yankee Gothic," New Statesman, January 20, 1967, pp.76-77.

1913. SCHLEIFER, Ronald. "Rural Gothic: The Stories of Flannery O'Connor," Modern Fiction Studies, 28 (1982): 475-485.

1914. SCHWEITZER, Darrell, ed. Discovering Stephen King. Mercer Island, WA : Starmont House, 1985.

1915. ______. Discovering Modern Horror Fiction. Mercer Island, WA : Starmont House, 1985.

1916. SHIMURA, Masao. "The Gothic Tradition and American Literature in the Forties," in American Literature in the 1940's. Tokyo, Japan : Tokyo Chapter, American Literary Society of Japan, 1976, pp.33-39.

1917. SIDNEY-FRYER, Donald. "Francis Marion Crawford: A Neglected But Not a Forgotten Master," Romantist, 3 (1979): 43-50.

1918. SNOW, Ollye T. "The Functional Gothic of Flannery O'Connor," Southwest Review, 50 (1965): 286-299.

1919. ST. ARMAND, Barton Levi. "'I Must Have Died at Ten Minutes Past One': Posthumous Reverie in Harriet Prescott Spofford's 'The Amber Gods,'" in The Haunted Dusk: American Supernatural Fiction, 1820-1920, eds. Howard Kerr, John W. Crowley, Charles L. Crow. Athens, GA : Georgia UP, 1983, pp.101-119.

1920. STONE, Laurie. "Secret Rooms, Secret Obsessions," New York Times Book Review, July 27, 1975, pp.7-8.

1921. SULLIVAN, Jack. "Two Ways to Write a Gothic: Little Angie and The Shining," New York Times Book Review, February 20, 1977, p.8.

1922. TORSNEY, Cheryl B. "The Vampire Motif in Absalom, Absalom!" Southern Review, 20 (1984): 562-569.

1923. WAGENKNECHT, Edward. "Whittier and the Supernatural--A Test Case," in Memorabilia of John Greenleaf Whittier, ed. John B. Pickard. Emerson Society Quarterly, 50 (1968): 8-11.

1924. WALL, Richard J. and Carl L. Craycraft. "A Checklist of Works About Truman Capote," Bulletin of the New York Public Library, 71 (1967): 165-172.

1925. WEINSTEIN, Lee. "Chambers and The King in Yellow," Romantist, 3 (1979): 51-57.

1926. WHAN, Edgar W. "Absalom, Absalom! As Gothic Myth," Perspective, 3 (1950): 192-201.

1927. WILSON, William. "Riding the Crest of the Horror Craze," New York Times Magazine, May 11, 1980, p.42.

1928. WITHERINGTON, Paul. "Albee's Gothic: The Resonance of Cliché," Comparative Drama, 4 (1970): 151-165.

George Lippard
(1822-1854)

1929. BUTTERFIELD, Roger. "George Lippard and His Secret Brotherhood," Pennsylvania Magazine of History and Biography, 79 (1955): 285-309.

1930. DE GRAZIA, Emilio. "Poe's Devoted Democrat, George Lippard," Poe Studies, 6, number 1 (1973): 6-8.

1931. EHRLICH, Heyward. "The 'Mysteries' of Philadelphia: Lippard's Quaker City and 'Urban' Gothic," ESQ: A Journal of the American Renaissance, 18 (1972): 50-65.

1932. FIEDLER, Leslie. Introduction to The Quaker City; or, The Monks of Monk Hall by George Lippard. New York : Odyssey Press, 1970.

1933. JACKSON, Joseph. "George Lippard: Misunderstood Man of Letters," Pennsylvania Magazine of History and Biography, 49 (1935): 376-391.

1934. ______. "A Bibliography of the Works of George Lippard," Pennsylvania Magazine of History and Biography, 54 (1940): 130-154.

1935. REYNOLDS, David S. George Lippard. Boston : Twayne; Twayne United States Authors Series Number 417, 1982.

1936. ______. George Lippard: Prophet of Protest. Cambridge, MA : Harvard UP, 1986.

1937. RIDGELY, J.V. "George Lippard's The Quaker City: The World of the American Porno-Gothic," Studies in the Literary Imagination, 7 (1974): 77-94.

1938. WYLD, Lionel D. "George Lippard: Gothicism and Social Consciousness in the Early American Novel," Four Quarters, 5, number 3 (1956): 6-12.

Howard Phillips Lovecraft
(1890-1937)

1939. BILLY, André. "Lovecraft: Edgar Poe du XXe Siècle," Figaro Littéraire, October 28, 1961, p.4.

1940. BUHLE, Paul. "Dystopia as Utopia: Howard Phillips Lovecraft and the Unknown Content of American Horror Literature," Minnesota Review, 6 (1976): 118-131.

1941. BURLESON, Donald R. "Humor Beneath Horror: Some Sources for 'The Dunwich Horror' and 'The Whisperer in Darkness,'" Lovecraft Studies, 1, number 2 (1980): 5-15.

1942. ———. "H.P. Lovecraft," in Supernatural Fiction Writers, ed. E.F. Bleiler. New York : Charles Scribner's Sons, 1985, II, 853-859.

1943. COCKROFT, T.G.L. "Some Notes on 'The Shadow Over Innsmouth,'" Lovecraft Studies, 1, number 3 (1980): 3-4.

1944. DE CAMP, L. Sprague. Lovecraft: A Biography. Garden City, NY : Doubleday, 1975.

1945. EMMONS, Winfred S. Jr. "A Bibliography of H.P. Lovecraft," Extrapolation, 3 (1961): 2-25.

1946. FISCHER, Jens Malte. "Produktiver Ekel. Zum Werk Howard Phillips Lovecrafts," in Phatastik in Literatur und Kunst. eds. Christian W. Thomsen, Jens Fischer Malte. Darmstadt, West Germany : Wissenschaftliche Luchgesellschaft, 1980, pp.314-332.

1947. FULWILER, William. "Reflections on 'The Outsider'," Lovecraft Studies, 1, number 2 (1980): 3-4.

1948. JOSHI, S.T., ed. H.P. Lovecraft: Four Decades of Criticism. Athens, OH : Ohio UP, 1980.

1949. ———. "Sources for the Chronology of Lovecraft's Fiction," Lovecraft Studies, 1, number 2 (1980): 21-29.

1950. ———. "Reality and Knowledge: Some Notes on the Aesthetic Thought of H.P. Lovecraft," Lovecraft Studies, 1, number 3 (1980): 17-27.

1951. ———. Lovecraft and Lovecraft Criticism: An Annotated Bibliography. Kent, OH : Kent State UP, 1981.

1952. ———. "Further Notes on Lovecraft and Music," Romantist, 4-5 (1980-1981): 47-49.

1953. MC INNIS, John Lawson III. "H.P. Lovecraft: The Maze and the Minotaur," Dissertation Abstracts International, 36 (1975): 2207A (Louisiana State University).

1954. MEIKLE, Jeffrey L. "'Other Frequencies': The Parallel Worlds of Thomas Pynchon and H.P. Lovecraft," Modern Fiction Studies, 27 (1981): 287-294.

1955. MENEGALDO, Gilles. "Le Statut du Narrateur dans le Récit Lovecraftien," in Poétique(s): Domaine Anglais, ed. Alain Bony. Lyon, France: PU de Lyon, 1983, pp.75-88.

1956. MOSIG, Dirk W. "Lovecraft: The Dissonance Factor in Imaginative Literature," Gothic: The Review of Supernatural Horror Fiction, 1 (1979): 20-26.

1957. ONDERDONK, Matthew H. "Charon in Reverse: or H.P. Lovecraft Versus the 'Realists' of Fantasy," Lovecraft Studies, 1, number 3 (1980): 5-10.

1958. OWINGS, Mark and Irving Binkin. A Catalogue of Lovecraftiana; The Grill/Binkin Collection. Baltimore, MD : Mirage Press, 1975.

1959. SELLEY, April. "Terror and Horror in 'The Case of Charles Dexter Ward,'" Nyctalops, 3, number 1 (1980): 8-14.

1960. SHEA, J. Vernon. "On the Literary Influences Which Shaped Lovecraft's Works," in H.P. Lovecraft: Four Decades of Criticism, ed. J.T. Joshi. Athens, OH : Ohio UP, 1980, pp.113-139.

1961. SHREFFLER, Philip A. "H.P. Lovecraft and an American Literary Tradition," in The H.P. Lovecraft Companion. Westport, CT : Greenwood Press, 1977, pp.1932; Rpt. in Literature of the Occult: A Collection of Critical Essays, ed. Peter Messent. Englewood Cliffs, NJ : Prentice-Hall, 1981, pp.156-170.

1962. SOLON, Ben. "Lovecraft on the Doorstep," Haunted: Studies in Gothic Fiction, 1 (1968): 87-88.

1963. ST. ARMAND, Barton Levi. "H.P. Lovecraft: New England Decadent," Caliban, 12 (1975): 127-155.

1964. _______. The Roots of Horror in the Fiction of H.P. Lovecraft. Elizabethtown, NY : Dragon Press, 1977.

1965. WHEELOCK, Alan S. "Dark Mountain: H.P. Lovecraft and the 'Vermont Horror,'" Vermont History, 45 (1977): 221-228.

1966. WILSON, Colin. "H.P. Lovecraft, 1890-1937," in Science Fiction Writers: Critical Studies of the Major Authors from the Early Nineteenth Century to the Present Day. New York : Charles Scribner's Sons, 1982, pp.131-137.

Herman Melville
(1819-1891)

1967. ARVIN, Newton. "Melville and the Gothic Novel," New England Quarterly,

22 (1949): 33-48; Rpt. in American Pantheon. New York : Delacorte Press, 1966.

1968. BOUDREAU, Gordon V. "Herman Melville: Master Mason of the Gothic," Dissertation Abstracts, 28 (1968): 5007A-5008A (University of Indiana).

1969. ______. "Of Pale Ushers and Gothic Piles: Melville's Architectural Symbology," ESQ: A Journal of the American Renaissance, 18 (1972): 67-82.

1970. COOK, Richard M. "The Grotesque in the Fiction of Herman Melville," Dissertation Abstracts International, 33 (1973): 6304A (University of Michigan).

1971. ______. "Evolving the Inscrutable: The Grotesque in Melville's Fiction," American Literature, 49 (1978): 544-559.

1972. FURROW, Sharon. "The Terrible Made Visible: Melville, Salvator Rosa, and Piranesi," ESQ: A Journal of the American Renaissance, 19 (1973): 237-253.

1973. HUTCHINSON, William H. "Demonology in Melville's Vocabulary of Evil," Dissertation Abstracts, 27 (1967): 2132A-2133A (Northwestern University).

1974. KOSOK, Heinz. Die Bedeutung der Gothic Novel für das Erzählwerk Herman Melvilles. Hamburg, West Germany : Cram, de Gruyter, 1963.

1975. MAGISTRALE, Anthony. "'More Demon Than Man': Melville's Ahab as Gothic Villain," Extrapolation, 27 (1986): 203-207.

1976. MANDEL, Ruth B. "Herman Melville and the Gothic Outlook," Dissertation Abstracts, 30 (1970): 3015A-3016A (University of Connecticut).

1977. MC ALEER, John J. "Poe and the Gothic Elements in Moby Dick," Emerson Society Quarterly, 27 (1962): 34.

1978. ROSENTHAL, Bernard. "Melville, Marryat, and the Evil-Eyed Villain," Nineteenth-Century Fiction, 25 (1970): 221-224.

1979. SHETTY, Nalini V. "Melville's Use of the Gothic Tradition," in Studies in American Literature: Essays in Honour of William Mulder. Delhi, India : Oxford UP, 1976, pp.144-153.

1980. TRIMPI, Helen P. "Melville's Use of Demonology and Witchcraft in Moby Dick," Journal of the History of Ideas, 30 (1969): 543-562.

Isaac Mitchell
(1759-1812)

1981. DAVIDSON, Kathy N. "Isaac Mitchell's The Asylum; or, Gothic Castles in the New Republic," Prospects: An Annual Journal of American Cultural Studies, 7 (1982): 281-299.

1982. PEARSON, Edmund. "Isaac Mitchell's The Asylum; or, Alonzo and Melissa (1811)," in Queer Books. Garden City, NY : Doubleday, 1928.

Edgar Allan Poe
(1809-1849)

1983. ALLEN, Bruce. "Delight and Terror," Hudson Review, 26 (1973): 735-742.

1984. ALLEN, Michael. Poe and the British Magazine Tradition. New York : Oxford UP, 1969.

1985. BENNETT, Maurice J. "'The Madness of Art': Poe's 'Ligeia' as Metafiction," Poe Studies, 14, number 1 (1981): 1-6.

1986. BERRYMAN, Charles. "Hawkes and Poe," Modern Fiction Studies, 29 (1983): 643-654.

1987. BIANCHI, Ruggiero, ed. E.A. Poe dal Gotico all Fantascienza: Saggi di Letteratura Comparata. Milan, Italy : Mursia, 1978.

1988. BLOCH, Robert. "Poe and Lovecraft," in H.P. Lovecraft: Four Decades of Criticism, ed. J.T. Joshi. Athens, OH : Ohio UP, 198, pp.158-160.

1989. BLYTHE, Hal and Charlie Sweet. "Poe's Satiric Use of Vampirism in 'Berenice,'" Poe Studies, 14, number 2 (1981): 23-24.

1990. BODY, Lois Maurine. "The Influence of the Gothic Novel on the Works of Edgar Allan Poe," Unpublished Master's Thesis, University of Illinois, 1940.

1991. BUDICK, Emily. "Gothic Idealism in the Works of Edgar Allan Poe," Dissertation Abstracts International, 33 (1972): 1136A-1137A (Cornell University).

1992. BUDICK, E. Miller. "Poe's Gothic Idea: The Cosmic Geniture of Horror," Essays in Literature, 3 (1976): 73-85.

1993. BURT, Donald C. "Poe, Bradbury, and the Science Fiction Tale of Terror," Mankato State College Studies, 3 (1968): 76-84.

1994. BUTLER, David W. "Usher's Hypochondriasis: Mental Alienation and Romantic Idealism in Poe's Gothic Tales," American Literature, 48 (1976): 1-12.

1995. CAIRNS, William B. "Poe's Use of the Horrible," Dial, 50 (1911): 251-252.

1996. CARLSON, Eric W. "'William Wilson': The Double as Primal Self," Topic, 16, number 30 (1976): 35-40.

1997. CARTER, Boyd. "Poe's Debt to Charles Brockden Brown," Prairie Schooner, 27 (1953): 190-196.

1998. CLARK, David Lee. "Sources of Poe's 'The Pit and the Pendulum,'" Modern Language Notes, 44 (1929): 349-356.

1999. COALE, Samuel. "The Primitive Poe: The Radical Awareness of His Gothic Art," Epistęmonikę Epetērida Philosophikēs Scholēs Aristoteleiou Panepistēmiou Thessalonikēs, 17 (1978): 35-51.

2000. COBB, Palmer. The Influence of E.T.A. Hoffmann on the Tales of Edgar Allan Poe. Chapel Hill, NC : North Carolina UP, 1908.

2001. _______. "Poe and Hoffmann," South Atlantic Quarterly, 8 (1909): 68-81.

2002. COLLINS, John H. "Critique of William Mudford," American Notes & Queries, 3 (1943): 8.

2003. CRONIN, James E. "Poe's Vaults," Notes & Queries, 198 (1953): 395-396.

2004. DAMERON, J. Lasley. Edgar Allan Poe: A Checklist of Criticism: 1942-1960. Studies in Bibliography. Charlottesville, VA : Bibliographical Society of the University of Virginia, 1966.

2005. DAMERON, J. Lasley. and Irby B. Cauthen, Jr. Edgar Allan Poe: A Bibliography of Criticism, 1827-1967. Charlottesville, VA : Virginia UP, 1974.

2006. DAMERON, J. Lasley, Thomas C. Carlson, John E. Reilly, Benjamin Franklin Fisher IV. "Currrent Poe Bibliography," Poe Studies, 13 (1980): 29-34.

2007. "The Detached Terrorism of Poe," Times Literary Supplement, January 22, 1971, pp.95-96.

2008. ESTREN, Mark James. "Horrors Within and Without: A Psychoanalytic Study of Edgar Allan Poe and Howard Phillips Lovecraft," Dissertation Abstracts International, 39 (1978): 1565A (SUNY at Buffalo).

2009. FISHER, Benjamin Franklin IV. "Gothic Techniques in Poe's Short Stories," Dissertation Abstracts International, 31 (1969): 2342A (Duke (Duke University).

2010. _______. "Poe's 'Metzengerstein': Not a Hoax," American Literature, 42 (1971): 487-494.

2011. _______. "Blackwood Articles à la Poe: How To Make a False Start Pay," Revue des Langues Vivantes, 39 (1973): 418-443.

2012. _______. "Fugitive Poe References: A Bibliography," Poe Studies, 13 (1980): 34-36.

2013. _______. "Playful Germanism in 'The Fall of the House of Usher': The Storyteller's Art," in Ruined Eden of the Present: Hawthorne, Melville, Poe, eds. G.R. Thompson, Virgil L. Lokke, Chester E. Eisinger. West Lafayette, IN : Purdue UP, 1981, pp.355-374.

2014. FORCLAZ, Roger. "A Source for 'Berenice' and a Note on Poe's Reading," Poe Newsletter, 1 (1968): 25-27.

2015. FRANK, Frederick S. "The Aqua-Gothic Voyage of 'A Descent into the Maelström," American Transcendental Quarterly, 29 (1976): 85-93.

2016. _______. "Poe's House of the Seven Gothics: The Fall of the Narrator in 'The Fall of the House of Usher,'" Orbis Litterarum, 34 (1979): 331-351.

2017. _______. "The Gothic at Absolute Zero: Poe's Narrative of Arthur Gordon Pym," Extrapolation, 21 (1980): 21-30.

2018. _______. "Neighborhood Gothic: Poe's 'Tell-Tale Heart,'" The Sphinx: A Magazine of Literature and Society, 3, number 4 (1981): 53-60.

2019. _______. "Polarized Gothic: An Annotated Bibliography of Poe's Narrative of Arthur Gordon Pym," Bulletin of Bibliography, 38 (1981): 117-127.

2020. _______. "Introduction to the Special Poe Issue," The Sphinx: A Magazine of Literature and Society, 4, number 4 (1985): 223-225.

2021. _______. "Poe's Gothicism: An Analytic Bibliography," The Sphinx: A Magazine of Literature and Society, 4, number 4 (1985): 277-301.

2022. GALLOWAY, David. "Introduction," to Edgar Allan Poe: Selected Writings. Baltimore, MD : Penguin Books, 1967, pp.9-47.

2023. GARGANO, James W. "The Question of Poe's Narrators," College English, 25 (1963): 177-181.

2024. GARRISON, Joseph M. Jr. "The Function of Terror in the Work of Edgar Allan Poe," American Quarterly, 18 (1966): 136-150.

2025. GRANGER, Byrd Howell. "Devil Lore in 'The Raven,'" Poe Studies, 5 (1972): 53-54.

2026. GRIFFITH, Clark. "Poe's 'Ligeia' and the English Romantics," University of Toronto Quarterly, 24 (1954): 8-25.

2027. _______. "Poe and the Gothic," in Papers on Poe: Essays in Honor of John Ward Ostrom. Springfield, OH : Chantry Music Press at Wittenberg University, 1972, pp.21-27.

2028. GRUENER, Gustav. "Notes on the Influence of E.T.A. Hoffmann upon Edgar Allan Poe," Publications of the Modern Language Association, 19 (1904): 1-25.

2029. GUILDS, John C. "Poe's Vaults Again," Notes & Queries, 202 (1957): 220-221.

2030. HALLIBURTON, David G. "The Grotesque in American Literature: Poe, Hawthorne, and Melville," Dissertation Abstracts, 27 (1967): 3840A-38-41A (University of California at Riverside).

2031. HELLER, Terry. "Poe's 'Ligeia' and the Pleasures of Terror," Gothic: The Review of Supernatural Horror Fiction, 2 (1980): 39-48.

2032. HIROTA, Minoru. "The Elements of American Romance in Wuthering Heights; Concurrent Origin and Themes Found in Wuthering Heights and 'The Fall of the House of Usher,'" Studies in English Language and Literature, 30 (1980): 57-75.

2033. HIRSCH, David H. "The Pit and the Apocalypse," Sewanee Review, 76 (1968): 632-652.

2034. _______. "Another Source for 'The Pit and the Pendulum,'" Mississippi Quarterly, 23 (1970): 35-43.

2035. HOFFMAN, Daniel. "Poe's Obsessive Themes," in The Origins and Originality of American Culture, ed. Tibor Frank. Budapest, Hungary : Akadémiai Kiadó, 1984, pp.105-111.

2036. HOFFMAN, Michael J. "The House of Usher and Negative Romanticism," Studies in Romanticism, 4 (1965): 158-168.

2037. HYNEMAN, Esther F. Edgar Allan Poe: An Annotated Bibliography of Books and Articles in English 1827-1973. Boston : G.K. Hall, 1974.

2038. KELLY, Thomas B. "Poe's Gothic Masques," Dissertation Abstracts International, 32 (1972): 5187A-5188A (University of Connecticut).

2039. KEMPER, Steven E. "Poe, Twain, and Limburger Cheese," Mark Twain Journal, 21 (1981-1982): 13-14.

2040. KENDALL, Lyle H. Jr. "The Vampire Motif in 'The Fall of the House of Usher,'" College English, 24 (1963): 450-453.

2041. KENNEDY, J. Gerald. "Phantasms of Death in Poe's Fiction," in The Haunted Dusk: American Supernatural Fiction, 1820-1920, eds. Howard Kerr, John W. Crowley, Charles L. Crow. Athens, GA : Georgia UP, 1983, pp.39-65.

2042. KERLIN, R.T. "Wieland and 'The Raven,'" Modern Language Notes, 31 (1916): 503-505.

2043. LAWES, Rochie. "The Dimensions of Terror: Mathematical Imagery in 'The Pit and the Pendulum,'" Poe Studies, 16 (1983): 5-7.

2044. LAWSON, Lewis A. "Poe's Conception of the Grotesque," Mississippi Quarterly, 19 (1966): 200-205.

2045. LÉVY, Maurice. "Edgar Poe et la Tradition 'Gothique,'" Caliban, 5, number 1 (1968): 35-51.

2046. _______. "Poe and the Gothic Tradition," ESQ: A Journal of the American Renaissance, 18 (1972): 19-28.

2047. LEWIS, Paul. "Laughing at Fear: Two Versions of the Mock Gothic," Studies in Short Fiction, 15 (1978): 411-414.

2048. ______. "The Intellectual Functions of Gothic Fiction: Poe's 'Ligeia' and Tieck's 'Wake Not the Dead,'" Comparative Literature Studies, 16 (1979): 207-221.

2049. LIND, Sidney E. "Poe and Mesmerism," Publications of the Modern Language Association, 62 (1947): 1077-1094.

2050. LJUNGQUIST, Kent P. "Uses of the Daemon in Selected Works of Edgar Allan Poe," Interpretations, 12 (1980): 31-39.

2051. MABBOTT, Thomas O. "Poe's Vaults," Notes & Queries, 198 (1953): 542-543.

2052. MAINVILLE, Stephen. "Language and the Void: Gothic Landscapes in the Frontiers of Edgar Allan Poe," Genre, 14 (1981): 347-362.

2053. MAROVITZ, Sanford E. "Poe's Reception of C.W. Webber's Gothic Western, 'Jack Long; or, The Shot in the Eye,'" Poe Studies, 4 (1971): 11-13.

2054. MARRS, Robert L. "'The Fall of the House of Usher': A Checklist of Criticism Since 1960," Poe Studies, 5 (1972): 23-24.

2055. MATTHIESSEN, F.O. "Poe," Sewanee Review, 54 (1946): 175-205.

2056. MERIVALE, Patricia. "The Raven and the Bust of Pallas: Classical Artifacts and the Gothic Tale," Publications of the Modern Language Association, 89 (1974): 960-966.

2057. MOONEY, Stephen L. "Poe's Gothic Waste Land," Sewanee Review, 70 (1972): 261-283.

2058. MORRISON, Claudia C. "Poe's 'Ligeia': An Analysis," Studies in Short Fiction, 4 (1967): 234-244.

2059. MOSIG, Dirk W. "Poe, Hawthorne, and Lovecraft: Variations on a Theme of Panic," Romantist, 4-5 (1980-81): 43-45.

2060. NEWLIN, Paul A. "The Uncanny in the Supernatural Short Fiction of Poe, Hawthorne, and James," Dissertation Abstracts, 28 (1968): 5064A-5065A (University of California at Los Angeles).

2061. PITCHER, Edward W.R. "Beyond 'Gothic Flummery': A Cosmoramic View of Poe's Symbolism and Ideas," The Sphinx: A Magazine of Literature and Society, 4, number 4 (1985): 241-249.

2062. POLLIN, Burton R. "Poe and Godwin," Nineteenth-Century Fiction, 20 (1965): 237-253.

2063. ______. "Bulwer-Lytton and 'The Tell-Tale Heart,'" American Notes & Queries, 4 (1965): 7-9.

2064. ________. "More on Lippard and Poe," Poe Studies, 7, number 1 (1974): 22-23.

2065. RICHMOND, Lee J. "Edgar Allan Poe's 'Morella': Vampire of Volition," Studies in Short Fiction, 9 (1972): 93-94.

2066. RIDDEL, Joseph N. "The 'Crypt' of Edgar Poe," Boundary, 7, number 2 (1979): 117-144.

2067. RIGGIO, Thomas P. "American Gothic: Poe and An American Tragedy," American Literature, 49 (1978): 515-532.

2068. RINGE, Donald A. "Poe's Debt to Scott in 'The Pit and the Pendulum,'" English Language Notes, 18 (1981): 281-283.

2069. SALZBURG, Joel. "The Gothic Hero in Transcendental Quest: Poe's 'Ligeia' and James' 'The Beast in the Jungle,'" ESQ: A Journal of the American Renaissance, 18 (1972): 108-114.

2070. SENELICK, Laurence. "Charles Dickens and 'The Tell-Tale Heart,'" Poe Studies, 6 (1973): 12-14.

2071. SHELDEN, Pamela J. "Poe's Urban Nightmare: 'The Man of the Crowd' and the Gothic Tale," Studies in the Humanities (Indiana, PA), 4, number 2 (1975): 31-35.

2072. ________. "'True Originality': Poe's Manipulation of the Gothic Tradition," American Transcendental Quarterly, 29 (1976): 75-80.

2073. SIEGEL, Gerald. "The Poe-esque Tale in American Magazines, 1830-1860," Dissertation Abstracts International, 32 (1972): 6943A-6944A (George Washington University).

2074. SLOANE, David E.E. "Gothic Romanticism and Rational Empiricism in Poe's 'Berenice,'" American Transcendental Quarterly, number 19, parts 1-2 (1973): 19-26.

2075. SLOANE, David E.E. and Benjamin Franklin Fisher IV. "Poe's Revisions in 'Berenice': Beyond the Gothic," American Transcendental Quarterly, 24, supplement 2 (1974): 19-23.

2076. SMITH, Allan Gardner. "Edgar Allan Poe, the Will, and Horror Fiction," in American Fictions: New Readings, ed. Richard Gray. Totowa, NJ : Barnes & Noble, 1983, pp.53-63.

2077. ST. ARMAND, Barton Levi. "The 'Mysteries' of Edgar Poe: The Quest for a Monomyth in Gothic Literature," in The Gothic Imagination: Essays in Dark Romanticism, ed. G.R. Thompson. Pullman, WA : Washington State UP, 1974, pp.65-93.

2078. STEIN, William Bysshe. "The Twin Motif in 'The Fall of the House of Usher,'" Modern Language Notes, 75 (1960): 109-111.

2079. STEPP, Walter. "The Ironic Double in Poe's 'The Cask of Amontillado,'" Studies in Short Fiction, 13 (1976): 447-453.

2080. STOEHR, Taylor. "Unspeakable Horror in Poe," South Atlantic Quarterly, 78 (1979): 317-332.

2081. STONE, Edward. "Usher, Poquelin, and Miss Emily: The Progress of Southern Gothic," Georgia Review, 14 (1960): 433-443.

2082. SULLIVAN, Ruth. "William Wilson's Double," Studies in Romanticism, 15 (1976): 253-263.

2083. THOMPSON, G.R. "Poe's 'Flawed' Gothic: Absurdist Techniques in 'Metzengerstein' and the Courier Satires," Emerson Society Quarterly, 60 (1970): 38-58.

2084. _______. "'Proper Evidences of Madness': American Gothic and the Interpretation of 'Ligeia,'" ESQ: A Journal of the American Renaissance, 18 (1972): 30-49.

2085. _______. "The Face in the Pool: Reflections on the Doppelgänger Motif in 'The Fall of the House of Usher,'" Poe Studies, 5, number 1 (1972): 16-21.

2086. _______. Poe's Fiction: Romantic Irony in the Gothic Tales. Madison, WI : Wisconsin UP, 1973.

2087. _______. "Poe and the Paradox of Terror: Structures of Heightened Consciousness in 'The Fall of the House of Usher,'" in Ruined Eden of the Present: Hawthorne, Melville, and Poe, ed. G.R. Thompson and Virgil L. Lokke. West Lafayette, IN : Purdue UP, 1981, pp.313-340.

2088. TUCKER, B.D. "'The Tell-Tale Heart' and the 'Evil Eye,'" Southern Literary Journal, 13, number 2 (1981): 92-98.

2089. VAUGHAN, Larry. "Poe and the Mystery of Things: A Remembrance," Sub-Stance, 13 (1984): 95-98.

2090. _______. "Explanation in 'The Fall of the House of Usher,'" Studies in Short Fiction, 23 (1986): 419-428.

2091. VON DER LIPPE, George B. "The Figure of E.T.A. Hoffmann as Doppelgänger to Poe's Roderick Usher," Modern Language Notes, 92 (1977): 525-534.

2092. _______. "The Fictionalization of Hoffmann: Three Articles Considering the Literary Relationship of Edgar Allan Poe to the Figure of E. T.A. Hoffmann," Dissertation Abstracts International, 30 (1979): 61-54A (Brown University).

2093. _______. "Beyond the House of Usher: The Figure of E.T.A. Hoffmann in the Works of Poe," Modern Language Studies, 9, number 1 (1978-1979): 33-41.

2094. _______. "La Vie de l'Artiste Fantastique: The Metamorphosis of the Hoffmann-Poe Figure in France," Canadian Review of Comparative Literature, 6 (1979): 46-63.

2095. WALKER, I.M. "The 'Legitimate Sources' of Terror in 'The Fall of the House of Usher,'" Modern Language Review, 61 (1966): 585-592.

2096. WHITT, Celia. "Poe and The Mysteries of Udolpho," University of Texas Studies in English, 17 (1937): 124-131.

2097. ZEYDEL, Edwin H. "Edgar Allan Poe's Contacts with German as Seen in His Relations with Ludwig Tieck," in Studies in German Literature of the Nineteenth and Twentieth Centuries: Festschrift for Frederic E. Coenen, ed. Siegfried Mews. Chapel Hill, NC : North Carolina UP, 19-71, pp.47-54.

VII. THE FRENCH GOTHIC NOVEL OR ROMAN NOIR

2098. ANGENOT, Marc. "La Littérature Populaire Française au Dix-Neuvième Siècle," Canadian Review of Comparative Literature, 9 (1982): 307-333.

2099. BERMAN, Lorna. "The Marquis De Sade and His Critics," Mosaic, 1, number 2 (1968): 57-73.

2100. ______. The Thought and Themes of the Marquis De Sade. Kitchener, Ontario : Ainsworth, 1972.

2101. BROMBERT, Victor. "Pétrus Borel, Prison Horrors, and the Gothic Tradition," Novel, 2 (1969): 143-152.

2102. BRUNEAU, Jean. "Madame de Genlis, William Beckford et Vathek," Nineteenth-Century French Studies, 5 (1977): 34-38.

2103. CERRUTI, Giorgio. "Il Marchese di Sade: La Sua Recente Fortuna et gli Ultimi Studi Critici (1958-1968)," Studi Francesi, 13 (1969): 420-441.

2104. CHANOVER, E. Pierre. The Marquis De Sade: A Bibliography. Metuchen, NJ : Scarecrow Press, 1973.

2105. CHIÉNIEUX-GENDRON, Jacqueline. "Lectures Surréalistes du Roman Noir," Europe, 659 (1984): 133-146.

2106. DAWSON, Robert L. "Baculard d'Arnaud (1718-1805): Life and Prose Fiction," Dissertation Abstracts International, 33 (1972): 2367A (Yale University).

2107. DEENEN, Maria. Le Merveilleux dans l'Oeuvre de Villiers de L'Isle-Adam, Paris : Librairie Georges Courville, 1939.

2108. FINK, Beatrice C. "Sade and Cannibalism," L'Esprit Créateur, 15 (19-75): 403-412.

2109. FOSTER, James R. "The Abbé Prévost and the English Novel," Publications of the Modern Language Association, 42 (1927): 443-464.

2110. FOWLER, Albert. "Sensibility Since Sade," Southwest Review, 45 (1960): 240-250.

2111. GILBERT, Claire P. "The Theme of the Double in the Work of Gérard de Nerval," Dissertation Abstracts International, 32 (1972): 6974A-69-75A (Johns Hopkins University).

2112. GILLET, Jean. "Ducray-Duminil, Le Gothique et la Révolution," Europe, 659 (1984): 63-72.

2113. GOARD, Robert R. "Baculard d'Arnaud (1718-1805): A Novelist of the Middle Way," Dissertation Abstracts International, 31 (1971): 5362A (University of Wisconsin).

2114. GORER, Geoffrey. "The Marquis De Sade," Encounter, 18, number 4 (19-62): 72-78.

2115. GOULEMOT, Jean Marie. "Un Roman de Révolution: Le Voyageur Sentimental en France sous Robespierre de François Vernes," Europe, 659 (1984): 80-88.

2116. GRIEDER, Josephine. "The Prose Fiction of Baculard d'Arnaud in Late Eighteenth-Century England," French Studies, 24 (1970): 113-124.

2117. HAYMAN, Ronald. De Sade: A Critical Biography. New York : Thomas Y. Crowell, 1978.

2118. HEINE, Maurice. Le Marquis De Sade et le Roman Noir. Paris : Nouvelle Revue Française, 1933.

2119. ______. "Promenade à Travers le Roman Noir," Minotaure, 5 (May, 19-34): 1-4.

2120. HUMPHREY, George. "Victor, ou l'Enfant de la Forêt et la Roman Terrifiant," French Review, 33 (1959): 137-145.

2121. IVKER, Barry. "On the Darker Side of the Enlightenment: A Comparison of the Literary Techniques of Sade and Restif de la Bretonne," Studies on Voltaire and the Eighteenth Century, 79 (1971): 199-218.

2122. JOSEPHS, Herbert. "Diderot's La Réligieuse: Libertinism and the Dark Cave of the Soul," Modern Language Notes, 91 (1976): 734-755.

2123. LABORDE, Alice M. L'Oeuvre de Madame de Genlis. Paris : Nizet, 1966.

2124. LACOMBE, Anne. "Les Infortunes de la Vertu, le Conte et la Philosophie," L'Esprit Créateur, 15 (1975): 425-437.

2125. LADEN, Richard A. "Terror, Nature, and the Sacrifice in the Comtesse De Ségur's Les Petites Filles Modèles," Modern Language Notes, 94 (1979): 742-756.

2126. LEVAYER, Paul-Edouard. "Le 'Noir' au Théâtre: Les Victimes du Clôitrées au Mélodrame," Europe, 659 (1984): 88-96.

2127. LEVY, Maurice. "Une Nouvelle Source d'Anne Radcliffe: Les Memoires du Comte de Comminge," Caliban, 1 (1964): 149-156.

2128. ______. "Le Roman Noir et la Société Anglaise à la Fin du Dix-Huitième Siècle," Etudes Anglaises, 23 (1964): 98-108.

2129. ______. Images du Roman Noir. Paris : Eric Losfeld, 1973.

2130. LUND, Mary Graham. "The Century of De Sade," Modern Age, 8 (1963-1964): 38-44.

2131. MARIE-ISOLINE, Françoise Marsaud. "The Notion of the Monster in the Works of De Sade and Flaubert," Dissertation Abstracts International, 37 (1977): 4401A (University of California at San Diego).

2132. MARTIN, Angus. "Baculard d'Arnaud et la Vogue des Séries de Nouvelles en France au XVIIIe Siècle," Revue d'Histoire Littéraire de la France, 73 (1973): 982-992.

2133. NASH, Suzanne. "Transfiguring Disfiguration in L'Homme Quit Rit: A Study of Hugo's Use of the Grotesque," in Pre-Text/Text/Context: Essays on Nineteenth-Century French Literature, ed. Robert L. Mitchell. Columbus, OH : Ohio State UP, 1980, pp.3-13.

2134. OLIVIER, Jean-Michel. Lautréamont: Le Texte du Vampire. Paris : L'Age d'Homme, 1982.

2135. O'REILLY, Robert F. "Cazotte's Le Diable Amoureux and the Structure of Romance," Symposium, 31 (1977): 231-242.

2136. PORTER, Laurence M. "The Seductive Satan of Cazotte's Le Diable Amoureux," L'Esprit Créateur, 18, number 2 (1978): 3-12.

2137. PRAZ, Mario. "An English Imitation of Diderot's La Réligieuse," Review of English Studies, 6 (1930): 1-8.

2138. PRICE, Lawrence M. "The Relation of Baculard d'Arnaud to German Literature," Monatsheft für Deutsche Unterricht, 37 (1945): 151-160.

2139. REBOUL, Pierre. "Villiers de l'Isle-Adam et le Melmoth de Maturin," Revue de Littérature Comparée, 25 (1951): 479-481.

2140. ROSENTHAL, A.S. "Mérimée and the Supernatural: Diversion or Obsession?" Nineteenth-Century French Studies, 1 (1973): 138-154.

2141. ROUDAUT, Jean. "Les Demeures dans le Roman Noir," Critique, 15 (1959): 147-148.

2142. RUDWIN, Maximillian. "Balzac and the Fantastic," Sewanee Review, 38 (1925): 1-24.

2143. SIVERT, Eileen B. "The Theme of Fear in Prosper Mérimée's Narrative Fiction," Dissertation Abstracts International, 33 (1973): 5200A

(University of California at Riverside).

2144. ______. "Fear and Confrontation in Prosper Mérimée's Narrative Fic-Fiction," Nineteenth-Century French Studies, 6 (1978): 213-230.

2145. STEINMETZ, Jean-Luc. "La Vérité sur Madame Putiphar," Europe, 659 (19-84): 112-123.

2146. THIERFELDER, William R. III. "Zola's Thérèse Raquin," Explicator, 41, number 3 (1983): 33-34.

2147. TURNELL, Martin. "The Novels of Prévost," Sewanee Review, 61 (1953): 582-601

2148. VAIL, Marilyn Irene. "Transformation of Narrative Structure in Relation to the Role of the Female Protagonist in the Eighteenth-Century Novel," Dissertation Abstracts International, 39 (1978): 313A (Cornell University).

2149. VIROLLE, Roland. "Madame de Genlis, Mercier de Compiègne: Gothique Anglais ou Gothique Allemand?" Europe, 659 (1984): 29-38.

2150. WAHBA, Magdi. "Madame de Genlis in England," Comparative Literature, 13 (1961): 221-238.

2151. WARD, Patricia A. "The Political Evolution of Victor Hugo's Gothic Vision," Modern Language Quarterly, 34 (1973): 272-282.

2152. WERNER, Stephen. "Diderot, Sade, and the Gothic Novel," Studies on Voltaire and the Eighteenth Century, 114 (1973): 273-290.

2153. WINANDY, Rita N. "Sensibility in the Novels of Abbé Prévost," Dissertation Abstracts International, 30 (1970): 3961A (University of Pittsburgh).

VIII. THE GERMAN GOTHIC NOVEL OR SCHAUERROMAN

2154. BARINE, Arvède. Poètes et Névrosés: Hoffmann, De Quincey, Edgar Poe, G. de Nerval. Paris : Hachette, 1908.

2155. BEAUJEAN, Marion. "Frauen,--Familien,--Abenteuer und Schauerromane," in Zwischen Revolution und Restauration: Klassik, Romantik, 1786-1815, ed. H.A. Glaser. Reinbek, West Germany : Rowohlt, 1980, pp. 216-228.

2156. BLEILER, E.F. Introduction to The Best Tales of Hoffmann by E.T.A. Hoffmann. New York : Dover Publications, 1967, pp.v-xxxiii.

2157. BREITLINGER, Eckard. Der Tod in Englischen Roman um 1800: Untersuchungen zum Englischen und Deutschen Schauerroman. Göppingen, West Germany : Kümmerle, 1971.

2158. CRAMER, Karin. "Bewusstseinsspaltung in E.T.A. Hoffmanns Die Elixiere des Teufels," Mitteilungen der E.T.A. Hoffmann-Gesellschaft, 16 (1970): 8-18.

2159. DAEMMRICH, Horst. "The Devil's Elixirs: Precursor of the Modern Psychological Novel," Papers on Language and Literature, 6 (1970): 374-376.

2160. DOSE, Claus D. "The Reception of E.T.A. Hoffmann in the United States, 1940-1976," Dissertation Abstracts International, 41 (1980): 1050A (New York University).

2161. DUFNER, Max. "Volksmärchen der Deutschen of Johann Karl August Musäus," Arizona Quarterly, 31 (1975): 149-164.

2162. EWTON, Ralph W. Jr. "Childhood Without End: Tieck's Der Blonde Eckbert," German Quarterly, 46 (1973): 410-427.

2163. FRIES, Thomas. "Ein Romantisches Märchen: Der Blonde Eckbert von Ludwig Tieck," Modern Language Notes, 88 (1973): 1180-1211.

2164. GUTHKE, Karl S. "Johann Karl August Musäus und das Übernatürliche im

Sensationsroman," Archiv für das Studium der Neueren Sprachen und Literaturen, 195 (1958): 129-138.

2165. HADLEY, Michael. "A Critical Puzzle: A Search for the German Gothic Novel," Transactions of the Samuel Johnson Society of the Northwest, 7 (1974): 58-72.

2166. ______. The Undiscovered Genre: A Search for the German Gothic Novel. Berne, Switzerland, Frankfurt am Main, West Germany, Las Vegas, NE : Peter Lang, 1978.

2167. HANSON, James C. "Style and Structure in Schiller's Der Geisterseher," Dissertation Abstracts, 28 (1968): 3183A (University of Michigan).

2168. HEIDERICH, Manfred W. The German Novel of 1800: A Study of Popular Prose Fiction. Berne, Switzerland : Lang, 1982.

2169. HYDE, Virginia M. "From the 'Last Judgment' to Kafka's World: A Study in Gothic Iconography," in The Gothic Imagination: Essays in Dark Romanticism, ed. G.R. Thompson. Pullman, WA : Washington State UP, 1974, pp.128-149.

2170. KENT, Leonard J. and Elizabeth C. Knight. Introduction to The Tales of Hoffmann. Chicago : Chicago UP, 1959.

2171. LANGE, James A. "The Levels of Suspense in E.T.A. Hoffmann's Die Elixiere des Teufels," Dissertation Abstracts, 28 (1967): 683A (University of Wisconsin).

2172. LAZARE, Christopher. Introduction to The Tales of Hoffmann. New York : Grove Press, 1946, pp.9-36.

2173. LIEDKE, Otto K. "Tiecks Der Blonde Eckbert: Das Märchen von Verarmung und Untergang," German Quarterly, 44 (1971): 311-316.

2174. LOKKE, Kari E. "Magic of Imagination: The Romantic Supernatural--A Study of Tieck, Coleridge, Arnim, and Nerval," Dissertation Abstracts International, 40 (1980): 4021A (Washington University).

2175. MARGRAF, Ernst. Der Einfluss der Deutschen Litteratur auf den Englischen Schauerroman. Leipzig, Germany : Schmidt, 1901.

2176. MC GLATHERY, James M. "Demon Love: E.T.A. Hoffmann's Elixiere des Teufels," Colloquia Germanica, Internationale Zeitschrift für Germanische Sprach-und-Litteraturwissenschaft, 12 (1979): 61-76.

2177. MENHENNEY, A. "Schiller and the 'Germanico-Terrific' Romance," Publications of the English Goethe Society, 51 (1981): 27-47.

2178. MITCHELL, Brean. "Ghosts from the Dungeon of the World Within: Franz Kafka's 'Ein Brudermord,'" Monatshefte, 73 (1981): 51-61.

2179. MUELLER, Ilze Klavins. "Spatial Imagery in E.T.A. Hoffmann's Die Elixiere des Teufels," Dissertation Abstracts International, 40 (1980): 5068A (University of Minnesota).

2180. MURPHY, Agnes Genevieve. *Banditry, Chivalry, and Terror in German Fiction 1790-1830*. Chicago : Photolithograph by University of Chicago Chicago Libraries, 1935.

2181. NEGUS, Kenneth. "The Allusions to Schiller's *Der Geisterseher* in E.T. A. Hoffmann's *Das Majorat*: Meaning and Background," *German Quarterly*, 32 (1959): 341-355.

2182. ______. "The Family Tree in E.T.A. Hoffmann's *Die Elixiere des Teufels*," *Publications of the Modern Language Association*, 73 (1978): 516-520.

2183. NEHRING, Wolfgang. "E.T.A. Hoffmann: *Die Elixiere des Teufels*," in *Romane und Erzählungen des Deutschen Romantik; Neue Interpretationen*, ed. Paul Michael Lützeler. Stuttgart, West Germany : Reclam, 1981, pp.325-350.

2184. OLSON, Susanne. "E.T.A. Hoffmann's *Elixiere des Teufels* als Schauerroman," *Dissertation Abstracts International*, 34 (1973): 3423A (University of California at Los Angeles).

2185. ______. "Das Wunderbare und Seine Psychologische Funktion in E.T.A. Hoffmanns *Die Elixiere des Teufels*," *Mitteilungen der E.T.A. Hoffmann-Gesellschaft*, 24 (1978): 26-35.

2186. OTTO, Linda M. "A Study of Evil and Insanity in Tieck's Early Works," *Dissertation Abstracts International*, 34 (1974): 4277A (Northwestern University).

2187. PASSAGE, Charles E. "E.T.A. Hoffmann's *The Devil's Elixirs*: A Flawed Masterpiece," *Journal of English and Germanic Philology*, 75 (1976): 531-545.

2188. REBER, Natalie. *Studien zum Motiv des Doppelgängers bei Dostojevskij und E.T.A. Hoffmann*. Marburg, West Germany : Wilhelm Schmitz, 1964.

2189. SUCHER, Paul. *Les Sources du Merveilleux chez E.T.A. Hoffmann*. Paris : Alcan, 1912.

2190. THIERGARD, Ulrich. "Schiller und Walpole: Ein Beitrag zu Schillers Verhältnis zur Schauerliteratur," *Jahrbuch der Schiller-Gesellschaft*, 3 (1959): 102-117.

2191. TRAINER, James. "The Incest-Theme in the Works of Tieck," *Modern Language Notes*, 86 (1961): 819-824.

2192. ______. *Ludwig Tieck: From Gothic to Romantic*. The Hague, Netherlands : Mouton; Anglica Germanica VIII, 1964.

2193. TYMMS, Ralph. "Hoffmann: The Climax of 'Horror-Romanticism,'" in *German Literature*. London : Methuen, 1955, pp.347-366.

2194. ______. "Ludwig Tieck," in *German Romantic Literature*. London : Methuen, 1955, pp.52-120.

2195. VON GLEICHEN-RUSSWURM, A. "Der Schwarze Roman," Die Litteratur, 27 (1924): 441-442.

2196. WILLSON, A. Leslie. "Hoffmann's Horrors," in Literature and the Occult: Essays in Comparative Literature, ed. Frank Luanne. Arlington, TX : Texas at Arlington UP, 1977, pp.264-271.

IX. OTHER NATIONAL GOTHICS AND COMPARATIVE GOTHICISM

2197. BLACK, Casey Bjerregaard. "The Fantastic in Karen Blixen's Osceola Production," Scandanavian Studies, 57 (1985): 379-389.

2198. COLAHAN, Clark and Alfred Rodríguez. "Lo 'Gótico' como Fórmula Creativa de Los Pazos de Ulloa," Modern Philology, 83 (1986): 398-404.

2199. COLUMBUS, Claudia Kemper. "The Heir Must Die: One Hundred Years of Solitude as a Gothic Novel," Modern Fiction Studies, 32 (1986): 397-416.

2200. CONGER, Syndy Mc Millen. "Matthew G. Lewis, Charles Robert Maturin, and the Germans: An Interpretive Study of the Influence of German Literature on Two Gothic Novels," Dissertation Abstracts International, 37 (1977): 7733A (University of Iowa).

2201. ______. Matthew G. Lewis, Charles Robert Maturin, and the Germans: An Interpretive Study of the Influence of German Literature on Two Gothic Novels. New York : Arno Press, 1980.

2202. CRAMPTON, Hope. "Melmoth in La Comédie Humaine," Modern Language Review, 61 (1966): 42-50.

2203. FINNÉ, Jacques. "Jan Potocki et le Gothic Novel," Revue des Langues Vivantes, 36 (1970): 141-165.

2204. ISHIMATSU, L.C. "Camilo Castelo Branco and the Gothic Tradition: Three Early Works," in La Chispa '85: Selected Proceedings, ed. Gilbert Paolini. New Orleans, LA : Tulane UP, 1985, pp.171-180.

2205. JAMES, Sibyl. "Gothic Transformations: Isak Dinesen and the Gothic," in The Female Gothic, ed. Juliann E. Fleenor. Montreal, Canada : Eden Press, 1983, pp.138-152.

2206. KADIR, Djelal. "Other Tombs: Structures of Mexican Gothic," Twentieth-Century Literature, 1 (1976-1977): 47-64.

2207. MERIVALE, Patricia. "Learning the Hard Way: Gothic Pedagogy in the

Modern Romantic Quest," *Comparative Literature*, 36 (1984): 146-161.

2208. MEWS, Siegfried. "Sensationalism and Sentimentality: Minor Victorian Prose Writers in Germany," *Modern Language Notes*, 84 (1969): 776-788.

2209. MILLER, Robin Feuer. "Dostoevsky and the Tale of Terror," in *The Russian Novel from Pushkin to Pasternak*, ed. John Garrard. *New Haven, CT : Yale UP, 1983*, pp.103-121.

2210. MOROZOV, A.A. "Zagadka Lermontovskogo Shtossa," *Russkaia Literatura*, 1 (1983): 189-196.

2211. MURATOVA, K.M. "Russkie Pisatelli Kontsa XVIII--Pervoĭ Poloviny XIX Veka o Zapadnoevropeĭskoĭ Gotike," *Voprosy Russkoĭ Literatury*, 1 (1972): 45-53.

2212. PEARSON, Alfred J. "The Gothic School in Swedish Literature," Unpublished Doctoral Dissertation, Yale University, 1896.

2213. PÉREZ, Gracia César. "Isak Dinesen y la Novela Gótica (Con Motivo de su Centenario)," *Insula*, 40 (1985): 17.

2214. PEYRONIE, André. "Julien Gracq et le Roman Noir," in *Julien Gracq: Actes du Colloque International d'Angers (21, 22, 23 Mai, 1981)*. Angers, France : PU d'Angers, 1981, pp.219-243.

2215. PHILLIPS, Delbert D. *Spook or Spoof? The Structure of the Supernatural in Russian Romantic Tales*. Washington, DC : UP of America, 1982.

2216. PINSKER, Sanford. "Isaac Bashevis Singer and Joyce Carol Oates: Some Versions of Gothic," *Southern Review*, 9 (1973): 895-908.

2217. RICHARDS, P.L. "The Italian Novel as Influenced by English Gothic Fiction," Unpublished Doctoral Dissertation, Harvard University, 1942.

2218. SCARI, Robert M. "Horacio Quiroga y los Fenómenos Parapsicológicos," *Cuadernos Hispanoamericanos*, 397 (1983): 123-132.

2219. SHEEHY, Maureen Elizabeth. "Fear as Prime Mover: A Study of Gothic Conventions in the Italian Historical Novel from 1818 to 1828," *Dissertation Abstracts International*, 34 (1974): 4286A (University of California at Los Angeles).

2220. SINKO, Zofia. "La Mode 'Gothique' en Pologne dans le Contexte Europeen," in *Proceedings of the 8th Congress of the International Comparative Literature Association*, eds. Bela Kopeczi, Gyorgy M. Vajda. Stuttgart, West Germany : Bieber, 1980, pp.399-405.

2221. SOUSA, Maria Leonor Machado de. "O Elemento 'Negro' na Novelística de Mário de Sá-Carneiro," *Bulletin des Etudes Portugaises et Bresiliennes*, 39-40 (1978-79): 393-430.

2222. STÉPHANE, Nelly. "Un Gothique Tardif: *Le Golem* de Gustav Meyrink," *Europe*, 659 (1984): 124-133.

2223. STEVENS, L. Robert and G. Roland Vela. "Jungle Gothic: Science, Myth, and Reality in _One Hundred Years of Solitude_," _Modern Fiction Studies_, 26 (1980): 262-266.

X. SPECIAL GOTHIC THEMES

The Evil Eye, Spontaneous Combustion, Science Fiction Gothic, Prominent Gothicists,Writing the Gothic Novel

2224. BLASINGAME, Wyatt. "Plotting and Writing the Terror Story," Writer's Digest, July, 1936, pp.12-15.

2225. BLOUNT, Trevor. "Dickens and Mr. Krook's Spontaneous Combustion," Dickens Studies Annual, 1 (1970): 183-211.

2226. BOOTH, Michael R. English Melodrama. London : Herbert Jenkins, 1965.

2227. BRANTLINGER, Patrick. "The Gothic Origins of Science Fiction," Novel, 14 (1980): 30-43.

2228. BREITLINGER, Eckhard. Der Tod im Englischen Roman um 1800. Göppingen, West Germany : Kümerle, 1971.

2229. BRISSENDEN, Robert F. Virtue in Distress: Studies in the Novel of Sentiment from Richardson to Sade. London : Macmillan, 1974; New York : Harper & Row, 1974.

2230. BROSE, Patricia B.D. "An Analysis of the Functioning of Gothic Themes in the Folklore and Writing of Children in the Second and the Fifth Grades," Dissertation Abstracts, 34 (1973): 2154A (University of Ne-Nebraska).

2231. BYRD, Max. "The Madhouse, the Whorehouse, and the Convent," Partisan Review, 44 (1977): 268-278.

2232. CARNOCHAN, W.B. Confinement and Flight: An Essay on English Literature of the Eighteenth Century. Berkeley, Los Angeles, London : California UP, 1977.

2233. CLAYBOROUGH, Arthur. The Grotesque in English Literature. New York : Oxford UP, 1965.

2234. CONRAD, Horst. Die Literarische Angst: Das Schreckliche in Schauerromantik und Detektivgeschichte. Düsseldorf, West Germany : Bertelsmann, 1974.

2235. DARNTON, Robert. *Mesmerism and the End of the Enlightenment in France*. Cambridge, MA : Harvard UP, 1968.

2236. DAVIS, Richard. *The Octopus Encyclopedia of Horror*. London : Octopus Books, 1981.

2237. "Detection and Terror Supplement," *Times Literary Supplement*, February 25, 1955, pp.i-xii.

2238. DIEDERICHS, Benno. *Von Gespenster Geschichten, Ihre Technik und Ihre Literatur*. Leipzig, Germany : Schmid & Spring, 1903.

2239. DUPERRAY, Max. "Idéologie et Irréel Littérature," *Cahiers de Centre d'Etudes et des Recherches dur les Littéraires de l'Imaginaire*, 9 (1984): 9-15.

2240. ELLWORTHY, Frederick T. *The Evil Eye*. London : Collier, 1958.

2241. FARRAG, Aida. "Zola, Dickens, and Spontaneous Combustion," *Romance Notes*, 19 (1978): 190-195.

2242. FERGUSON, J. Delancey. "Death by Spontaneous Combustion," *Colophon*, 9 (1932): no page numbers.

2243. FIEDLER, Leslie. *Freaks: Myths and Images of the Secret Self*. New : York : Simon and Schuster, 1978.

2244. GADWAY, John F. "The Castle in the Bildungsroman," *Dissertation Abstracts International*, 33 (1973): 4341A (Tulane University).

2245. GAUNT, William. *Bandits in a Landscape: A Study of Romantic Painting from Caravaggio to Delacroix*. London : The Studio, 1937.

2246. GOODRICH, Norma L. "Gothic Castles in Surrealist Fiction," in *Proceedings of the Comparative Literature Symposium, From Surrealism to the Absurd*. Lubbock, TX : Texas Technological UP, 1970, pp.143-162.

2247. GRANT, Marcus. *Horror: A Modern Myth*. London : Heinemann, 1974.

2248. HAINING, Peter. *Terror! A History of Horror Illustrations from the Pulp Magazines*. London : Souvenir Press, 1976; New York : A&W Visual Library, 1976.

2249. HALLIE, Philip. *Horror and the Paradox of Cruelty*. Middletown, CT : Wesleyan UP, 1969.

2250. HAYCRAFT, Howard. *Murder for Pleasure: The Life and Times of the Detective Story*. New York : Appleton-Century-Crofts, 1941; London : Davies, 1942.

2251. HAYS, Peter. *The Limping Hero: Grotesques in Literature*. New York : New York UP, 1971.

2252. HOWATCH. Susan. "Realism in Modern Gothics," *The Writer*, 87 (May, 19-74): 11-13.

2253. INGLIS, Fred. "Gentility and Powerlessness: Gentility and the New Class," in J.R.R. Tolkien: This Far Land, ed. Robert J. Giddings. London : Vision, 1983; Totowa, NJ : Barnes & Noble, 1983, pp.25-41.

2254. JEROME, Joseph [Brocard Sewell]. Montague Summers: A Memoir, foreword by Dame Sybil Thorndike. London : Cecil & Amelia Woolf, 1965.

2255. JONES, Robert. The Shudder Pulps. West Linn, OR : FAX Collector's Editions, 1975.

2256. KAPLAN, Fred. Dickens and Mesmerism: The Hidden Springs of Fiction. Princeton, NJ : Princeton UP, 1975.

2257. KEELING, Thomas H. "Science Fiction and the Gothic," in Bridges to Science Fiction, eds. George E. Slusser, George R. Guffey, Mark Rose. Carbondale, IL : Southern Illinois UP, 1980; London : Feffer, 1980, pp.107-119.

2258. KELLY, Catherine. "In the Vague Spaces of Duncan Campbell Scott's Poetry," Studies in Canadian Literature, 8 (1983): 61-92.

2259. KENNEDY, Mopsy Strange. "How To Write a Gothic Novel," New England-Boston Sunday Globe, October 8, 1979, 11, 14-15.

2260. KERR, Howard. "'Ghosts and Ghost Seeing': Spiritualism in American Occult Fiction," in Mediums, and Spirit-Rappers, and Roaring Radicals: Spiritualism in American Literature, 1850-1900. Urbana, IL : Illinois UP, 1972, pp.55-79; Rpt. in Literature of the Occult: A Collection of Critical Essays, ed. Peter Messent. Englewood Cliffs, NJ : Prentice-Hall, 1981, pp.78-88.

2261. KIESSLING, Nicholas J. "Demonic Dread: The Incubus Figure in British Literature," in The Gothic Imagination: Essays in Dark Romanticism, ed. G.R. Thompson. Pullman, WA : Washington State UP, 1974, pp.22-41.

2262. KNOEPFLMACHER, U.C. "Private Allegory: The Unveiling of Horror," in George Eliot's Early Novels: The Limits of Realism. Berkeley, CA : California UP, 1968, pp.139-143.

2263. LEE, Elsie. "When You Write a Gothic," The Writer, 86 (May, 1973): 17-19, 35.

2264. LEE, Grace Farrell. "The Grotesque: A Demonic Tradition," Dissertation Abstracts, 40 (1980): 4012A (Brown University).

2265. LEIBER, Fritz. "The Changing Faces of Horror," Fantasy Review, 73 (1984): 19-20.

2266. LIGOTTI, Tom. "The Consolations of Horror," Dark Horizons, 27 (1984): 26-32.

2267. MARSHALL, Roderick. Italy in English Literature, 1755-1815; Origins of the Romantic Interest in Italy. New York : Columbia UP; Columbia

University Studies in English and Comparative Literature, 1934.

2268. MASTERS, R.E.L. Perverse Crimes in History: Evolving Concepts of Sadism, Lust-Murder, and Necrophilia--From Ancient to Modern Times, Including a Historical Survey of Sexual Savagery in the East by Allen Edwardes. New York : Julien Press, 1963.

2269. MATTHEWS, J.H. "Anticipation," in Surrealism and the Novel. Ann Arbor, MI : Michigan UP, 1966.

2270. MESSENT, Peter B., ed. Literature of the Occult: A Collection of Critical Essays. Englewood Cliffs, NJ : Prentice-Hall, 1981.

2271. METCALFE, Robin. "Dr. Varma and Mr. Hyde," Books in Canada, June/July, 1986, pp.4-5.

2272. MÖBIUS, Hans. Die Englischen Rosenkreuzer Romane und Ihre Vorläufer: Eine Studie die Entwicklung der Phantastisch-Romantischen Erzählungsart in England während des 18. und 19. Jahrhunderts. Hamburg, Germany : Lüctke & Wulff, 1911.

2273. NOSKE, Frits. "Sound and Sentiment: The Function of Music in the Gothic Novel," Music & Letters, 62 (1981): 162-175.

2274. PALMER, Jerry. Thrillers: Genesis and Structure of a Popular Genre. New York : St. Martin's Press, 1979.

2275. PATERNA, Wilhelm. Übersinnliche im Englischen Roman (Von Horace Walpole bis Walter Scott). Hamburg, Germany : Lüctke & Wulff, 1915.

2276. PEDERIN, Ivan. "Na Izvorištima Trivijalne Književnosti: Njemačka Sablasna Pripovedka (Geistergeschichte) i Engleska Gotska Pripovedka (Gothic Story) Prema Kriminalističkom Romanu," Izraz, 22 (1978): 15-17-1533.

2277. PERKINS, George. "Death by Spontaneous Combustion in Marryat, Melville, Dickens, Zola, and Others," Dickensian, 60 (1964): 57-63.

2278. PETERS, Elizabeth. "Modern Gothics . . . The Willing Suspension of Disbelief," The Writer, 87 (February, 1974): 15-17.

2279. ______. "Character and Humor in the Gothics," The Writer, 89 (November, 1976): 15-17.

2280. RABKIN, Eric S. "The Fantastic and Literary History," in The Fantastic in Literature. Princeton, NJ : Princeton UP, 1976.

2281. RAWCLIFFE, D.H. Illusions and Delusions of the Supernatural and the Occult: The Psychology of the Occult. New York : Dover Publications, 1959.

2282. RICHARDSON, Maurice. "The Psychoanalysis of Ghost Stories," Twentieth Century, 166 (1959): 419-431.

2283. ROBERTS, Janet Louise. "Writing and Selling the Gothic Novel," Writer's Digest, 53 (January, 1973): 25-27.

2284. ROGAN, Helen. "How to Write a Gothic Novel," Harper's Magazine, May, 1975, pp.45-47.

2285. ROTTENSTEINER, Franz. The Fantasy Book: The Ghostly, the Gothic, the Magical, the Unreal. New York : Macmillan, 1978.

2286. RUDWIN, Maximilian. The Devil in Legend and Literature. Chicago : Open Court, 1931.

2287. SAURAT, Denis. Literature and Occult Tradition: Studies in Philosophical Poetry, trans. D. Bolton. London : G. Bell, 1930.

2288. SCHÄFER, Martin. "The Rise and Fall of Antiutopia: Utopia, Gothic Romance, Dystopia," Science-Fiction Studies, 6 (1979): 287-295.

2289. SCHUCHARD, Ronald. "Eliot and the Horrific Movement," Southern Review, 21 (1985): 1045-1056.

2290. SCOTT, George Ryley. The History of Torture Throughout the Ages. London : Torchstream Books, 1954.

2291. SCOTT, Sutherland. Blood in Their Ink; The March of the Modern Mystery Novel, foreword by Beverly Baxter. London : Stanley Paul, 1953.

2292. SEDGWICK, Eve Kosofsky. "Toward the Gothic: Terrorism and Homosexual Panic," in Between Men: English Literature and Homosocial Desire. New York : Columbia UP, 1985, pp.83-96.

2293. SEWELL, Brocard. "The Reverend Montague Summers," Romantist, 4-5 (1980-1981): 1-6.

2294. SHANNON, Edgar F. Jr. "'The Thews of Anakim': Postulations of the Superhuman in Tennyson's Poetry," Virginia Quarterly Review, 59 (1983): 587-608.

2295. SHUMAKER, Wayne. Literature and the Irrational: A Study in Anthropological Backgrounds. Englewood Cliffs, NJ : Prentice-Hall, 1960.

2296. SPENCE, Lewis. An Encyclopedia of Occultism. London : Routledge, 1920; Rpt. New Hyde Park, NY : University Books, 1960.

2297. STADE, George. "Thrillers," Columbia Forum, 13, number 1 (1970): 34-37.

2298. STEIG, Michael. "Defining the Grotesque: An Attempt at Synthesis," Journal of Aesthetics and Art Criticism, 29 (1970): 253-260.

2299. STOCK, R.D. "Spiritual Horror in the Novel: Richardson, Radcliffe, Beckford, Lewis," in The Holy and the Daemonic from Sir Thomas Browne to William Blake. Princeton, NJ : Princeton UP, 1982, pp.259-313.

2300. SULLIVAN, T.R. The Ghost in Fiction. New York : Riverside Press, 19-

06.

2301. SUMMERS, Montague. *The History of Witchcraft and Demonology*. New York: Alfred A. Knopf, 1926; Rpt. New Hyde Park, NY : University Books, 1965.

2302. THOMPSON, Leslie M. "'Childe Roland to the Dark Tower Came' and the Gothic Tradition in Literature," *Browning Newsletter*, 9 (1973): 17-22.

2303. THORSLEV, Peter Jr. "Incest as Romantic Symbol," *Comparative Literature Studies*, 2 (1965): 41-58.

2304. TODOROV, Tzvetan. "The Uncanny and the Marvelous," in *The Fantastic: A Structural Approach to a Literary Genre*, trans. Richard Howard. Cleveland, OH : Case Western UP, 1973; Rpt. in Literature of the Occult: A Collection of Critical Essays, ed. Peter Messent. Englewood Cliffs, NJ : Prentice-Hall, 1981, pp.17-30.

2305. TOOKER, Richard. "Writing the Terror Story," *Author and Journalist*, June, 1936, pp.17-18.

2306. TROUSSON, Raymond. *Le Thème de Prométhée dans la Littérature Européene*. Genève, Switzerland : Librairie Droz, 1964.

2307. UTTER, Robert Palfrey and Gwendolyn Bridges Needham. *Pamela's Daughters*. New York : Macmillan, 1936.

2308. VARMA, Devendra P. "Montague Summers: A Gothic Tribute," *Miscellany (Vine Press, London)*, April, 1984, pp.1-12.

2309. WEBB, James. *The Occult Underground*. La Salle, IL : Open Court, 1974.

2310. WHITMORE, Charles Edward. *The Supernatural in Tragedy*. London : Oxford UP, 1915; Cambridge, MA : Harvard UP, 1915.

2311. WHITNEY, Phyllis A. "Writing the Gothic Novel," *The Writer*, 80 (February, 1967): 9-13, 42-43.

2312. WILEY, Elizabeth. "Four Strange Cases," *Dickensian*, 58 (1962): 120-125.

2313. WILSON, Colin. *The Strength to Dream: Literature and the Imagination*. Westport, CT : Greenwood Press, 1973.

2314. WILSON, James D. "Incest and American Romantic Fiction," *Studies in the Literary Imagination*, 7 (1974): 31-50.

2315. WILT, Judith. "Imperial Month: Imperialism, the Gothic and Science Fiction," *Journal of Popular Culture*, 14 (1981): 618-628.

2316. WOOD, Chris. "Close Up: Devendra Varma, Connoisseur of Horror," *Maclean's Magazine*, April 14, 1986, pp.6, 10.

XI. THE WANDERING JEW AND THE DOUBLE FIGURE

2317. ANDERSON, G.K. "The Wandering Jew Returns to England," Journal of English and Germanic Philology, 45 (1946): 237-250.

2318. ________. "The Neo-Classical Chronicle of the Wandering Jew," Publications of the Modern Language Association, 63 (1948): 199-213.

2319. ________. The Legend of the Wandering Jew. Providence, RI : Brown UP, 1965.

2320. ANDREWS, S.G. "The Wandering Jew and The Travels and Adventures of James Massey," Modern Language Notes, 72 (1957): 39-41.

2321. BAYLISS, Linda Sue Singer. "Mirrors: Literary Reflections as Psychic Process," Dissertation Abstracts International, 46 (1985): 416A (Michigan State University).

2322. BRIGGS, Katharine M. "The Legends of Lilith and of the Wandering Jew in Nineteenth-Century Literature," Folklore, 92 (1981): 132-140.

2323. CHIZHEVSKY, Dmitri. "The Theme of the Double in Dostoevsky," in Dostoevsky, ed. René Wellek. Englewood Cliffs, NJ : Prentice-Hall, 1962, pp.112-129.

2324. FLETCHER, Robert Pearson. "The Convention of the Double-Self in Nineteenth-Century English Fiction," Dissertation Abstracts International, 37 (1976): 2195A (University of Delaware).

2325. FREESE, Peter. "Das Motiv des Doppelgängers in Truman Capotes 'Shut a Final Door' und E.A. Poes 'William Wilson,'" Literatur in Wissenschaft und Unterricht (Kiel), 1 (1968): 40-48.

2326. FROSCH, Mary Alfred. "Narcissus: The Negative Double," Dissertation Abstracts International, 37 (1976): 1562A (City University of New York).

2327. FULMER, Oliver B. "The Wandering Jew in English Romantic Poetry," Dissertation Abstracts International, 27 (1966): 455A-456A (Tulane University).

2328. ______. "The Ancient Mariner and the Wandering Jew," Studies in Philology, 66 (1969): 797-815.

2329. GAER, Joseph. The Legend of the Wandering Jew. New York : New American Library, 1961.

2330. GUERARD, Albert. "Concepts of the Double," in Stories of the Double, ed. Albert Guerard. New York : J.B. Lippincott, 1967.

2331. HALLAM, Clifford Barry. "The Double as Incomplete Self: Studies in Poe, Melville, and Conrad," Dissertation Abstracts International, 40 (1979): 4026A-4027A (Miami University).

2332. KANZER, Mark. "Freud and His Literary Doubles," American Imago, 33 (1976): 231-243.

2333. KEPPLER, C.F. The Literature of the Second Self. Tucson, AZ : Arizona UP, 1972.

2334. KILLEN, A.M. "L'Evolution de la Légende du Juif Errant," Revue de Littérature Comparée, 5 (1925): 5-36.

2335. MILLER, Karl. Doubles: Studies in Literary History. New York : Oxford UP, 1985.

2336. MIYOSHI, Masao. The Divided Self: A Perspective on the Literature of the Victorians. New York : New York UP, 1969.

2337. MONTGOMERY, Marion. "Of Cloaks and Hats and Doublings in Poe and Flannery O'Connor," South Carolina Review, 11, number 1 (1978): 60-69.

2338. PALMS, Rosemary H.G. "The Double Motif in Literature: From Origins to an Examination of Three Modern American Novels," Dissertation Abstracts International, 33 (1972): 321A (University of Texas at Austin).

2339. PORTER, Laurence M. "Devil as Double in Nineteenth-Century Literature: Goethe, Dostoevsky, and Flaubert," Comparative Literature Studies, 15 (1978): 316-335.

2340. RANK, Otto. "Der Doppelgänger," Imago, 3 (1914); Rpt. as "The Double: A Psychoanalytic Study," trans. and ed. Harry Tucker, Jr. Chapel Hill, NC : North Carolina UP, 1971.

2341. ROGERS, Robert. A Psychoanalytic Study of the Double in Literature. Detroit, MI : Wayne State UP, 1970.

2342. ROSENFIELD, Claire. "The Shadow Within: The Conscious and Unconscious Use of the Double," Daedulus: Journal of the American Academy of Arts and Sciences, 92 (1963): 326-344.

2343. SHIRLEY, Ralph. The Mystery of the Human Double: The Case for Astral Projection. New Hyde Park, NY : University Books, 1972.

2344. ST. ARMAND, Barton Levi. "Harvey Birch as the Wandering Jew: Literary Calvinism in James Fenimore Cooper's The Spy," American Literature, 50 (1978): 348-368.

2345. TAKAHASHI, Norikane. "The Wandering Jew Densetsu to Romanha no Shi," Eigo Seinen, 129 (1983): 210-214.

2346. TERRAS, Rita. "The Doppelgänger in German Romantic Literature," in Symposium on Romanticism: An Interdisciplinary Meeting, eds. P. Deguise, R. Terras. New London, CT : Connecticut College, 1977, pp.13-20.

2347. THUR, Robert. "Longing for Union: The Doppelgänger in Wuthering Heights and Frankenstein," Dissertation Abstracts International, 37 (1977): 4172B (California School of Professional Psychology, San Francisco).

2348. TYMMS, Ralph. Doubles in Literary Psychology. Cambridge, England : Bowes & Bowes, 1949.

2349. WAIN, Marianne. "The Double in Romantic Narrative: A Preliminary Study," Germanic Review, 36 (1961): 257-268.

2350. WALDECK, Peter B. The Split Self: From Goethe to Broch. Lewisburg, PA: Bucknell UP, 1979.

2351. ZIRUS, Werner. Der Ewige Jude in der Dichtung Vornehmlich in der Englischen und Deutschen. (Leipzig, Germany : Mayer & Müller, 1928.

XII. WEREWOLFERY AND VAMPIRISM

2352. ALDRIDGE, A. Owen. "The Vampire Theme: Dumas Pére and the English Stage," Revue des Langues Vivantes, 39 (1973): 312-324.

2353. BABENER, Liahana Klenman. "Predators of the Spirit: The Vampire Theme in Nineteenth-Century Literature," Dissertation Abstracts International, 36 (1976): 6668A-6669A (University of California at Los Angeles).

2354. BARAN, Henryk. "Some Reminiscences in Blok: Vampirism and its Antecedents," in Aleksandr Blok Centennial Conference, eds. Walter N. Vickery, Bogdan B. Sagatov. Columbus, OH : Slavica, 1984, pp.43-60.

2355. BLACK, George F. A List of Works Relating to Lycanthropy. New York : New York Public Library, 1920.

2356. BLEILER, E.F. Introduction to Wagner the Wehrwolf by G.W.M. Reynolds. New York : Dover Publications, 1975.

2357. BREENE, R.S. "An Irish Vampire," Occult Review, 38 (October, 1925): 242-245.

2358. CARTER, Margaret. Shadow of a Shade: A Survey of Vampirism in Literature. New York : Gordon Press, 1977.

2359. COPPER, Basil. The Vampire in Legend, Fact, and Art. London : Robert Hale, 1973.

2360. ________. The Werewolf in Legend, Fact, and Art. New York : St. Martin's Press, 1977.

2361. EAVES, A. Osborne. Modern Vampirism. Harrogate, England : Talisman, 1904.

2362. EISLER, Robert. Man into Wolf. New York : Philosophic Library, 1952.

2363. FRAYLING, Christopher. "Vampires," London Magazine, 14 (June/July, 1974): 94-104.

2364. GRILLOU, Jean-Louis. "Loup-Garou, Mandorle et Mandala: Le Motif de Loup-Garou dans les Nouvelles d'Algernon Blackwood," Caliban, 16 (1979): 65-76.

2365. HAMEL, Frank. Human Animals. London : W. Rider, 1915.

2366. HOCK, Stefan. Die Vampyrsage und Ihre Verwertung in der Deutschen Literatur. Berlin : Forschungen zur Neueren Literatur, Band 17, 1900.

2367. HOYT, Olga. Lust for Blood: The Consuming Story of Vampires. New York: Stein and Day, 1984.

2368. KAPLAN, Stephen. Vampires Are. Palm Springs, CA : ETC Publications, 1984.

2369. KITTREDGE, George Lyman. "Metamorphosis," in Witchcraft in Old New England. Cambridge, MA : Harvard UP, 1928, pp.174-184.

2370. KRAUSS, Friedrich Salomon. "Der Werwolf," in Slavische Volkforschungen; Abhandlungen über Glauben, Gewohnheitsrechte, Sitten, Bräuche, und die Guslarenlieder der Südslaven, Vorwiegand auf Grund Eigener Erhebungen. Leipzig, Germany : W. Heims, 1908, pp.137-144.

2371. "Lycanthropy," Occult Review, 25 (April, 1917): 214-217.

2372. MARIGNY, Jean. "Dialectique de l'Échange dans les Histoires de Vampires," in Société des Anglicistes de l'Enseignement Supérieur; Échanges Actes du Congrès de Strasbourg, foreword by G. Laprevotte. Paris : Marcel Didier, 1982, pp.309-319.

2373. MASTERS, Anthony. The Natural History of the Vampire. New York : G.P. Putnam's Sons, 1972; London : Rupert Hart-Davis, 1972.

2374. MC NALLY, Raymond. Dracula: A Biography of Vlad the Impaler, 1431-1476. New York : Hawthorn Books, 1973.

2375. _______. A Clutch of Vampires. These Being Among the Best From History and Literature. New York : New York Graphic Society, 1974.

2376. MURGOCI, Agnes. "The Vampire in Roumania," Folk-Lore, 37, number 4 (1926): 320-349.

2377. O'DONNELL, Elliott. Werewolves. New York : Longrue Press, 1965.

2378. OINAS, Felix J. "Heretics as Vampires and Demons in Russia," Slavic and East European Journal, 22 (1978): 433-441.

2379. _______. Introduction to Werewolf in The Golden Steed: Seven Baltic Plays, ed. Alfreds Straumanis. Prospect Heights, IL : Waveland Press, 1979.

2380. OLIVIER, Jean-Michel. "Le Texte du Vampire," Etudes Littèraires, 11 (1978): 113-159.

2381. OTTEN, Charlotte, ed. The Lycanthropy Reader: Werewolves in Western Culture. Syracuse, NY : Syracuse UP, 1986.

2382. PERKOWSKI, Jan L. Vampires of the Slavs. Cambridge, MA : Slavica, 1976.

2383. RICCARDO, Martin V. Vampires Unearthed: The Vampire and Dracula Bibliography of Books, Articles, Movies, Records, and Other Material. New York : Garland Publishing, 1983.

2384. SENF, Carol Ann. "Daughters of Lilith: An Analysis of the Vampire Motif in Nineteenth-Century English Literature," Dissertation Abstracts International, 39 (1979): 7363A (SUNY at Buffalo).

2385. SMITH, Kirby Flower. "An Historical Study of the Werewolf in Literature," Publications of the Modern Language Association, 9 (1894): 1-42.

2386. SPENCE, Lewis. "The Cult of the Werewolf in Europe," Occult Review, 34 (October, 1921): 221-226.

2387. STEWART, Caroline Taylor. "The Origin of the Werewolf Superstition," University of Missouri Studies (Social Science Series), 2, number 3 (1909): 1-22.

2388. SUMMERS, Montague. The Vampire, His Kith and Kin. London : Kegan Paul, Trench, and Trubner, 1928; Rpt. New Hyde Park, NY : University Books, 1964.

2389. _______. The Vampire in Europe. Kegan Paul, Trench, Trubner, 1929; Rpt. New Hyde Park, NY : University Books, 1965.

2390. _______. The Werewolf. London : Kegan Paul, Trench, and Trubner, 1933; Rpt. New Hyde Park, NY : University Books, 1966.

2391. TWITCHELL, James. "The Vampire Myth," American Imago, 37 (1980): 83-92.

2392. _______. The Living Dead: A Study of the Vampire in Romantic Literature. Durham, NC : Duke UP, 1981.

2393. "Vampire Lolly," The Listener, 92 (1974): 275.

2394. WHITTON, Charlotte. "Lord Byron on Vampires," Queen's Quarterly, 57 (1950): 474-478.

2395. WRIGHT, Dudley. Vampires and Vampirism. London : W. Rider, 1924.

XIII. THE GOTHIC FILM
A SELECTIVE LISTING

2396. ACKERMAN, Forrest J., ed. Boris Karloff: The Frankenscience Monster. New York : Ace Books, 1969.

2397. AMIS, Kingsley. "Dracula, Frankenstein, Sons & Co.," in What Became of Jane Austen? And Other Questions. New York : Harcourt, Brace, Jovanovich, 1970, pp.125-135.

2398. AYLESWORTH, Thomas G. Monsters from the Movies. Philadelphia : Lippincott, 1972.

2399. BECK, Calvin. Heroes of the Horrors. New York : Collier, 1975.

2400. BEDFORD, Michael and Bruce Dettman. The Horror Factory. New York : Pergamon Press, 1978.

2401. BOUJUT, Michel. "Preface and Filmography," to Frankenstein by Mary Shelley. Levallois-Perret (Hauts-de-Seine), France : Cercle du Bibliophile, 1969.

2402. BOUYXOU, Jean-Pierre. "Frankenstein". Lyon, France : Société d'Etudes Recherches et Documentation Cinématographiques, 1969.

2403. BRITTON, Andrew. "The Devil, Probably: The Symbolism of Evil," in American Nightmare: Essays on the Horror Film. Ottawa, Canada : Canadian Film Institute, 1981, pp.34-42.

2404. BROSNAN, John. The Horror People. New York : St. Martin's Press, 1976.

2405. BRUSTEIN, Robert. "Reflections on Horror Movies," Partisan Review, 25 (1958): 288-296; Rpt. in Thought in Prose, eds. Richard S. Beal, Jakob Korg. Englewood Cliffs, NJ : Prentice-Hall, 1966, pp.363-371.

2406. BUNNELL, Charlene. "The Gothic: A Literary Genre's Transition to Film," in Planks of Reason: Essays on the Horror Film, ed. Barry Keith Grant. Metuchen, NJ : Scarecrow Press, 1984, pp.79-100.

2407. BUTLER, Ivan. *The Horror Film*. New York : A.S. Barnes, 1967; London : A. Zwemmer, 1967.

2408. CARROLL, Noel. "Nightmare and Horror Film: The Symbolic Biology of Fantastic Beings," *Film Quarterly*, 34 (1981): 16-25.

2409. CLARENS, Carlos. *An Illustrated History of the Horror Film*. New York : G.P. Putnam's Sons, 1967.

2410. DADOUN, Roger. "Fetishism in the Horror Film," *Enclitic*, 1, number 2 (1979): 39-63.

2411. DANIELS, Les. *Living in Fear: A History of Horror in the Mass Media*. New York : Charles Scribner's Sons, 1975.

2412. DERRY, Charles. *Dark Dreams: The Horror Film from Psycho to Jaws*. London : Thomas Yoseloff, 1977.

2413. DILLARD, R.H.W. "Even a Man Who is Pure in Heart: Poetry and Danger in the Horror Film," in *Man and the Movies*, ed. W.R. Robinson. Baltimore : Penguin Books, 1967, pp.60-96.

2414. ________. *Horror Films*. New York : Monarch Books, 1976.

2415. DOUGLAS, Drake. *Horror!* New York and Toronto : Collier-Macmillan, 1969.

2416. DYER, Peter John. "Some Nights of Horror," *Films and Filming*, 4, number 10 (1958): 13-15.

2417. ________. "The Roots of Horror," in *International Film Annual Number 3*, ed. William Whitebair. New York : Taplinger Press, 1959, pp.69-75.

2418. EDWARDS, Roy. "Movie Gothick," *Sight and Sound (British Film Institute)*, Autumn, 1957, pp.16-18.

2419. EISNER, Lotte H. *The Haunted Screen: Expressionism in the German Cinema and the Influence of Max Reinhardt*. Berkeley, CA : California UP, 1969.

2420. ELLISON, Harlan. "Three Faces of Fear: A Theory of Film Horror from the Works of Val Lewton," *Cinema*, 3, number 2 (1966): 4-8, 13-14.

2421. EVANS, Walter. "Monster Movies: A Sexual Theory," *Journal of Popular Film*, 2 (1973): 353-365.

2422. ________. "Monster Movies and Rites of Initiation," *Journal of Popular Film*, 4, number 2 (1975): 124-142.

2423. EVERSON, William K. "Horror Films," *Films in Review*, 5 (1954): 12-23.

2424. ________. "The Monsters," in *The Bad Guys: A Pictorial History of the Movie Villain*. New York : Citadel Press, 1964, pp.94-113.

2425. ______. Classics of the Horror Film. New York : Citadel Press, 1974.

2426. EYLES, Allen. The House of Horror: The Story of Horror Films. London : Lorrimer, 1973.

2427. FOX, Julian. "The Golden Age of Terror," Films and Filming, 22, number 9 (1976): 16-23.

2428. FRANK, Alan G. Horror Movies: Tales of Terror in the Cinema. London : Octopus Books, 1974.

2429. ______. Monsters and Vampires. London : Octopus Books, 1976.

2430. ______. The Horror Film Handbook. Totowa, NJ : Barnes & Noble, 1982.

2431. GIFFORD, Denis. Movie Monsters. London : Studio Vista, 1969; New York: E.P. Dutton, 1970.

2432. ______. A Pictorial History of Horror Films. London : Hamlyn, 1973.

2433. GLUT, Donald F. The Frankenstein Legend: A Tribute to Mary Shelley and Boris Karloff. Metuchen, NJ : Scarecrow Press, 1973.

2434. ______. Classic Movie Monsters. Metuchen, NJ : Scarecrow Press, 1978.

2435. ______. The Frankenstein Catalogue. Jefferson, NC : Mc Farland, 1979.

2436. "Gothic Horror," Parade: A Pageant of Personalities and Events (Sydney, Australia), November 1958, pp.38-39.

2437. GRANT, Barry Keith, ed. The Planks of Reason: Essays on the Horror Film. Metuchen, NJ : Scarecrow Press, 1984.

2438. HALLIWELL, Leslie. "The Baron, the Count and Their Ghoul Friends," Films and Filming, 15, number 9 (1969): 13-16; number 10, (1969): 12-16.

2439. HAMMOND, Paul. "Melmoth in Norman Rockwell Land . . . on The Night of the Hunter," Sight and Sound, 48, number 2 (1979): 105-109.

2440. HILL, Derek. "The Face of Horror," Sight and Sound, 28 (Winter, 1958-1959): 6-11.

2441. HUSS, Roy and T.J. Ross, eds. Focus on the Horror Film. Englewood Cliffs, NJ : Prentice-Hall, 1972.

2442. HUTCHINSON, Tom. Horror and Fantasy in the Cinema. London : Studio Vista, 1974.

2443. ISHERWOOD, Christopher and Don Bachardy. Frankenstein: The True Story. New York : Avon Books, 1973.

2444. JANION, Maria. "Films, Demons, and Romanticism," Polish Perspectives, 18, number 4 (1975): 57-67.

2445. JENSEN, Paul. "On Frankenstein," Film Comment, 6 (1970): 42-46.

2446. KENNEDY, Harlan. "Kubrick Goes Gothic," American Film, 5, number 8 (1980): 49-52.

2447. KEROUAC, Jack. "Nosferatu," in Film and the Liberal Arts. New York : Holt, Rinehart, and Winston, 1970, pp.354-357.

2448. KRACAUER, Siegfried. "Hollywood's Terror Films: Do The Reflect an American State of Mind?" Commentary, 2, number 2 (1946): 132-136.

2449. ______. From Caligari to Hitler: A Psychological History of the German Film. Princeton, NJ : Princeton UP, 1971.

2450. LAVERY, David. "The Horror Film and the Horror of Film," Film Criticism, 7, number 1 (1982): 47-55.

2451. LEE, Walt. Reference Guide to Fantastic Films: Science Fiction, Fantasy, & Horror. Los Angeles : Chelsea-Lee, 1972-1974.

2452. LOSANO, Wayne A. "The Horror Film and the Gothic Narrative Tradition," Dissertation Abstracts International, 34 (1973): 5221A (Rensselaer Polytechnic Institute).

2453. ______. "The Vampire Rises Again in Films of the Seventies," Film Journal, number 2 (1973): 60-62.

2454. LUHR, William. "Nosferatu and Postwar German Film," Michigan Academician, 14 (1982): 453-458.

2455. MANK, Gregory W. "It's Alive!" The Classic Cinema Saga of Frankenstein. San Diego : A.S. Barnes, 1981.

2456. MC CONNELL, Frank. "Rough Beast Slouching: A Note on Horror Movies," Kenyon Review, 32 (1970): 109-120.

2457. ______. Terrors of the Screen. Englewood Cliffs, NJ : Prentice-Hall, 1970.

2458. MONACO, James. "Aaaieeeaarrggh! Horror Movies," Sight and Sound, 49, number 2 (1980): 80-81.

2459. NAHA, Ed. Horrors: From Screen to Scream. New York : Avon Books, 1975.

2460. NESTRICK, William. "Coming to Life: Frankenstein and the Nature of Film Narrative," in The Endurance of Frankenstein: Essays on Mary Shelley's Novel, eds. George Levine and U.C. Knoepflmacher. Berkeley, CA : California UP, 1979, pp.290-315.

2461. PATTISON, Barrie. The Seal of Dracula. New York : Crown Publishers,

1975; London : Lorrimer, 1975.

2462. PIRIE, David. *A Heritage of Horror: The English Gothic Cinema 1946-1972*. London : Gordon Fraser, 1973; New York : Avon Books, 1973.

2463. ______. *The Vampire Cinema*. Feltham, England : Hamlyn Group, 1977.

2464. PITTS, Michael R. *Horror Film Stars*. Jefferson, NC : Mc Farland, 1981.

2465. PRAWER, Siegbert S. *Caligari's Children: The Film as Tale of Terror*. New York : Oxford UP, 1980.

2466. REED, Ellis. *A Journey into Darkness: The Art of James Whale's Horror Films*. New York : Arno Press, 1980.

2467. RINGEL, Harry. "Hammer Horror: The World of Terence Fisher," in *Graphic Violence on the Screen*, ed. Thomas R. Atkins. New York : Monarch Press, 1976, pp.35-45.

2468. ROCKETT, W.H. "The Door Ajar: Structure and Convention in Horror Films That Would Terrify," *Journal of Popular Film and Television*, 10, number 3 (1982): 130-136.

2469. ______. "Landscape and Manscape: Reflection and Distortion in Horror Films," *Post Script*, 3, number 1 (1983): 19-34.

2470. ROMER, Richard Ira. "The Cinematic Treatment of the Protagonists in Murnau's *Nosferatu*, Browning's *Dracula*, and Whale's *Frankenstein*," *Dissertation Abstracts international*, 46 (1985): 2A-3A (Columbia University Teachers College).

2471. ROTH, Lane. "Dracula Meets the Zeitgeist: *Nosferatu* (1922) as Film Adaptation," *Literature/Film Quarterly*, 7 (1979): 309-313.

2472. SCHWEITZER, Darrell. *Lovecraft in Cinema*. Baltimore : T-K Graphics, 1977.

2473. SEVASTAKIS, Michael G. "Death's Love Songs: The American Horror Film (1931-1936) and its Embodiment of Romantic Gothic Conventions," *Dissertation Abstracts International*, 40 (1979): 2308A-2309A (New York University).

2474. SIEGEL, Joel. *Val Lewton: The Reality of Terror*. London : Secker and Warburg/British Film Institute, 1972.

2475. SILVER, Alain and James Ursini. *The Vampire Film*. New York : Wiley, 1972; San Diego, CA : A.S. Barnes, 1976.

2476. STEIGER, Brad. *Monsters, Maidens, and Mayhem: A Pictorial History of Horror Film Monsters*. New York : Merit, 1965.

2477. STRICK, Philip. "*Nosferatu*--The Vampyre," *Sight and Sound*, 48, number 2 (1979): 127-128.

2478. TELOTTE, J.P. "A Photogenic Horror: Lewton Does Robert Louis Stevenson," Literature/Film Quarterly, 10 (1982): 25-37.

2479. TODD, Janet M. "The Class-ic Vampire," in The English Novel and the Movies, ed. Michael Klein. New York : Frederick Ungar, 1981, pp.197-210.

2480. TURNER, George E. and Michael H. Price. Forgotten Horrors: Early Talkie Chillers from Poverty Row. South Brunswick, NJ and New York : A. S. Barnes, 1979.

2481. UNDERWOOD, Peter. Horror Man: The Life of Boris Karloff. London : Drake, 1972.

2482. WALDMAN, Diane. "Horror and Domesticity: The Modern Gothic Romance Film of the 1940's," Dissertation Abstracts International, 42 (1982): 4627A (University of Wisconsin).

2483. WALLER, Gregory A. The Living and the Undead: From Stoker's Dracula to Romero's Dawn of the Dead. Urbana, IL : Illinois, UP, 1986.

2484. WELSH, Jim and John Tibbetts. "Visions of Dracula," American Classic Screen, 5, number 1 (1980): 12-16.

2485. WHITE, Denis. "The Poetics of Horror: More Than Meets the Eye," Cinema Journal, 10 (Spring, 1971): 1-18.

2486. WILLIS, Donald C. Horror and Science Fiction Films: A Checklist. Metuchen, NJ : Scarecrow Press, 1972.

2487. WOLF, Leonard. "In Horror Movies, Some Things Are Sacred," New York Times Book Review, April 4, 1976, pp.6-7.

2488. WOOD, Robin. "Burying the Undead; The Use and Obsolescence of Count Dracula," Mosaic, 16, numbers 1-2 (1983): 175-187.

2489. WOOD, Robin and Richard Lippe, eds. The American Nightmare: Essays on the Horror Film. Toronto : Festival of Festivals, 1979.

ADDENDA

2490. GOULDER, Nancy Harriet. "The Legacy of the Gothic Novel: The Uncanny and the Logic of the Law," Dissertation Abstracts International, 47 (1987): 3761A-3762A (Columbia University).

2491. PATTERSON, Mary K. The Monster in the Mirror: Gender and the Sentimental Gothic Myth in Frankenstein. Ann Arbor, MI : UMI Press, 1987.

INDEX OF CRITICS

INDEX OF AUTHORS AND ARTISTS